Lancashire,

Where Women Die of Love

CHARLES NEVIN

MAINSTREAM
PUBLISHING

EDINBURGH AND LONDON

For Jack and Jean Nevin, and all Lancastrians everywhere,
whether native, adopted or just by inclination.

Reprinted 2007

Copyright © Charles Nevin, 2004
All rights reserved
The moral right of the author has been asserted

First published in Great Britain in 2004 by
MAINSTREAM PUBLISHING COMPANY (EDINBURGH) LTD
7 Albany Street
Edinburgh EH1 3UG

ISBN 9781845960377

This edition, 2006

A catalogue record for this book
is available from the British Library

Typeset in Apollo and Stone Sans

Printed and bound in Great Britain by
Cox & Wyman Ltd

Contents

INTRODUCTION

The County of Romance

Lancashire. Beyond the Trent, up a bit, left-hand side. Cotton and coal and clogs and caps and chimneys and chippies and all the rest of it: people who speak as they find, but friendly with it, come in, sit down and have a cup of tea, love, life's as hard as my vowels. Rains a lot, too.

I was born in Lancashire. I can do a bit of that: dark winter afternoons, the coughing on the top deck, the smell of damp gaberdine mixing with the tobacco and whatever particular piece of pungency was coming out of the chimneys that day, the yellow in the lamplight; or, if you prefer, I can give you the dust hanging in a summer's day, the smuts on the privets.

Smuts on the privets! There's hard. No, we weren't poor; in fact, we were rather well off. My father had a string of grocery shops, mostly passed down from his father, son of a man from Louth who left 'because my father wouldn't let me keep racehorses'. An Irish joke. St Helens, where he settled, was a good walk from Liverpool, where the boat came in. My mother, daughter of another self-made man, came, by way of the War, from London, a sparrow's hop from the East End; but she somehow found an altogether worse grime and uncouthness in south-west Lancashire, and worked very hard on our vowels.

I left, as you do, although I really hadn't joined very much, and went to London, change at Oxbridge, holding on to a bit of stage Northernness for distinction and identification purposes among the metropolitan middle classes.

We who play this game keep a close eye on our references. We know what is expected of us. Northerners should display two principal characteristics: no-nonsense, down-to-earth, spade-a-spadery, resolutely unimpressed by any fancy modishness; and that famously droll sense of humour, deemed essential to survive the accident, and accent, of birth.

The humour bit is interesting and crucial to the really important Northern distinction, easily grasped but so often ignored by outsiders: that between Lancashire and Yorkshire. (The North-east? Sui generis. North-easterners, not Northerners, fetching folk, with an affecting faith in the ability of their quaint accent to lend an intrinsic wit, wisdom and interest to anything they might care to say. And have you ever seen one in an overcoat? Exactly. Cumbria? Much of it used to be in Lancashire; most of it should have been. I should also add that anywhere south of Lancashire and Yorkshire is in the Midlands.)

I tell you, Lancashire and Yorkshire is the thing. The Pennines: a boundary far more significant than the Trent. On the one side lives a warm and whimsical race, ever ready to chuckle, even laugh, in the face of the sheer ridiculousness of life; on the other, a sad and surly people, unable to understand why they haven't been let in on the joke.

Unable to understand, too, why their importance, so clear, obvious and evident to them, remains so stubbornly unrecognised by everyone else. Little wonder that they feel so impelled to insist upon it, very loudly and very regularly. And to trumpet their virtues, which have so similarly failed to travel. Cast your eye over this summary, contained in the old Yorkshire rhyme:

> You must hear all; you must say nothing.
> You must sup all; you must pay nothing.
> And if ever you do anything for nothing
> Do it for yourself.

Hmm. My purpose, though, is not to judge, but to distinguish: to beg you not to confuse them with us; to rescue Lancashire lightness and wit from the smothering gloom that has fallen upon it from over there. And they will thank me for it: they've never liked us, you know. J.B. Priestley, from Bradford, of course, thought us noisy, frivolous spendthrifts, and joined in the general headshaking at our 'annual goings on' in Blackpool. They didn't call him Jolly Jack for nothing. He was a professional Yorkshireman, but, as Paul Routledge, the estimable political commentator and biographer, also from over there, has put it: 'Have you ever heard of an amateur Yorkshireman?' Consider this list: Arthur Scargill, Roy Hattersley, Michael Parkinson, Fred Trueman, Geoffrey Boycott, Alan Titchmarsh, David Blunkett. And now this one: George Formby, Gracie Fields, Stan Laurel, Frank Randle, Robb Wilton, Tommy Handley, Ken Dodd, Les Dawson, Eric Morecambe, Victoria Wood, Steve Coogan, Johnny Vegas, Caroline Aherne, Peter Kay. It is an essential truth that comics come from Lancashire and don't come from Yorkshire. Forget the ten famous Belgians, ask a Yorkshireman to name a famous Yorkshire comic. Actually, as it happens, Frankie Howerd was born in York, but I think we'll let that pass. And Ernie Wise.

Why is this? Well, I have tended to toy with the Scandinavian influence on the east and the Celtic influence on the west, but it is careful toying, as my wife is half-Norwegian. And then, not long ago, I came upon a guidebook to Lancashire written by Walter Greenwood, author of the classic Lancs romance *Love on the Dole*. It was Walter who provided that old Yorkshire rhyme. Here he is on the difference:

> These two great counties, as every schoolboy knows, are divided by the Pennines, the backbone of old England. Yorkshire faces the full blast of the easterly wind which may account for the Yorkshire character . . . [whereas] The boisterous wind that buffets the land of the Red Rose is born in the tumbling wastes of the Atlantic. A wild, warm, amorous wind wenching with fat clouds and leaving them big with rain of which they deliver themselves on the Pennines' westerly slopes.

Terrific, Walter, thank you. On the one side, a land exposed, under attack from the elements and whatever else Europe can hurl at it; on the other, even the wind is more fun. No wonder we're different. Very different. I also recommend A.J.P. Taylor's *Essays in English History*, and in particular the one on Manchester, which has a fascinating excursion into Lancashire and Lancashireness. He agreed about the Pennines, and the wind:

> Cultivated Englishmen who never go further than Stratford-on-Avon or perhaps Lichfield regard all 'the North' as one in character and scenery – hard, bleak, rugged. Yorkshiremen are hard all right – living in stone houses and sharpened by the east wind. But . . . Lancashire people are the very opposite from those in Yorkshire. This is the land of the south-west wind, bringing an atmosphere that is always blurred and usually gentle.

The finest, though, is yet to come. Taylor had read *Le Lys dans la vallée* by Honoré de Balzac, in which the hero, Félix de Vandenesse, is seduced by the beautiful Lady Arabella Dudley, a Lancastrian, who tells him that Lancashire is 'the county where women die of love'. Well. The county where women die of love! That is something, is it not? Can Surrey, Sussex, Gloucestershire, Shropshire or even Essex make such a boast?

It is true that Balzac's authority on England, Sarah Lovell, his lover, came from Bath; and that, in the book, Lady Arabella does not die of love, despite being spurned by Félix: these, though, are minor quibbles. Taylor himself thought Lancashire women more likely to say, 'Come on, lad, let's get it over,' but then he was a bit dry, even though he came from Birkdale. He is better on the whimsicality of the Lancastrian male, that talent for not taking things too terribly seriously evidenced by all those comics cited above, which he blames on the benign and blurring breeze. His father, he wrote, was incapable of going out of the house without coming back with some fantastic tale of what had happened to him. This chimed with my own father, who, while not a 'romancer', as he called people like Alan's dad, certainly had his whimsical side.

His account of service life between 1939 and 1945, for example, was not a routine one, despite an unswerving admiration for Churchill and 'Monty', and distinguished service in Egypt and Europe. The only shot of any significance he claimed to have fired, for example, seemed to have gone through a wall at the Rose and Crown, Colchester, nearly killing an American officer in the next bedroom. Otherwise, by his account, he managed to rise quite peaceably from private to major in the Royal Army Service Corps (Run Away Someone's Coming, as he loved to put it) because his superiors decided, rightly as it turned out, that a Lancashire grocer would be rather better at supplying the Eighth Army than any of their regular chaps. The high-ups, he said, seemed to think a Lancashire accent the outward sign of an inward trustworthiness. This belief proved particularly useful during their visits to his depots, which tended to involve groups of men moving the same stock to different points on the inspection route to disguise irregularities (not of his making, I stress). And he never did get to go back to the Western Desert to find all that sugar they had stored there, under the sand, away from Rommel, and which, he claimed, seeing as it was uncontaminated by Hiroshima, would now be worth a bloody fortune, if he could remember where he put it.

His memories of all this, including the Indian Army CO sitting down to lunch in a tent in the middle of the desert and sending the plates back because they hadn't been warmed, would more often than not lead to the set piece of his war time: the embarkation from North Africa of 500 Italian prisoners of war followed by their immediate disembarkation and re-embarkation when he mistakenly counted only 499. I can see him now, hugging his small but generously sized self over this, feet up, whisky in hand, and hear his giggling exclamation at the daftness of it all: 'Oooh, bloody hell!', or, as he elided it, 'Oooh, bloody'ell!'

Whimsical, you see. Very whimsical, Lancashire. Where else, for example, would a bull actually find its way into a china shop? Lancaster. Where else, for another, would a man end a 12-hour siege after police gave in to his one demand, an egg and mayonnaise sandwich? Blackpool. The 68-year-old pensioner caught breaking the speed limit four times in three days? Accrington. Three times World Salsa Champion? Southport. Australian rugby Test centre collapses with sunstroke? Wigan. Lord Lucan traced to Goa? No, it was a banjo-player from St Helens called Barry. Exactly. And always so. Something in the water as well as the wind, perhaps. And wherever you go. I was in Bury not long ago, admiring the town's striking Whitehead

12

Clock Tower, which bears the legend about time and tide waiting for no man, and features, high up, a life-size bronze figure of fleeting Time. And as I looked, I noticed that someone had climbed up and neatly hung a pair of trainers on the figure's arm.

What I'd like to do is explore the source, the spring of this whimsy, and sift the stories that flow from it: stories of lost lands and dreams and laughter and kings and weavers, including the top hand, the Bard himself.

Indeed. Shakespeare spent much time in Lancs, at Hoghton Tower, in the service of the Hoghtons, ready to write, drawing his inspiration. It must have been at Hoghton that Will found his Lancashire-like passion for abroad, that sympathy for sunshine and warm earth and exotic passions that touches the people of this land as surely as its rain (which is probably why).

Go on, sneer: that will account for Benidorm and Tenerife. But, consider: there is a Lancashire toreador, Frank Evans, a kitchen-fitter from Salford. It was also long the habit around Barrow to name children Ferdinando in tribute to the doomed, romantic fifth Earl of Derby. Plato was a popular choice, too. And, as it happens, in a whimsical gesture of fellow feeling, the Greeks offered their throne to a later Earl of Derby, the nineteenth-century prime minister and translator of the *Iliad*. He turned it down, of course, preferring, as Disraeli put it, 'Lancashire to the Attic Plains'. And who should blame him? Another version has the Greeks bearing their gift to his son, Lord Stanley, provoking the response, 'Don't they know I'm going to be the Earl of Derby?'

Balzac obviously sensed these affinities and fancies. Stand at Hoghton Tower, looking west, and you will see that other great erection: Blackpool! Has there ever been a more breathtaking monument to whimsy and romance, this homage by the Irish Sea to Monsieur Eiffel and La Belle France? And the compliment is returned: further south, down the coast, is Southport, where the youthful, pre-imperial Napoleon III found inspiration for his new Paris.

So why should this not be the county where women die of love? After all, did Jung not have a famous dream that Liverpool was the pool of life? He did. And while we're dealing in deep thought and this great county's international influence, can it really be mere coincidence that Frank Zappa and Captain Beefheart grew up in the small town of Lancaster in the Californian desert?

You should know, too, that, according to the Ordnance Survey, the exact centre of Great Britain, taking into account the mainland and the 401 islands, lies in Lancashire, just near Dunsop Bridge, a charming place, cupped by the gently grand green hills of Bowland, watered by the sweet Hodder and the stream that lends it its name. Ignore rival claimants and desperate tourist boards: Lancashire is The True Heart of Britain.

I do not say that there can be no seriousness here. There weren't that many laughs, on the whole, during the Industrial Revolution. And whimsy does have its sober moments. How else would you describe the decision to turn Manchester into a seaport by building a canal 35 miles long, 120 feet wide and 28 feet deep? Or, indeed, the decision of the Lancashire cotton workers to support Abraham Lincoln's fight against slavery despite his blockade of the South's cotton, the blockade which had thrown them out of work? Lincoln called this 'an instance of sublime Christian heroism which has not been surpassed in any age or in any country'. Well, he would, wouldn't he? But I'm pushed to find any matching acts of such, well, high-minded gormlessness. It strikes me as a bit like having George Formby in charge of foreign policy, and rather splendid.

Anyway, having thought about all this, it seemed to me that, even though the mines and the mills had gone, there was still some digging and spinning left to do: I wanted to see if the County of Romance was still there, whether the Spring of Whimsy had survived, and if women could still die of love; to find out if Paris really was based on Southport and whether Lancastrians were still named after Ferdinando. I wanted to look for the Grail near Ince, to dance in the Tower Ballroom, experience longing in Liverpool and wistfulness in Oldham, and convince you of the truth and beauty of rugby league; go bullfighting from Salford; briefly encounter Carnforth; and play Earsy, Kneesy, Nosey in Wigan. And, perhaps, too, Walter Greenwood's dream had come true, and boys were fishing again in the Irwell, a river which, someone once told me, 'You don't fall in twice'. Coming?

Chapter One

Vive La Blackpool!

Chips, Casinos, and Cross-dressing

> Of course, Lancashire is quite a place – with the best
> country in the world to my mind, and the nicest people
> . . . The men are independent without being aggressive:
> tolerant, affectionate, sentimental – almost mawkish.
> Balzac describes Lancashire as 'the county where women
> die of love'. I think this very unlikely. I have always
> assumed, though with little first-hand experience, that
> Lancashire women are as brisk and businesslike in love-
> making as in everything else. The men provide the
> romantic atmosphere. It delights them to imagine that
> the women die of love. In reality a Lancashire woman
> would reply: 'Come on, lad. Let's get it over!'
>
> A.J.P. Taylor, *Essays in English History*

On the platform at Blackpool North, Claire was wearing a plastic
tiara. Claire was a management consultant in London, but she
was also from Blackburn and had brought her London friends to

Blackpool for her hen party, to show them how these things were done properly, in Lancs. Her fiancé was from Yorkshire and, with a typically eastern lack of imagination, was having his stag party in Paris. Still, at least it has a tower. I asked Claire if she knew that Lancashire was the county where women died of love. 'I thought it was from the cold, or too many chips,' she said.

It was raining hard, so I took shelter under a pawnbroker's canopy, not far from the Winter Gardens, Blackpool's first indoor entertainment centre, opened in 1878 but continuing to fulfil a clear and pressing need. Whimsically entitled, too. Waiting, in early September, for a change in intensity from the vertical to the merely angled slashing, I had a look in the pawnbroker's window at the rows and rows of gold rings, on sale at 'giveaway prices', ranging from the delicately diamonded to those clunky ones with the gold coins. They were all 'unredeemed pledges'. In more ways than one: quite a lot of dead love for sale there, I thought. All right, all right, but that's the way it is when you have a theme and it's raining.

There is this plan for Blackpool: to turn it into Las Vegas. Resort casino hotels, four, five, maybe six; hundreds of tables, thousands of slot machines, themed restaurants, conference and exhibition space, open 24 hours a day, first hotel expected as soon as the endlessly protracted and contested legislation to liberalise the gaming laws gets through. The Lancashire Las Vegas.

A lot of people laugh at this, of course. But people laughed at the Winter Gardens and, 10 years later, at the idea for a tower just like Eiffel had put up in Paris. Even Eiffel laughed when they asked him for help. But it got built, which is more than can be said for the one they tried in London, at Wembley. And, I'll have you know, Atlantic City used to advertise itself as the Blackpool of America. It did.

The most testing time for the visionary, though, must be a wet Saturday in the Winter Gardens, just after they've gone into

18

the theatre for Danny La Rue, with a few elderly couples in the amusement arcade on the Twopenny Nudgers and more in the Victoria Bar, which is resting between the live entertainment efforts of Wayne and Jackie, a vocal duo in their eighth consecutive season, and Hats Off, a band featuring two members 'direct from Freddie and the Dreamers'. Except perhaps for a Monday night, when Jackie is having a break at the bar and you watch Wayne working the audience with a beaming determination that is almost undone by his eyes and you wonder if the previous seven seasons have been like this, too; or down at the Tower Lounge, right underneath it, where a beautiful, groomed black girl, who looks as if she thought she was going to Las Vegas, is smiling too bright a smile and singing 'A hot time baby tonight' and on the dance floor below a Glaswegian with a moustache and a football shirt dances with a bald elderly uncle, also in a football shirt, while everybody else watches, sort of. I wondered if I should tell her that Sarah Bernhardt walked out of the Winter Gardens in disgust even before the end of her first act, but decided against it. I remembered that my father had always been very keen on Blackpool, and that my mother couldn't stand it, and I agreed with both of them.

Anyway, whatever, and at any rate, it was, without a doubt, the maternal instinct which kicked in on the Saturday afternoon as I walked south along the Golden Mile in the rain and the wind and the cold, and the delightfully whimsical notion of staying with a real old-fashioned Blackpool landlady began to beckon ever less brightly in the face of thoughts of an en-suited establishment with stars and a trouser press and ungrudged amounts of hot water.

Even the most deterred researcher, though, perks up at the prospect of a bit of expert input. Gypsy Petulengro seemed fairly convinced that Las Vegas would be a goer, and that it would sit comfortably alongside Blackpool's traditional attractions. She had been in her booth on the Golden Mile for 40 years, she said.

19

Recently, though, it had not been so good: the families were staying away, put off by all these stag parties. 'There were some lads outside here earlier with not a stitch on them,' she said. Well. I don't know what struck me more about this: such astounding hardiness, or the discovery that there were things that could be a bit much even for a gypsy. I asked her about Lancashire and women dying of love. She didn't know anything about that, she said; she was from Skegness.

A bit further along, Gypsy Levengro was non-committal on the Vegas question, even though she did agree that Blackpool had 'been going down for years'. And, on the general topic of gypsy consultation over seaside developments, I should tell you that, carrying out a similar mission some years ago, I got a very firm and favourable prediction about the possibilities of a new pier in Bognor, and nothing has happened yet.

The sun shone for a bit, then it started raining again. I turned off the prom before the South Pier and began to look for a boarding house. Blackpool has more beds for hire than the whole of Portugal; I know this because it's one of those facts that you see reported time and again, in the same way that Birmingham has more canals than Venice and, size-wise, countries are always a multiple of Wales. Finding the right bed, though, was not easy. What I wanted was not just a suitably fearsome landlady but a suitably fearsome landlady who was running an enterprise with a title affording a touch of irony, or at least a cheap joke opportunity. And I have to say that the spirit of innovation and fun that has always run through Blackpool like ... no, I promised myself, no rock similes ... let us just say that Blackpool's spirit of innovation and fun doesn't extend to the names of its boarding houses. Cliftons, Ocean Views, Sunny This, Sunny That, all manner of Banks and Braes and Denes and Sides, but nothing that really grabbed and shouted, 'Come in here, we're good for at least two paragraphs of wry and whimsical humour.'

I stopped a taxi and asked the driver if he knew where I'd find an old-fashioned, no-nonsense landlady; he wasn't really interested. I got to the door of The Haven, but the sound of a stag party in full voice with the 'Why, Why, WHY' chorus of 'Delilah' at half past four in the afternoon put me off. It shouldn't have done, I know: a real reporter would have gone right in there and spent the weekend with them, and that, I suppose, is why I'm not a Fleet Street legend. More of a footnote, really, or one of those small entries at the bottom of the obituary pages known in the trade as 'nuggets', the ones that journalists tend to get in their own or former newspapers when they meet the last deadline, and then only if it's been a slow day for death.

Sorry, I'll be strong and get on with it now. The Haven passed up, I followed a woman into one called after its proprietors, Tomarosa, Jeffasharon, something like that. The woman asked if there was a room available for the night. 'I've only got a family room and you wouldn't be able to afford it,' said Rosasharon, clearly believing the woman and me to be a couple. Insulted? This was the landlady I was after, except that she was Irish and wasn't about to part with a room. The landlady at the San Remo told me The Calypso might have a room, but the Irish landlady there didn't think I was worth it for one night, either.

So: rejected in Blackpool, no room for the night, and this my heritage, too. But then, just like in *A Taste of Honey* or *Saturday Night and Sunday Morning* or another of those gritty, black-and-white 1960s britfilms, the landlady from the San Remo came out onto the pavement and shouted down the street that she had a room after all. She was from Eastbourne, but it was still raining.

The room was small, clean, nylon, floral, briskly clashing, bathroom ex-suite, down the corridor. I went out. It was dusk, turning dark. There are, you should know, two great Blackpool sights. One is the Golden Mile: the Tower, the prom and the piers and the people, deckchairs and donkeys and sands stretching out along to the wheels and dippers of the Pleasure Beach. The other sight is the one I was now experiencing: Blackpool by night, the Illuminations, 'The Greatest Free Show on Earth', six miles of winking, flashing tableaux and giant faces and figures, and trams lit up as gondolas, lifeboats and battleships, with the Tower traced in light above it all.

The Lights were another great Blackpool wheeze, taken up enthusiastically in the 1920s to extend the season right through September into October. They're now Blackpool's biggest draw, attracting more than three million visitors, most of them driving in their cars, very slowly, bumper to bumper, along the route. Watching them on that Saturday night, on the South Shore, going into town, with the hens and the stags weaving their way along, I began to see that this Las Vegas thing might not be so daft after all. If Tom Wolfe could bang on about Vegas being the shining light of American popular working-class culture, a flash-brash confection of fun and games and ready cash out there in the middle of the desert away from the prissy elegance of European ideas about architecture and the right way to enjoy yourself, what price Blackpool, a roar of drink and chips and tits and lights and silly outfits and songs and shouts up here out of the way on a rainy night in September while the rest of the country was watching *Casualty*?

I was on my way to Funny Girls, the throbbing, quivering heart of the stag and hen industry. It's called Funny Girls because the floor show, the bar staff and the waiters are all transvestites. It was packed with various parties, from Birmingham, Chesterfield, Cardiff, Wrexham and Glasgow, all drinking at a ferocious pace. There were girls dressed as policewomen and nurses, and lads in cowboy outfits. For the girls, minimalism and plenty of protrusion seemed to be the dress code; the blokes weren't wearing much, either. T-shirts featuring the name of the hen or the stag or the birthday person – Martina, Neil, Lisa, Rachel – were big, too. You get used to the groups after a bit; later, though, out on the street, when some of them have got separated, it does still give you a bit of a pause to see a lone priest, in soutane, with crucifix and wide-brimmed hat, staggering past, followed minutes later by a man in full combat gear moving deliberately.

The floor show in Funny Girls was slick, mimed, beautifully costumed and with the odd bit of rudery, which seemed mostly to go ignored in the partying. The MC was Zoe, who won't forgive me if I describe her as a kind of Lily Savage. 'You can tell I used to work at Manchester Airport,' (s)he rasped. 'I wasn't on the check-in staff, I used to sniff the luggage.'

Watching all this, I began to work on another great Lancashire theory, to do with big dominant women, whimsical men and the emergence of Manchester and Blackpool as major gay venues. Zoe, on a break, wasn't impressed, and she didn't think much of women dying of love, either. Mind you, (s)he said, on Wednesday and Thursday nights, they got loads of pensioners in, from places like Bolton and Southport, and they absolutely loved it, roared away. So, Lancashire, the county where old people go to watch men dressed up as women.

Zoe was from Bradford and his real name was Adrian. 'How old are you?' I asked. He replied, 'Zoe's 28, Adrian's marginally older.' Just then, a big bloke, stubbly and T-shirted, approached. 'Can I just ask you one question?' he said, loudly, looking at Zoe's lower parts. Oh dear, I thought, here we go. And then he asked his question: 'How the fuck do you walk in those shoes?' Marvellous.

I went back to my banquette and my theory, but it was difficult to concentrate, what with Sharon from Birmingham walking past in her bridal veil carrying a large inflatable penis. Louise from Bolton was in the men's loo because of the queue for the women's. A man coming in did a double-take. 'All right, petal?' said Louise. At the end of the bar, what I took to be a big, blonde woman in her early forties, with short hair, tattoo, denim and cleavage, was laughing and being generally uproarious. Now that, I thought, is the type of woman who should be very good for a quote on the dying of love question. And the woman over there with the short grey hair who was still wearing her anorak. I went up to the blonde. Her name was Helen and she was from Worksop, in Nottinghamshire, she told me. I asked her if she was aware that Lancashire was the county where women died of love. She laughed a bit more. 'I can't really comment on that, love,' she said, 'because I haven't had a shag yet.' I couldn't find the woman in the anorak.

After Funny Girls closes, a lot of people go up to the Pink Flamingo, the big gay club, behind the Flying Handbag pub. All three, and more, are owned by Basil Newby, the Queen of Blackpool, as he likes to style himself. On a good night, more than 7,000 people pass through Basil's establishments. Basil calls his company In The Pink and is one of those gays who would giggle at the mention of 'Basil's establishments'. Basil describes himself as 'a child entrepreneur', never reveals his age and hasn't been to bed before three in the morning in the 20-odd years since he opened the Pink Flamingo: he has that 24-hour casino complexion, an interesting hair arrangement and one of the biggest rings I've ever seen. And he won't let you down. When you ask him about his ring, he lifts a buttock and looks at his bottom. The diamonds, though, are very big, and real. Basil is worth quite a few million.

Basil is the son of a Blackpool hotelier who used to put up the likes of Shirley Bassey and the Kaye Sisters, he will tell you. He did his time as a Bluecoat at Pontin's and nowadays addresses dinners hosted by the Chief Constable of Lancashire and tells stories involving him being in Amman (you have to pronounce that last 'a' shortly). When he took over the Pink Flamingo, it was the kind of establishment, with girls, that had its busiest period over Blackpool's renowned Pigeon Fanciers' Weekend in February. (Pigeon Fanciers' Weekend!) When he started Funny Girls, the licensing magistrate, a female Justice of the Peace,

24

asked him, 'Are you sure this will be all right, Basil?' People predicted all sorts of trouble, but now nobody bats an eye when one of Basil's 'girls' passes by in the street, and there are advertisements at the local job centre: 'Have you got the balls to work at Funny Girls?'

So there I was, eager with my theory about Lancashire's whimsicality and other native features making it the natural premier location for the gay community, but Basil wasn't particularly convinced. He could see that Blackpool's postcard and panto qualities provided a rich and sustaining setting for cross-dressing, but he felt Gay Blackpool was more to do with himself than anything in the air or the water. I was tempted to say, 'Cometh the hour, cometh the man', but decided not to give Basil the opportunity. We parted, after I'd satisfied myself on one thing that had been bothering me: the safety of all these approximately clad girls staggering around Blackpool all night. 'Don't worry about that,' said Basil. 'They're much rougher than the men.'

The next morning, a bell rang at the San Remo for breakfast. Mrs Harris was doing the cooking and Mr Harris was doing the serving. Mr Harris was from Ashton-under-Lyne, even if Mrs Harris was from Eastbourne. The front room was pretty full, with several families, a couple of young lads, another on his own, and me. Mr and Mrs Harris kept up a flow of chat in the manner which has been adopted, rather more self-consciously, by the proprietors of those middle-class boarding houses, small country house hotels. They'd had the San Remo for 24 years, they said, came to it through a family connection. It was hard work and getting harder: weekly stays were in steep decline and a lot of places had gone bust, the ones that had borrowed. A lot of people saw 24 sitting down for evening dinner at a tenner a head, but mostly it wasn't that easy.

Mr Harris asked the young lad on his own where his dad was; the lad explained that he had met someone last night and gone off with her. 'So he just left you in the lurch, like?' said Mr Harris. The lad said it had been late on, so it wasn't too bad. There was a bit more joshing. I asked Mrs Harris what had happened to the battleaxe Blackpool landlady of legend. 'A myth!' said Mrs Harris. Just then, the lad's father drew up outside in his car. 'I hope he's not come for his breakfast, because it's cold!' said Mrs Harris.

They were finding themselves getting more and more irritated with people, said Mrs Harris. The English were always whingeing and whining about this and that – 'Somebody told me that their 12 year old should be half-price the other night. I said "Are you telling me what I should charge?".' But the Scots and the Irish were all right. 'Some places complain the Scots don't eat the food,' said Mrs Harris, 'but so what if they pay for it?' Next weekend was Glasgow weekend, for the Lights, one of the few remnants of the old en masse descents from the same place – the Wakes Weeks. 'Girls and lads from the same town used to start their courting in the Tower Ballroom,' said Mr Harris. They had some old friends in Blackpool, they said, Eileen and Denis, from Leigh, that's how they'd met.

The front room was empty now. Mr and Mrs Harris confided that, as it happened, this was their last weekend. Some people from down south had bought the San Remo for less than they had got for their house. They'd be there next weekend to help them get started. The new people hadn't any experience, but neither had they when they started. They were off to Canada to join their daughter, who was living in Calgary. Mrs Harris had been to a spiritualist years ago who had told her she would cross the water and wear a uniform, and this seemed pretty close, as her daughter had worn a kind of uniform when she had worked for a spell as a hotel receptionist in Lytham.

They'd just got tired, really. They should have been converting the rooms into en suites, that's what everybody wanted now. And televisions. Although nobody watched the television in the lounge. Hadn't been on at all this last week, except for the old lady who wanted to watch her soap at teatime. I went to get my bag. I didn't mention that I was in desperate need of an en suite and a telly myself. When I came back down, Mrs Harris gave me a little gift, a tape with a song on it about the *Blackpool Belle*, the train that used to run into the old Central Station, and a cover version of George Formby's 'With My Little Stick of Blackpool Rock'. They told me they would miss Blackpool and I could see that they would. I told Mrs Harris about Lancashire, women and love, and she said that in Eastbourne they died of boredom.

I went off to the Tower. I'd somehow got this idea that the Ballroom was up at the top of it somewhere. It isn't, but don't let that put you off. 'See Naples and Die, but See Torquay First', went the old slogan, and I'd put the Tower Ballroom right up there with the Palmed Paradise of the West Country. What a place! Rococo? I should cocoa! Louis Quinze, Borromini, Bernini? Frank Matcham did more than that: columns, arches, twiddly bits, friezes and frescos, garlands, gold, scalloped and embossed tiers, painted ceiling, cherubs, gods, goddesses, lovers, clowns, clouds, chandeliers, the names of the great composers emblazoned along its length. Louis and the Italians would have been begging for mercy, but Frank, who'd done a few theatres in his time, including the London Coliseum and the Hackney Empire, pressed on. A palace, a temple for the people, and impossible to look at without thinking of all those people, like Eileen and Denis from Leigh, whose lives were set by a meeting on that mighty sprung floor, to the music of Bertini, or Jack Hylton or Ivy Benson. Duke Ellington played there, too, which doesn't seem quite right. In 1956, the Ballroom was badly damaged in a fire. The Wurlitzer had to be rebuilt and Matcham's work restored. When the Ballroom was reopened, the guests of honour were the people who had danced at its opening, nearly 60 years before. I rather liked the idea of that.

There weren't that many there the day I went. But it was sunny outside. The rain brings them in. Ballroom dancing during the day, big bands at night. Ballroom dancing to, of course, the Mighty Wurlitzer, the organ that comes up out of the stage, beneath the proscenium arch and its legend 'Bid Me Discourse and I Will Enchant Thine Ear'. Once, of course, it came up along with Reginald Dixon, Mr Blackpool, organist at the Tower for 40 years, whose signature tune was 'Oh, I Do Like to Be Beside the Seaside'. Today it was Phil Kelsall, who has quite a following, including Willie and Julia.

Willie and Julia were retired, from Manchester, and tiny. Willie was dressed in black shirt and trousers. Julia was in a long black skirt and a black-and-white patterned blouse. They hadn't met there, but they'd been coming for years, usually at the weekend, sometimes for a week, in at ten, out at five. Why? 'Everything,' said Julia. 'There's a nice atmosphere, and it's the music, it's music you want to dance to, and after 30 or 40 years, it's still the same.' Willie said you could catch them in the background, 'just a flash', on a film made to celebrate the Ballroom's centenary in 1994.

I asked Julia if I could have a dance. I don't remember much about it, probably because of the embarrassment; I remember that Phil was playing 'Are You Lonesome Tonight?' and that it was a waltz and we seemed to be going round in circles and that Julia was very good about it. 'You did very well,' she said. 'I've seen some terrible rows between couples out there,' said Willie. 'You didn't look down, which is good. Look down and you're lost.' Phil moved on to the Harry Lime Sequence Foxtrot. Behind the bar, a young waitress, dressed in the old Nippie fashion, black dress, white apron, began to dance on the spot. The next time I looked, she was out there on the floor, in uniform, dancing with a distinguished-looking silver-haired chap to 'Young At Heart'. Blimey, I thought, we're all in a Gracie Fields film!

28

Her name was Michelle and she was 24. She'd been working in the Ballroom for 18 months and she loved it. 'I like it here. It's nice, isn't it? Everyone's dead nice. They teach me to dance. There's Fred and Sandra, and a lovely old bloke called Joe, he's 85, he comes on his own since his wife died. It's great when they have the big events, too, like the world championships. They come from all over the world for that, the Far East, the lot. What do you want, love? Salmon and soft cheese? Just the one?' The last bit was to a customer. I went to have a chat with Michelle's recent partner, Roy. He was with his wife, Sophie. Roy had been born in Blackpool but had been away for 40 years, design engineering. But they'd come to the Ballroom and were hooked. 'You only have to walk in here and look at it,' said Sophie. 'It's a magical place, like something out of a fairy tale.' Now they were regulars, and Roy had learnt to dance. They had a son, they said, who was a record label manager, who looked after Dido, Faithless, people like that. What did he make of the parental passion? 'He thinks we're crackers,' said Roy.

There were a few people sitting on their own, widows and widowers, mostly widows, made even more lonely by all the empty seats around them and the sun outside. Like Joe, they used to come with their partners, and now they just sit. Sophie said it was a shame no one ever asked them to dance, very sad. I suppose I should have taken the hint, but I'm not sure that moving round in a shuffling circle with me would have added much to their memories, particularly if I stumbled all over them with my typically adroit questions as well. I told you I had my limitations as a journalist. My moment of truth came in the Azores, rushing to cover the honeymoon of the Duke and Duchess of York, when I had to stop to think about knocking a nun out of the way.

Michelle was doing the food and soft beverages. Ian was doing the bar. At night, he was a trumpeter in the big band. I asked him about Lancashire and women and love. 'That's a difficult one, that is,' he said. 'I've killed a few,' said a man at the side of the bar in a black leather jacket. Michelle said she wasn't sure that people believed in romance like that any more. Then the man in the leather jacket went up on stage, sat down and took over at the organ from Phil.

I swapped the San Remo for the Imperial, Blackpool's premier hotel, host to many a prime minister at party conference time, and more besides. Ah, the Imperial. Charles Dickens stayed there, you know. And Bill Clinton: 'I like Blackpool. The weather's great. And the town's . . . kinda sleazy, isn't it?' The Imperial has a bar dedicated to the prime ministers, with big pictures, framed newspapers, the lot. More to the point for me, it also has lots of en suite rooms with tellies and trouser presses, with taps and buttons just waiting.

First, though, I wanted to see a proper comic. Roy Chubby Brown was on at one of the piers, but I wasn't feeling quite strong enough for his Rabelaisian tendencies; and besides, he's from Yorkshire, and rather spoils my theory about there never having been any successful Yorkshire funny men. (All right, then, Keith Waterhouse, Barry Cryer and the *Bo Selecta* bloke as well. But the League of Gentlemen are a quarter Lancastrian, you know.) So, as recommended by Mr and Mrs Harris, I went off to the Number One Club in Bloomfield Road, near the football ground, where Brian Sharpe, from Rochdale, was doing his turn. The Number One was a working men's club and I had a slight difficulty with the man on reception about getting in without proof of affiliate membership. I wasn't too surprised when he told me he was a big fan of national identity cards.

Frank Matcham, I felt sure, would have liked the Number One, with its flecked, red, fitted carpet with 'Number One' woven into it, mirrored columns at the bar, ruched curtains, wallpaper and panels in varying shades and patterns of orange, red, green, blue, gold and beige ensuring that no space was left undecorated. There was a red dot-matrix announcement apparatus of a type I had also observed at Bernard Manning's Embassy Club in Manchester, with arrows pointing to a side room accompanied by the simple legend 'Pies'.

Ah, yes, pies. A word, here, perhaps, about Lancashire and food. There is certainly some excellent cuisine available, and you will travel far before you find a finer cheese than that on offer from Eric, very chatty, nice chap, at Ormskirk market every Thursday.

But there is also a generally robust attitude, a liking for the fast and unfussy fostered by generations of working women with limited cooking time; the first mass convenience food, fish and chips, appeared in Oldham before anywhere else; its first mate, the pie, particularly the meat and potato variety, remains revered, even though Europe now insists on it being called potato and meat to reflect more accurately the portion proportion. Wiganers are often referred to, slightlingly, as 'pie-eaters', but nobody seems quite sure why, as the rest of the county is equally keen on the individual piece of pastried paradise. There is some talk that the nickname's origin lies in the fact that Wiganers were the first back to work from the General Strike, and so had to eat humble pie, but that is confected. I do like, though, the way that the JJB stadium, the posh new ground for the rugby and soccer clubs, is known to everybody else as the Pie Dome.

And that's the thing about Lancs and food: they do like to laugh about it, probably because it helped a little when there wasn't much. You know about tripe; you might also know that the famous Liverpool stew is known as Blind Scouse when there isn't any meat in it. And black pudding, of course. 'I think it is a sacrilegious waste of good blood puddings,' said a horrified Frenchman witnessing the 141st World Black Pudding-Throwing Championships in Ramsbottom. They're making black-pudding ice cream now, too. But my favourite is still George Formby being asked at the Ritz in one of his films if he would like some salmon: 'All right, then, if you're opening a tin.'

Brian Sharpe came on stage. Brian, it was fair to say, belonged to the more aggressive Lancashire comic school typified by Bernard Manning rather than the whimsy of Formby or Laurel or Dodd. Hecklers, for example, were told, 'Hey, this isn't a double act. Shut it.' There were plenty of my-wife gags, mostly to do with her size: 'She wears a g-rope'; her domestic shortcomings: 'We haven't had a clean plate in the house since the dog died. I saw a cockroach in the kitchen the other day sucking a Rennie'; and her looks: 'She's a treasure. Someone asked me the other day where I'd dug her up from.'

There were some very old racist jokes, but nothing to match the Manning bravura in the offence department. When I saw him, a few years ago now, a well-known light entertainer was spending his last days bravely raising money for cancer research. Manning leant on the microphone stand, took a deep draw from his cigarette, paused for a beat, and then said, 'Fuck Roy Castle.' Michael Barrymore told me once that to be a really big success, the audience had to like you, a theory his subsequent career was to prove fairly spectacularly. I don't know where that leaves Manning. The comic who managed to combine his, how shall we say, blunt and direct approach with whimsy and loveability was Les Dawson, though, in the way of them all, not much of his act stands up to time. But Les would have understood about Balzac; Les had his time in a garret, in Paris, trying to become a great writer as well. No, it's true. I wasn't so sure about Brian. I asked him for a quick chat, but he was rushing off to his next spot, so I bought one of his tapes and said I would phone him. Then I went back to the Imperial. I wouldn't have said it was quiet, but, in the bar, one of the other three patrons was making a close study of the newspaper on the wall reporting the death of Churchill.

The Tower, the Winter Gardens, all the piers, and much else in the British leisure industry are owned by an ex-bricklayer and diesel grease-wiper of pensionable age from Chorley called

Trevor Hemmings, who is worth around £700 million, keeps a collection of vintage Rolls-Royces in a barn and loves racehorses almost as much as his privacy. Mr Hemmings, the rarely seen figure behind Blackpool, the new Las Vegas, follows in a line of slightly unorthodox Blackpool entrepreneurs with the requisite touch of whimsy. William Cocker, the first Mayor, who introduced the Illuminations and built the Winter Gardens, was a retired doctor; Sir John Bickerstaffe, who built the Tower, affected a white sailor's cap on most occasions, social and business.

But for poignancy, apt and as broad as the place itself, the palm must go to the Rev. William Thornber, the town's first vicar and enthusiastic populariser, who ended up in an asylum, unhinged by 'intemperance and the breaking of his marriage vows'. (Blackpool's most famous clergyman was, of course, Harold Davidson, the defrocked Rector of Stiffkey, who, wearing only a barrel, protested the innocence and evangelical intent of his association with London's ladies of the night right up until the day he was eaten by a lion. But that was in Skegness; he should have stayed in Lancs, much gentler.)

Nothing like that for Mr Hemmings, or his Leisure Parcs team, who operate from a warren up in the Winter Gardens and have a room with a mock-up of the plans for the front, complete with the Pharoah's Palace resort hotel, the first casino, 70 tables, 2,500 slot machines, 4,000-capacity conference facilities, a 3,000-seat theatre, 500 rooms, 2,000 new jobs, £100-million cost. I thought it looked terrific, lots of big Blackpooly sphinxes and that sort of thing.

There is also lots of talk of creating environments and holistic master plans, of alleviating unemployment and of spin-off benefits in tackling crime and deprivation. It is, Mr Hemmings and his people believe, time for a big gesture. Blackpool should lead British tourism into the future, showing once again the spirit of risk and adventure and innovation that had created and evolved Blackpool. There is all this affection for Blackpool, they believe, and it is time to cash in on it.

They point to Baltimore, Atlantic City and Biloxi, all places that have regenerated themselves through casinos; why, in Biloxi, so much money was coming into the place that they were now pressed to find new civic amenities to spend it on. And then there was the East, the Japanese: they will come. They already come for the ballroom-dancing championships, very big, and they love the golf at Lytham nearby; they have the right game for a laugh, karaoke, kiss me quick attitude.

It would have taken someone far more cynical than me to resist this rich concoction of statistics, jargon, vision and optimism. But I did manage to ask about the climatic differences between Blackpool and the North American role models. This, too, was not a problem: 'In Las Vegas, they go inside to escape the heat. Here, they will go inside to escape . . .' Of course!

I left the future and went off for a wander, still a little worried and sentimental for the old and present Blackpool, the one that is slowly dying. Blackpool Borough Council has its own regeneration plans, more concerned with family entertainment than casinos, with a giant aquarium and such, but I wasn't sure this would be any more welcoming for Petulengro and Levengro and the Pigeon Fanciers' Weekend; or the Ford Day, organised by a delivery driver from Preston, when all these owners of old Cortinas and Escorts and other such unregarded old numbers park their cars down on the lower prom; or the Deaf and Dumb Weekend, come to that, which is always good for a bit of trouble when they get in drink.

By now I was up among the slightly posher guest houses, with their illuminated fronts, and licensed lounges, and huge gilt-framed prints with fancy downlighters, and plaster columns and porticos, and busts, and lamps involving all manner of undraped females holding up all manner of torches, and hanging baskets and every kind of decking and crazy paving in the short space between front step and pavement, below the bright and rigid plastic awnings over each window decorated with messages offering different enticements: 'Small pets and guide dogs – all welcome', 'We just spoil you', 'Free showers'.

Back a bit of a way into the streets up from the Tower, opposite the Comrades' Club and next to the dentist's, was a terraced boarding house with a sign outside reading 'Shirley House. Fantasy Bedrooms. Visit Camelot, Japan, Morocco, Egypt, Pompeii and St Lucia'. And you can, you can. Stella, the landlady, took me round a jamboree of striking stencils and painted tracings, a pot-pourri of beads and drapings and converted Christmas trappings, a frantic bonanza of colour and car boot sales. Here was the wardrobe as mummy case, there as bathing hut. You could dream Arthurian dreams under mounted plastic armour in Camelot, or slumber under a sari-draped ceiling in old Baghdad ('Careful of the flying carpet, don't touch that old lamp!' cries Stella). Here and in another house full of holiday flats round the corner, her husband Geoff does the basics and Stella adds the crowning touches, often at four o'clock in the morning, to opera. 'Looking for something different? Stay in Blackpool and see the world!' says their brochure, but times are hard here, too, apart from the Lights Weekends and other special occasions, including, of course, the Pigeon Fanciers' Weekend: 'We've had £12,000 worth of pigeons going coo-coo in here,' said Geoff. 'I had to hide one in the cellar so as this bloke's wife wouldn't know he'd bought it.' Stella said, 'Tell them that if they could start building that Pharoah's Palace, we'd be bloody grateful!' They could do worse than take on Stella as design consultant.

I phoned Brian, the comic from the Number One Club. He might have been from Rochdale, but he was not a great analyst of his art. You did your stuff, and they either liked you or they didn't. Blackpool? Blackpool, he thought, was finished. He knew where he was going to be in ten years' time: in Benidorm, lots of work out there, that was the future. I walked back to the Imperial along the front. Somewhere along here was the souvenir shop where Harry Corbett bought Sooty. His wife dabbed the glove puppet's paws in the grate, hence the name. Did I say glove puppet? Harry kept him in a box with airholes, you know. He did. I went into a shop to buy, yes, finally, some rock. I asked the shopkeeper, a man of senior years, if it wasn't less popular these days, what with health consciousness and all that. 'It's more popular!' said the man. 'Full of lots of good stuff, like glucose!' And there was more: without changing the rest of a rather pokerish face, he suddenly leant forward and bared his teeth. 'Look at these,' he cried. 'All my own!' And they quite clearly were. Ah, Blackpool!

Chapter Two

The King and Ince

Our True History At Last Revealed

Camelot lies just off the M6. It's between Standish and Chorley, up from Wigan. If you're approaching from the south, you will pass the Xmas Light Centre, the Dream Angling, Tackle and Bait shop, Singleton's fish and chip shop, the Alison Arms – 'Grumpy Hour 5 till 7' – and a large display of conservatories.

Camelot near Wigan? Why not? It's a good spot for a theme park. And it seems a good theme park, too. My son reported that the Excalibur ride, a mighty revolving beam with giddying counterbalances, was terrific; and this, I should tell you, is a son who has braved the Dragon Falls at Chessington World of Adventures, and they're 60 feet high. I myself quite enjoyed the Holland's pies on offer and my other son was much taken with the Jousting Knights, presented in association with Rollover, 'the best hot dog in the world', featuring King Arthur, Sir Lancelot, Sir Percival, Sir Gawaine and Sir Mordred, and a couple of rude mechanicals, Jess and Mad Edgar.

King Arthur's accent was disappointingly non-Lancastrian,

but Mad Edgar more than compensated. Nor was he constrained by any slavish adherence to historical accuracy or dramatic integrity, seeing his role rather as that of compère. 'Where are you from?' he asked one of the female spectators sitting in the large grandstand alongside the lists, across from The Once And Future King. 'South Shields,' she replied. 'Really?' said Mad Edgar. 'My brother's working in South Shields. He's a burglar.' Jess and Mad Edgar did a spot of tumbling business. Jess fell to the ground. 'I've broken me bum,' he shouted. 'There's a big crack right down the middle!' I was enjoying myself. My wife said, 'There's nothing like a bit of Northern humour to get you going, is there?' And she was right, of course.

The tourney, billed as a battle of good against evil for the prize of the Sword of Avalon, pitted Lancelot and Percival against Mordred and Gawaine. I particularly admired the way Mordred picked a bit of debris out of his nose and flicked it into the audience. He was rude to Lady Juliana about her dancing horse, too: 'Dancing horses make me sick. There's only one thing worse than a dancing horse, and that's smelly, disgusting rancid little kids!' Nor did he fight fair; but to no avail. After some very ill treatment of Percival, much of it going against the groin, and some fine horsemanship on all sides, good triumphed. 'You know what you can do with your Sword of Avalon!' sneered Mordred, which I suppose we should have expected.

All good stuff. In the gift shop, they were selling plastic AK-47 assault rifles for three pounds. There were fridge magnets next to the rifles. One of them read, 'I feel like I'm parked in a parallel universe'. Indeed. The Arthurian tradition had not been entirely forgotten, though; there were some plastic swords for sale as well. A five-year-old girl seized one and approached her father, brandishing it. 'Say your prayers!' she shouted.

Why is the Camelot theme park called Camelot? The PR lady wasn't absolutely sure. She said it was all to do with the original owner, John Rigby. I got in touch with Mr Rigby. Years before, he said, this old professor from Manchester had contacted him about the early settlement of Benedictine monks on the site of the big leisure complex he was running, Park Hall; he'd told him, too, about the legend that Arthur had fought a famous battle here, on the River Douglas, which flows through Wigan. So when Mr Rigby decided to open a theme park, Camelot was the obvious name for it. But, no, he couldn't remember the name of the professor and he would be long dead now, in any event.

Thus do the mists of time cover and smother history in the course of just 25 years, in the Information Age. And how much more so must it be over the past 2,000 years? Rightly do historians point out that in the written histories of Britain, in the epic of these isles, Lancashire rarely receives even a passing nod until the wheels begin to turn and the smoke begins to curl and the Revolution is here.

Before that? A land of myth and magic, sheltered and bounded by hills and waters, where the Celts lingered, the Romans dallied, and even the Vikings dreamed; saved by a great King and his knights from the thump of the dull Saxon plod, ripe for Norman French nurturing and romance. Even the county's name is bewitching. Not that dissimilar, I would suggest, from 'Kashmir', the dying breath of regret for lost beauty that fell from the lips of the great Mogul emperor Jehangir. And consider this: that name, Lancashire, is derived from Lancaster, the Roman camp on the River Lune. Ignore those perverse people who would argue that Lune comes from the supposedly ancient British word 'Lon', meaning health-giving; it's not the River Lon, is it? No, Lune is Latin, from Luna, the Moon. Yes, this is the County of the Moon; the Lune is, of course, Moon River. And there is more, as you will discover.

Go on, mock if you like. They laughed at Von Daniken, too, didn't they? And at that chap who worked out that the Mayans believed that the world would end in 2012, and all the other people who've come up with fascinating theories about the

Pyramids, and Polynesia, and Atlantis. I've got evidence that is just as convincing as anything they've served up. I have. Stay, and wonder.

Little is known about Lancashire before the Romans arrived, except that it was fertile and, though this is scarcely believable, slightly warmer than it is today. Recorded history begins, fittingly, with a woman: Cartimandua, Queen of the Brigantes, the dominant northern tribe at the time of the third coming of the Romans, in 43 AD, designed to make Claudius look as good as the first Caesar, who had invaded twice, but inconclusively, despite all that flashy boat-burning. The Claudian invasion was the one so stoutly resisted by the brave Caractacus, who fought a stirring guerrilla campaign on the Welsh borders for more than six years before eventually being brought to battle and defeated. He then fled north, to urge Cartimandua to rise up and hurl the foreign invaders from our shores. Cartimandua handed him over to the Romans.

That's a fine way to behave, you might say. To me, though, this is the first recorded example of that strain of great common sense which distinguishes the women of Lancashire when confronted by some impractical male dreamer. Think of Gracie Fields, Thora Hird, Hilda Ogden, Mrs Pankhurst, Vera Duckworth, and you will see what I mean. A bedraggled and emotional Ancient Briton, woad running dreadfully, turns up and suggests that you take on the most impressive fighting machine the world has seen and will see for at least another 1,500 years: what would you do? Exactly. You'd tell him not to be so bloody daft. And Caractacus got his 15 minutes of fame in Rome, successfully and eloquently pleading for his life; and he lived there happily ever after. So?

But then, sadly, that other leading characteristic of the Lancashire woman, the inability to pick the right man (see Fields, Ogden, Duckworth) came into play. Cartimandua's husband, Venutius, seems to have been something of a bore, forever complaining about how ghastly the Romans were, notwithstanding the luxurious lifestyle that had become his as a result of his wife's eminently sensible decision to befriend the invaders. So, rather in the manner of the landlady taking up with the potman, the Queen cast Venutius to one side in favour of Vellocatus, his armour-bearer. Any of us, I think, could see that this would end in tears. Venutius rose up against the Queen; the Romans rescued her and took her to Chester; the great Agricola then subdued Venutius and took over the North. Nothing more is heard of them. I'd like to think that they ended up retired on the Fylde coast, still bickering, but affectionately and out of habit, about her fancy man and those bloody Romans. I fear, though, that she died of love, exiled in Chester, a dreadful fate for anyone.

I'll add a quick note here, if I may: there are those who would argue that Cartimandua was from Yorkshire, with her capital at Almondbury, or Aldborough, or York, or Ingleborough, or Stanwick. But it seems inconceivable that, given the choice, she would not have preferred the west. Certainly, current archaeological thinking supports this view, as the evidence found at those eastern sites is inconsistent with a major pre-Roman settlement. The surviving texts also suggest that her capital was close to Wales.

We owe this first Lancastrian insight to Tacitus, who was, of course, Agricola's son-in-law. After him, the mists close in again, although we can make some informed conjectures. Here is this fertile plain to the south, with plentiful woods and rivers to the north. But no reports, no news. It's the usual media thing, isn't it? Tacitus and the rest of them are buzzing round like anybody's business when it's death and battle and rebellion, but when it's peace, they don't want to know. They're off with Boudicca and people like that. And if you've got yourself a small piece of paradise in a very dodgy world, you're not going to broadcast it, are you?

Let me give you a couple of examples. The Parisi were a tribe to be found in the Humber area at the beginning of the second century AD. Little is heard of them thereafter. They were a branch of the Parisii, from the banks of the Seine, who have given their name to Paris. Have you been to Hull? And don't forget, too, that round there was about to get really very crowded, with incomers of all sorts pouring in, some of them, frankly, barbaric. Would a sophisticated tribe, keen on cuisine and that sort of thing, hang around? Whither would it make its way? I don't want to labour the obvious affinities, so I'll just say that a liking for big iron towers has got to be genetic. Next, the IX Legion, the legendary lost legion, the one which left York for an unknown but supposedly hideous fate beyond the Wall at the hands of the Picts, or the Scots, or possibly both. Historians now categorically dismiss the legend; so where did they all go? Sure, a few names appear on later rolls of other legions – but the rest of them? Precisely.

Then there is another legend: Valentia. This was the fifth Roman province in Britain, surrounded by all manner of doubt and mystery. No one knows for sure why it was founded, or even where it was, exactly. The orthodox view is that it was created in the fourth century in response to a failed revolt by Roman dissidents in Britain and that it was named after the Emperor Valentinian. There have been powerful arguments that it was located in what is now Cumbria.

My research, though, imaginatively interpreted, leads me to an entirely different conclusion. I believe that Valentia was the name given to an area slightly to the south and blessed with abundant natural resources and a harmonious but heterogeneous population attracted by its reputation and inspired by its unique ambience of fertile plain, magical woods, clear waters and bracing sea air. I believe it was named not for an emperor, but for a saint: St Valentine, fused Christian and Pagan symbol of love, both spiritual and worldly, his feast day an excuse to celebrate the old Roman mid-February fertility festival of Lupercalia. Lupercalia, Lancashire. The County of Love, home of Britain's first hippies – Britons, Romans, fey Hibernians from across one water, the gentler sort of European from across another – a kind of perpetual Woodstockish Wakes Week.

But even here, time passes. And now the Empire has fallen; large men with beards are everywhere. The noise, my dear, and the people. Where shines the last light of truth, beauty and acceptable personal habits? Scotland? Wales? The West Country? Surely not. Whence will spring a leader of noble valour, but a bit of a dreamer, with trouble at home? Where else?

Arthur. You won't need me to rehearse the legend yet again. And I think you will accept that it has some basis in fact, beneath the copious imaginings of Geoffrey of Monmouth, Wace, Layamon, Chrétien de Troyes, Malory and whoever wrote that dreadful film with Richard Gere in it. I must say, too, that Lerner and Loewe's *Camelot* is not one of their best. I yield to no one in my admiration of *My Fair Lady*, but, really, look at this, from the title song:

> In short, there's simply not
> A more congenial spot
> For happy ever aftering
> Than here in Camelot.

Quite. Anyway, we might agree that, around 500, a British leader mounted a spirited campaign against the invasion from Europe by Angles, Saxons and Jutes. He seems to have been a cavalry leader, implementing the nearly forgotten skills of the Roman auxiliaries at skirmishing and sudden strikes. Forget Geoffrey of Monmouth's fanciful twelfth-century chronicling of an Arthurian invasion of France and a defeat of the Roman Emperor, Lucius; instead we shall rely on Ptolemy of Alexandria and two other famed chroniclers, Gildas, the sixth-century monk, and Nennius, the ninth-century scholar. Ptolemy wrote of the Port of the Setantii, one of the native tribes based around the Ribble; he also mentioned one of their settlements, Camulodunum, a name with a familiar ring to it.

It is all too easy to wander ever more deeply into the fog of legend, the dark caverns of conjecture and the shifting sands of supposition. But the later Welsh bards referred to a warrior called Seithennin; this is now thought to be a misinterpretation of the name of the tribe, the Setantii; and this Seithennin had a son called 'Menestry', which, of course, means 'Cupbearer' in Brythonic Celt. How much more evidence do we need that Arthur was a chief of the Setantii, and that the Setantii were in possession of the Holy Grail? Exactly.

Gildas wrote of the crucial battle at Mount Badon which checked the Saxon encroachment; Nennius has Arthur fighting 12 battles against the invaders, the last of which was at Badon. The locations for the battles have been given: Gloucester, Wigan, Blackrod, Penrith, another site near Wigan on the banks of the River Douglas, Lincoln, Ettrick Forest, Caer Gwynion, Leith, Dumbarton, Brixham and Badon, which is said to have been near Bath. Many have commented on the huge geographical sweep of these battles and argued that Arthur was a restless, questing guerrilla leader; very few have noticed that they are quite clearly mounted from, and in protection of, one particular area: Lancashire. As the Lancashire author Stan Jones has pointed out, to very little acclaim, in an excellent book, most undeservedly out of print (my sister-in-law got me Skelmersdale Library's copy), the Port of the Setantii and Camulodonum, or Camunlodunum, or, most popularly, Camelot, are one and the same place: Lancaster, which was known by both names, Celtic and Latin, rather in the manner of modern Londonderry. Centuries of argument and fierce debate, theory and counter-theory, may be over. The only wonder is the question in Mr Jones's title: *Was Lancaster Camelot?*

Nor should we be too surprised at the prominence of Wigan. Over the years large numbers of ancient weapons have been unearthed in and around the town, particularly at Hasty Knoll and Poolbridge and Blackrod. Tradition still maintains that the first battle, at Blackrod, was so bloody that 'the Douglas was

44

crimsoned with blood all the way to Wigan', some five miles away. In the old Lancashire vernacular, to give a man a 'wigan' was to give him a good thrashing. Even today the form of greeting known as a 'Wigan Kiss' involves the enthusiastic contact of greeter's forehead with greetee's nose.

Less familiar to me was the research undertaken by the eighteenth-century Mancunian historian, the Rev. John Whitaker, into another aspect of the Nennius account, the chronicler's placing of the River Douglas in the region of Linuis. Scholars agree that 'Linuis' is a barbarous Latinisation of the Gaelic 'Linn', the Welsh 'Lyn' and the Anglo-Saxon 'Lin', meaning sea or lake. Whitaker posited the proximity to Wigan of the then far larger lake now known as Martin Mere; and pointed out, too, that the name Linuis survives as Ince, seven miles from Wigan. This led the Reverend to a conclusion even more germane to our purpose: Sir Lancelot of the Lake, one of the world's most notorious lovers, fabled swordsman and poly-balladed heart-breaker, was . . . from Lancashire!

One must be wary, though, of the enthusiasm that invades, rather than informs, scholarship. I have been to Martin Mere and, pleasant bird sanctuary though it now is, with numerous and varied avians on view, including the Abyssinian Blue-Winged Goose, the Bufflehead and the European Shoveller, it did not speak to me of noble dreams and sacred quests crushed by lust and frailty, nor of mystery, magic and mists, although the refreshment facilities are excellent. If, too, I were in search of the lost sea-girt lands of Lyonesse and Avalon, I would not necessarily start in Douglas, Isle of Man. I have seen passengers disembark from the Isle of Man ferries at the Pier Head, Liverpool, and they did not look as if they had partaken in a mystical experience. This, though, was before I knew. And I have not yet been to Ince. But I shall.

So now the King slept. His last great victory had checked the Saxon advance, channelled it away from his Lancashire heartland into other areas, and permitted the slow, gentle and tolerant assimilation that marked and distinguished the County of the Moon. The evidence is there. For example, historians have long regarded Aethelfrith of Northumbria's victory at Chester over the Britons of Wales in the early 600s as the moment when the English drove a wedge of conquered land between the Celts of the west and the north. But the place names of Lancashire suggest a quieter, longer and more peaceful process, with English and Celtic settlements jostled up against one another in larger numbers than anywhere else in England.

There are a lot of Norse names, too. But before you start conjuring up horns, pillage, bad breath and worse, I should remind you that my wife was born in Oslo and is forever telling me that the Vikings just had a bad press from bored monks with overactive imaginations; and that they were, in reality, merely peace-loving traders with a direct negotiating manner. In particular, I shall never forget the look on her face when she came to me brandishing a newspaper cutting reporting that a pair of spectacles had been found in a Viking grave.

Besides, the Norse in Lancs arrived from Ireland in the late ninth or early tenth century, fleeing the iron, unifying hand of Harald Fairhair, King of Norway. And, naturally, Irish Vikings were far more easy-going than the average straight-out-of-the-longboat-and-at-it Viking: 'Sure, you carry on now . . . '

Throughout all the clashes and struggles of Roman and Briton, Northumbrian and Mercian, Saxon and Viking, Saxon and Norman, the land that would become Lancashire remained just out of reach of the various power bases, untouched by anything more than the odd skirmish and raid. Lancashire, lacuna. Curious; some might even say magical.

It was the Conquest which saw Lancashire formally united for the first time, as a gift from the Conqueror to Roger of Poitou, third son of Roger de Montgomery, commander of a wing at Hastings. Unlike the rest of the country, the north-west had not been divided into shires before 1066; as late as 1182, a royal clerk was writing, '*Lancastra, quod non erat ei locus in Northumberland*' ('Lancashire, because there is no place for it in Northumberland'). The land beyond, unclassifiable. A Duchy with no Duke save the King or Queen, held directly by the Crown – unique.

Note, once again, the crucial French influence, to be echoed and imprinted over the years. We do not know much about Roger, but what we do displays much of the Lancastrian male talent for whimsical vacillation, often settled by a robust unilateral intervention from the distaff side, who are certainly likely to die of waiting for a firm decision. One moment he is in revolt against the king, the next he's not. Twice Lancashire was confiscated, before, finally, Roger seems to have returned to Poitou, where apparently they were, and still are, rather keen on the bagpipes, although how much that influenced his decision is not recorded. We clearly need to know more about Lady Poitou. And while we're talking about bagpipes, according to Lord Dacre, the eminent historian whom we shall meet again later, it was a Lancastrian who inspired the kilt. Thomas Rawlinson, the ironmaster from Furness with a furnace at Glengarry, around 1730 commissioned a regimental tailor in Inverness to design a less restrictive piece of dress for his workers. You will, I think, be less amazed by such things by the end of this book. Lancashire influences are all-pervasive. We invented the Teasmade, as well, you know.

The Red Rose is interesting, too. It was chosen by Edmund Crouchback, son of Henry III and younger brother of Edward I, as his emblem. There had been talk of his becoming King of Sicily, but far greater things beckoned: in 1276 he was created first Earl of Lancaster. He is said to have alighted upon the red rose after a visit to France, country of his mother, Eleanor of Provence. Whatever, it was an apt and inspiring selection, as the red rose is the flower of Aphrodite, of Venus, of Love, created from the tears of the goddess and the blood of her dying lover Adonis, acme of masculine beauty. Red roses garlanded the gardens of Babylon;

wreaths were laid and petals strewn on tombs in Persia, Egypt and India, most famously on those of Jehangir and Omar Khayyám, poet of the rose, employer of their ancient symbolism of mystery and magic, sacred and profane, taken up by shadowy and fanciful societies like the Knights of the Rosy Cross. Just the thing, as you will be beginning to learn, for Lancashire.

Right, let's get on. The important thing about this popular history and exciting new theory business, I've noticed, is the big sweep, the broad brush, and the repeated use of repetition as corroboration. So now I'm going to repeat my theory and sweep my brush back to the fifteenth century. Lancashire. Place apart. Magical. All comers welcomed, bewitched and beguiled. County of the Moon. Lost Roman province of Valentia, dedicated to peace and love. Arthur was from there. And Lancelot. Home of strong women and whimsical men. Big French influence.

I suppose, too, we'd better glance at the Wars of the Roses, although they do seem a bit difficult to grasp for popular historians such as myself. How come, for example, York was a Lancastrian stronghold? Tricky. And even I have noticed that not one battle in the Wars of the Roses took place in Lancashire. The last battle, though, does lead to one of my points, so we'll stop for a moment. Bosworth Field. Richard III has 10,000 men; Henry Tudor has 5,000. Then there is Thomas, Lord Stanley, the most powerful man in Lancashire, who, with his men, stands some distance away. Can he decide who he's going to fight for? Of course he can't, even though Richard threatens to execute his son. Eventually, when the battle is almost over, he throws in his lot with Henry, who makes him the first Earl of Derby. This is generally portrayed as the mark of a clever card-player, biding his time, but to me it is quite clearly an early example of the talent of the Lancashire male for dreamy dithering. You should also know that his wife, Margaret Beaufort, though not from Lancs, was a very strong woman indeed and, crucially, Henry's mother.

Contrast the behaviour of a later member of the family, who

steadfastly withstood a Roundhead siege for many months during the next civil war. But this, of course, was a woman, and French with it: Charlotte de Tremouille, Countess of Derby, daughter of the Duc de Thouars and Prince of Palmont, scorner of a Roundhead Colonel from Wigan, even if he did have a mighty mortar. Her husband, the Earl, meanwhile, managed to get his head chopped off at Bolton. Charlotte lived to see the Restoration. She didn't die of love, but she was buried next to the headless corpse.

So. I could go on. And I do. But that's in another chapter, in which I prove beyond the slightest doubt, the slightest doubt, that William Shakespeare owed everything to the years spent in this magical land of eclectic influence and unusual passions. Now, though, it is time to get the hands inky and the feet dirty and pester Lancastrians who have done absolutely nothing to deserve it as I pursue hard evidence to transform my persuasive theories into glorious fact. Now is the time for a spot of fieldwork. Now is the time to visit the fabled home of Lancelot. Now is the time to go to Ince.

I think it's fair to say that there wasn't much sign of troubadouring and the like on the afternoon I went. At first sight, Ince seemed much like any other of the red-bricked Lancashire towns that show all the signs of hard living and a harder past. The only thing separating it from Wigan now is the Leeds–Liverpool canal. I went into the library and asked the librarian behind the counter if she was aware that the mighty Lancelot might have hailed from here. 'I've not been around very long,' she said, 'so I'm not the best person to ask.' She went into the back to see if any of the other librarians might know. 'It doesn't seem to ring any bells with anybody,' she said, suggesting I had a look at the Local History section.

I did, but there was nothing about Lancelot, although I did learn that the Rose Bridge Colliery had been one of Britain's deepest. There was nothing, either, about the theory that the 'Makerfield' in Ince-in-Makerfield and Ashton-in-Makerfield derives from 'maserfeld', the Anglo-Saxon word for 'battlefield', and relates specifically to the great battle of 642 known as Maserfeld, in which the saintly Christian king of Northumbria, Oswald, was slain by the forces of the pagan Penda, King of Mercia. A great barrow south of Ince and Ashton was opened in 1843 and found to contain nothing but the imprint of a body, which some claimed had been that of Penda's brother, Eawa. Professional scruples insist on my noting that Oswestry – Oswald's Tree – over in Shropshire is a more favoured choice for the king's last stand (actually, they cut him down as he knelt in prayer). And I must say I agree, as I suspect the Lancs barrow may well have been the resting place of Arthur. (Local legend also nominates both Alfred the Great, in a golden crown and silver coffin, and Robin Hood, but I wouldn't like to attract accusations of overstating Lancashire's claims.)

A good rule of journalistic inquiry is never to neglect the local post office. I put the Lancelot theory to the lady behind the general counter. 'That would explain why they're always fighting round here,' she said. The postmaster, a genial man in glasses, was intrigued. 'It would be very good for the area if that turned out to be true,' he said, clearly following my train of thought, which had on board at least an annual Lancelot Festival, with visits from the lads up the road at Camelot. 'But,' he said, as wistfully as a postmaster gets, 'I've never heard of it.'

I wondered if he had heard of Poolbridge, in Wigan, where, in 1735, when they were linking the Douglas with a new canal, they found, the Rev. Whitaker wrote, 'The ground everywhere containing the remains of men and horses . . . the point of land on the south side of the Douglas, which lies immediately fronting the scene of the last engagement, is now denominated by the Parson's Meadow; and tradition very loudly reports a battle to have been fought in it.'

He hadn't heard of Poolbridge, but suggested I try Poolstock, where there was a bridge over the canal. I went to Poolstock and found a lock rather than a bridge. The man in the old lock-keeper's cottage said he was moving. He'd liked it there, he said, but he'd never heard of a battle or seen any ghosts. The next rule of journalistic inquiry is if the post office fails, try the local filling station. But no one there had heard of Parson's Meadow. I went to look at the maps for sale. A man who had been buying petrol came up and said he was a delivery driver in the area and wondered if he could help. That's what I mean about Lancs: they are warm, friendly people. I told him I was looking for the site of a battle King Arthur had fought in Wigan, and he said, 'Well, you learn something new every day,' and made himself scarce, rather quickly, I thought.

But it was there, on the large-scale map: Parson's Meadow, still a big piece of common, going down to the banks of the Douglas. Dusk was drawing in as I walked along, wondering that such an open area of scrubland so close to the town centre should have survived everything that the last two centuries could throw at it. It seemed pretty atmospheric, too, although I'm not great at that sort of thing. I once visited the Healthy Islands (Iles du Salut) off French Guiana, better and more justly known by the name of one of them, Devil's Island, where I stood in the ruins of the little sanatorium in which desperate men ended their days in crazed gibbering, and where, amid the bougainvillea and the noise that passes for tropical silence, I felt absolutely nothing. That night, in the Guianan capital, Cayenne, where the pepper comes from, I was dining off crocodile (not bad, as it happens) when the Foreign Legion marched smartly past, singing. 'They seem happy,' I remarked to my host. 'They're going to the brothel,' he said.

There was no one about on Parson's Meadow, although I could just make out something in the gloom, which turned out to be a tethered black-and-white horse. A horse grazing in the middle of Wigan: now will you believe me about the romance of Lancs? I got a little closer to check that it wasn't a unicorn, and then moved down to the bank where once mighty armies had clashed. Asda was at one end now, the bus station at the other. The Douglas swept round the bus station rather well, though, carrying a lone McDonald's container at quite a jaunty lick. I walked back. A two-carriage train trundled away to the right, up on an elevated section, and I remembered the Ray Bradbury story about the knights who charge the dragon at night and the train driver who sees two knights in his lights.

I interviewed Bradbury once, to very little effect. I don't think writers like to give too much away; they'd rather write it themselves. I can't remember anything of note that Lawrence Durrell, Mordecai Richler, Wilfred Thesiger or Anthony Burgess told me, except that Burgess asked me to be kind, which seemed a bit rich. I can remember Anita Brookner's unspoken but vivid reaction when I hurried in late and sat there sweating, but not much else. I remember Norman Mailer saying, as he showed me out of his hotel room and ushered *The Times* in, 'Gentlemen, now I know how a whore feels'; I remember Gore Vidal's reply when he was asked who was doing better in the election campaign, Labour or Tory: 'I did not come to Lilliputia with a measuring stick'; I remember, as well, much later, thinking that the two remarks might not have been entirely spontaneous. I'll tell you about Anthony Powell later. Meanwhile, I should also mention that I once interviewed A.J.P. Taylor, inspirer of this book, but it was before I read his bit about Balzac and Lancashire, and I can't recall anything he said, either, although I do remember his mix of crotchet and twinkle, as he sat hunched in a chair in a little house in north London. This might be the time, as well, to reveal that in my translation, Lady Arabella says it is the county where women can, rather than do, die of love, but that's obviously down to some cynical Southern translator.

George Orwell, though. I wonder if he would have been kinder to Wigan if he'd known about its Arthurian connections.

Probably not. Rather too earnest for me, George. And things were bad enough in Wigan, then, without having to pretend, as he did, that his ghastly lodgings over the tripe shop were typical. But Wigan has its revenge, with a fittingly good joke. Wigan Pier is now a themed experience and the headquarters of the North-West Tourist Board. Best of all, the pub there is called, yes, The Orwell. Did you know that Lionel Blair used to have a dog named Eric, in tribute? Amazing.

I was brought back to Parson's Meadow sharpish by a hooded figure cycling past in his tracksuit top. It was quite dark by now. The horse was still there. Two mallards suddenly took off from the water, honking with cartoon laughter. I recovered eventually. Forget Devil's Island, Parson's Meadow is the place.

My next stop, Blackrod, sounded much more Arthurianly promising than Wigan, but wasn't, although my visit was of some help to Mr and Mrs Hunt of Bolton, no longer in the prime of life, whose car had broken down just by the bridge over the Douglas. I was able to lend them my mobile so they could call for help from their garage. Not exactly top knight-errant stuff, I grant you, but the Douglas wasn't up to much, either – hardly the mighty stream which had been crimsoned with blood to Wigan, although I was pretty sure this was the right place, as it was called, with suitable echo, Grimeford Lane.

A woman was walking her dog down the lane, which is in the countryside between Blackrod (an old colliery town, whose name, meaning 'bleak clearing', is less apt than it was) and Grimeford. She hadn't heard about Arthur, but suggested trying her friend up the road, who knew all about local history. He had red cheeks, a flat cap, a stout stick and two collies, and he was about to take them all out for a walk. He wasn't impressed. 'That,' he said, 'is a lot of nonsense, absolutely. I'm sorry, I can't help you. I've never heard of it, and if I had, I wouldn't give it any credence. That's a lot of nonsense, is that.' I should have asked him if he was from Yorkshire, originally.

It can be hard, research, especially when the story is 1,500 years old. Old stories. I had a world exclusive once, you know: the true identity of Jack the Ripper, long before the recent rush, original documentation, pencilled note by the top policeman involved. Everyone at the *Daily Telegraph* was so impressed they didn't use it for two days, and then nobody took any notice, probably because it was a mad Pole no one had ever heard of. Ah, well. I telephoned Wigan Library to ask about Arthur. The charming lady I spoke to sounded a bit dubious, but said she would get back to me.

I, in the meantime, was off to the even more promisingly named Anglezarke, up beyond Blackrod and Grimeford. Part of the West Pennine Moors, it lies next to Rivington, former outpost of the domain of the Soap King, William Lever, Lord Leverhulme, of Unilever, Bolton, Wigan and the world, hard-seller, riser from nothing and at 4.30 in the morning until the day he died, begetter and purveyor of Sunlight Soap, philanthropist, model-village founder and, here, high above Lancs, constructor of follied gardens and a ruined reconstruction of Liverpool Castle. Here, too, are the reservoirs that help water Liverpool, with the extra calm that a seething, heaving final destination always lends.

My interest in the moor, though, predated the soap and water, and had been engaged by two particularly interesting pieces of information in Mr Kenneth Fields' fascinating book, *A Journey Through Lancashire*.

The first was that the Bronze Agers who had settled up here were from the Mediterranean. Of course! The second was that, much later, the Knights Hospitallers of St John of Jerusalem exercised jurisdiction and privileges in the area, including the working of some mines. Excellent. Just the sort of detail that a campaigning historical theorist with a book to sell likes, another piece of corroboration to pile on to a case that seems more and more obvious to me the more often I write it.

The Hospitallers were established at the same time as the Templars to protect and succour pilgrims to Jerusalem, and took a leading part in the Crusades. The Templars grew mighty, arrogant and rich, and were suppressed all over Europe amid accusations of heresy, sorcery and secrets, but that's quite enough Dan Brown, thank you. The Hospitallers had an equally colourful but more orthodox history, fighting their Christian way in and out of Cyprus, Rhodes and Malta; the important thing for our purpose is that they inherited the assets of the doomed Templars and have lately been attracting their share of best-selling opprobrium, accused of similar shadowinesses and secrecy. And why else would they have been involved in a remote part of Britain with a peculiarly suggestive name?

Mr Fields, clearly a man after my own heart, and a worthy successor to Rev. Whitaker, has seized the point, too. 'It does seem appropriate,' he writes, 'that this order, which became involved in the search for the Holy Grail together with many other strange events, should have associations with mysterious Anglezarke.' See?

The nice lady from Wigan Library, or, more properly, Wigan Leisure & Culture Trust's History Shop (thank you, George, that will do), had now been back in touch, sending me promptly and without charge a photocopy of the only mention she could find of Arthur and Wigan, a cutting from the *Evening Chronicle* in 1927, headlined 'When Knights Were Bold – At Wigan', and written by 'Historian'. There was some terrific stuff in it, including sightings of the legendary Mermaid of Martin Mere, considered by 'Historian' to be an obvious reference to The Lady of the Lake. And this: 'The name Martin is said to be a corruption of Merlin, which was originally spelt Myrrdhin. From "dh" to "t" is a well-known philological change, so that the theory seems plausible.' Well, well. Merlin Mere! What more do you want?

I travelled further onto the moor, mulling over later and recent legend, much of it based around the Round Loaf, a large and remote Bronze Age burial mound that has fostered the superstitions of the ages, from sorcerers to witches to their most favoured modern expression, UFOs, which, apparently, treat Anglezarke as some kind of intergalactic Crewe. As I went, my vision became clearer: post-industrial Lancs could become New Age Lancs, a shining grail again, visited by seekers from this world and beyond, home of romance and mystery, of Cartimandua and kings, Arthur, Lancelot and Merlin, once the necessary rebranding and signage was in place.

It was about then that I began to notice some mysterious writings at regular intervals on the road. Spotting an excellent opportunity for some original research, I stopped to have a look at one. 'Nina – Go Wales, Julia', it read. I was pondering on why alien visitors who had travelled light years from distant galaxies would need to communicate like this when a lone figure came striding down the hill towards me. It was Mr Derek Chesworth, out on a walk. 'I've just come down from Lead Mine Clough,' he said. 'It's so beautiful, with water cascading over these great rocks, breathtaking!'

He did a lot of walking in Lancs, said Mr Chesworth, especially since he'd retired: Darwen Moor, the Ribble area, spectacular. I asked him where he was from. 'St Helens,' he said. I told him that was a coincidence, since that's where I'm from, originally, too. I told him my name. Well, he asked, did I know a Miss Nevin? That was my Auntie Vera, I said. Well, he replied, he was a neighbour of hers, lived just round the back of her house. Small world. I told him about this book. He said he liked to think of himself as a Lancastrian, rather than a Scouser, even if St Helens was supposed to be in Merseyside now. And he certainly had the gentler-pitched Lancashire accent. Had he, I wondered, seen any UFOs? 'Not yet,' said Mr Chesworth. 'Mind you, they'd have to be pretty low-flying today, there's only a couple of hundred feet below the cloud.' We bade each other farewell. I asked him to give Auntie Vera my regards, and he said he'd shout over the fence.

Chapter Three

Scouse Dreams

Culture, Custard and Joan Collins

Liverpool. People, I think it's fair to say, tend to have an opinion about Liverpool. And it's also fair to say, I think, that these opinions are not always entirely positive. Let me attempt a description of the physical reaction I have most often encountered, particularly among the metropolitan middle classes, at the sound of that name: a rapid progress from curled lip to raised eyes to deep sigh. Try it yourself on one of them and see what I mean.

And then, depending on articulacy, intelligence, the time of day and the ingestion of artficial stimulants, they will be off, flat out, in top sneer, on a tour de Scouse that will take in the dreadful accent, the awful tracksuits, how they all think they're so bloody funny and how you call one in a tie the defendant, how they're always whinging and never working, and always blaming everybody else for everything, old Boris Johnson and *The Spectator* were absolutely bloody right to call them peculiar, deeply unattractive and and all the rest of it. Remarkable.

57

Unique. Where else provokes such instant exasperation and irritation, such vehemence? What, exactly, is this all about?

Perhaps I can help. Perhaps it is my destiny to effect the long-overdue reconciliation between this great city and the rest of the country. Perhaps it has been given to me to explain one to the other, to promote the understanding that is the first condition of appreciation, the first gear in the motor of affection.

I was, after all, born there, even if I did leave quickly for St Helens, with my mother, from the maternity hospital. I worked in Liverpool for a bit, too, and I've always liked it, the fizz and buzz and edge and action of it, the great grey grandeur. Think Woody Allen and the opening titles to *Manhattan* – that's me, although I'm fatter and not quite as funny and Gerry and the Pacemakers are not George Gershwin, and 'Ferry 'Cross the Mersey' is not 'Rhapsody in Blue' and the thrilled voice fawning over the silhouetted city would inevitably be punctured by somebody saying 'My arse'.

Being almost one, and despite it being desperately unfashionable, I've always liked Scousers, with the admiration of the timid for the daring, of the man below for the high-wire artist; in this case high-wire artists of the over-dramatic, the anarchic and the riskily sentimental. It's in and from the Mersey, a distillation of what happens when Irish whimsy meets Lancashire whimsy. It's in the obsession with soccer, red or blue, the refusal, to paraphrase Shankly, to take anything else as seriously. And nearly all of it is in the famous exchange between Cilla Black and her young audience during *Jack and the Beanstalk* at the Liverpool Empire: 'Now then, children, how are we going to kill the big bad giant?' 'Sing to him, Cilla!'

So. Declaration of interest entered impeccably early. Declaration of the love that barely dares speak its name. Seekers after impartiality, objectivity and cautious judgement should leave now. This is no place for cool heads. Liverpool is no place for cool heads. Liverpool is a place for wits and living on them, where only the normal is abnormal. The cliché, of course, is that Liverpool is apart because it's a port, has always been a port, where abroad is as important as home; an impermanent place of passage and beginnings and leavings, with all the accompanying baggage of high emotion and distraction, but there's more to it than that.

If, for instance, you were looking for a resident population to add some stability and stolidness as a balance to all these comings and goings, you would probably not choose a high proportion of incoming Irish. And then there are the old, added tensions between nomads and settlers, grasshoppers and ants, the sort of thing, apart from the girl, that caused all the trouble in *Oklahoma!*. Liverpool has always had lots of that. In the nineteenth century, its bosses, its 'Liverpool Gentlemen', didn't make things, like 'Manchester Men'; no, they were traders, chargers of dues, takers of tolls, while its workers were daily, dock and casual, not cog-tied and head-down at mine and mill.

Different. And, in its pomp, easy to envy. By the end of the nineteenth century, Liverpool owned one-third of Britain's shipping and one-seventh of the world's. It was Britain's second city and more. Its Victorian fathers saw it as the Florence of the North; the *Illustrated London News* thought it the New York of Europe; and nobody laughed, not even Southerners. Today it is a better place than any to marvel at the scale of Victorian and Edwardian monument-making, from the mighty classical form of St George's Hall and its surrounding buildings in the centre, to the famed Three Graces down by the river, the Liver, Cunard, and Docks and Harbour buildings. It is a better place than any to gaze upon the remains of Empire. Who would not be over-dramatic against a backdrop like that?

Ah, yes, the remains of Empire. The remains of an Empire that, for any number of reasons, few want to remember. How cheerful is all that to contemplate? Particularly when there's not much else to do, because your city has declined as rapidly and certainly as that Empire and all attempts at revival have failed, principally because where you are, once such a blessing, is now a curse and you are the last stop, the final service station, on an economy that has stalled. How much sympathy did the grasshopper get when the winter came? Precisely. Its polite protestations at its plight were immediately and callously characterised by the heartless ants as 'whinging'.

How am I doing so far? Just the faintest stirring of fellow-feeling, the merest incipience of regret for kicking a grasshopper when it's down? Come on. There are many worse things than a Scouser. What has enhanced more lives, do you think, Scouse sharpness or Yorkshire bluntness? Here's a diary entry from a Yorkshireman, Alan Bennett, on Liverpudlians: 'They all have the chat, and it laces every casual encounter, everybody wanting to do their little verbal dance.' The shame of it. And my, how everyone everywhere else laughed, jeered and teased when it turned out that the dead baby commemorated by a makeshift Liverpudlian street shrine of flowers, teddy bears and handwritten cards had been, in fact, a deceased chicken. The 'hooked on grief' jibes were reeled out again, along with the dread 'm' word: mawkishness. But, again, who would you more warm to, the well-intentioned, over-emotional, sympathetic and commiserating Scousers or the smart, sophisticated, cynical sneerers? Thank you. And lest we get too carried away, I should tell you that shortly afterwards, at Hallowe'en, two men turned up on a doorstep in Huyton, enquired of the man answering the door, 'Trick or treat?' and then shot him. That unmawkish enough for you? A study of the death notices in the *Liverpool Echo* might help, too; this one would be quite representative: 'Pull yourself together, Arthur, you've got over worse than this.'

Perhaps, though, you are of a more sensitive and contemplative turn of mind, and it is the association with failure and spent energies and dead times that you find unattractive. If so, prepare for revision.

Change is here. The Pier Head is not a bad place to contemplate it, sense it, almost smell it on that whippy breeze. Money! Oodles of it: several billions of it. Public money, private money, Government money, EU regeneration money. Getting ready for 2008, the date from which there is no escape, the year Liverpool will be European Capital of Culture, an investment-attracting, tourist-beckoning bonanza just waiting to happen, the title taken coming from behind against the likes of Newcastle and Birmingham. 'We just nicked it,' is the Liverpool joke. See, they can laugh at themselves, too.

Down there, the docks south of the successfully born-again Albert Dock are to be revamped and revived for watery events and activities and posh moorings; Kings Dock is to be the site of a sports stadium and conference centre. Just there, that's the site for the striking, some say startling, X-shaped new Museum of Liverpool, part of a multi-million-pound waterfront development to go with a new terminal for the fabled ferries to Birkenhead. And more: the liners, the big ships, the cruise ships are coming back. The liners! No more will old men have to sigh, 'Ay, doh, but you should have seen it when de liners were in.' Soon they will be sighing instead, 'Ay, doh, but you should have seen it before it was declared a World Heritage Site by Unesco.'

Landmark buildings are planned and opening all over the city, big works down at the docks. This is how it must have been in the days of Victoria. Economic output has increased by nearly half since 1995. Coutts have opened a branch, a 44 per cent increase in potential millionaires, house prices leading the country and the middle classes moving back into the long-spurned centre. There are plenty of shiny new bars about, all chrome and blond wood and people who say 'excuse me'; the Duke of Westminster is on his way with a £750-million development, a Harvey Nichols is promised, Vivienne Westwood has arrived. The vision beyond sees Liverpool in 2015 'as a major retail centre with the world-famous Mersey ferries carrying visitors between a string of visitor centres forming the backbone of the Mersey Waterfront Regional Park'. All this, and suburbs turned into science parks, new media and new technology ventures arriving, and the continuing rise of Liverpool as the Hollywood of the North, the 'most film-friendly city in the UK', with Liverpool Film Studios busier than Pinewood, a fitting use for a city filled with and fuelled by drama.

Liverpool, let me tell you, is going to be the big rediscovery of the century. That is my prediction, and I am, let me also tell you, the man who tipped four out of six winners at Newton Abbot the only time I stood in as Mercury of the *Liverpool Daily Post*, without doubt the highlight of my career there, unless you include meeting Joan Collins, but more on that later.

I have no wish to lull, though. Be reassured that Liverpool is not turning into just another pasteurised-modern regenerated old city, just another beguilingly glossy twenty-first-century axis of technology and art and tourism. Such things cannot be, here. Other things will, thank goodness, always prevent it. The city has too much of a past, too much strength in memory, too much celebration of wit and indulgence of whimsy, prime prerequisites of its glorious underlying anarchy. This is a city, after all, that has purple wheelie bins.

Some of the explanation lies in another forthcoming celebration: 2007, the 800th anniversary of the founding of the city by King John. Never underestimate the effect of owing your existence to someone regarded as perhaps the arch-villain, and certainly the panto baddie, of English history; a king, interestingly, who has been atrociously misrepresented, sneered at and slighted.

No one can deny that he was quite often in touch with his dark side: his brother, Richard the Lionheart, whom he serially betrayed, and his nephew and rival, Arthur of Brittany, whom he treacherously slayed, would swear to that. And no one can deny that Liverpool, too, has its dark side, caught in the shadow cast by poverty and by wealth based on slavery, often finding expression in strange and baleful ways: in casually murderous crime families; in fierce drugs wars of high, exotic violence, involving car bombs and hotlines to Colombian cartels; in the burying of an axe in the head of a black schoolboy; in attitudes which led, famously, during James Callaghan's Winter of Discontent, to the refusal by council workers to bury the dead. And in the series of stark and dark disasters – Hillsborough, Heysel, the awful execution of Kenneth Bigley in Iraq – which the city seems somehow, implacably, to attract.

John, like his new town, was complicated and misunderstood. He was a man at odds with his time, cynical, mischievous, never able to take things too seriously, always game for a laugh and a drink, modern, even anarchic. Conveniently familiar, you will agree. It's impossible not to warm to a man who retaliated to the papal bull of excommunication by raiding the houses of the clergy and holding their female 'housekeepers' to ransom; who entered into negotiations with the Sultan of Morocco to embrace Islam in return for a loan; who used to stay in bed with his new young queen until noon while his French possessions were disappearing all around him, saying there would be plenty of time to win them back later.

When the fleeing chancellor, Longchamp, disguised as a woman, was fumbled and rumbled by an amorous fisherman at Dover, it made John laugh so much that he let him go. When the hermit Peter of Pontefract prophesied that his reign would not last longer than 14 years, John held a great festival on the anniversary to mock the grumpy old Yorkshireman. No wonder Richard forgave and forgave his brother, even when, instead of ransoming the Lionheart from his Austrian castle prison, he offered money to keep him there (this being John, the sum was less than the ransom demand).

Go and look at John's effigy in Worcester Cathedral, where he was buried after over-feasting to forget Magna Carta and the loss of all that treasure in the Wash. Think of this, from John

Harvey's splendid essay: 'His temperament would have been called "French" in Victorian times; he loved to saunter through life, seeing and enjoying the surface of things; the best food, expensive drink, fine clothes, pretty women, amusing companions with whom he could while away the hours in chatter and endless games of backgammon', and try not to smile.

All, you will agree, entirely recognisable. And there is more. John hated the way Longchamp made servants serve on their knees. Remarkably, this distaste for an over-fawning approach to the service industry survives undimmed in Liverpool to this day, and is another reason why the city is unlikely ever to become the New Somewhere Else. Some of you may remember the entertaining fly-on-the-wall documentary about the Adelphi Hotel. Its producer got the idea when he dined there and complained that the soup was cold. The waitress put her finger in it and said, 'Dat's all right, dat.' More recently, a lady from Cambridge, arriving at Lime Street Station, approached the Liverpool Tourist Bureau there and asked for directions to her hotel. The tourist official was attentive, friendly and helpful. 'You could piss on it from here,' he said. Ah, Liverpool.

I'm not sure why the collision between Irish whimsy and Lancastrian whimsy should produce this kind of edge as well as the sentimentality. But it is still whimsy. Take the activities of the well-documented local phenomenon, the scally, short for scalliwag, youths who move round the city, dressed, of course, in tracksuits and trainers, as if ready to get away, hands plunged in jacket pockets, feet splayed in a rolling gait, en route to some unspecified income opportunity involving, true to the traditions of the city, little long-term commitment.

I followed Michael Heseltine round Liverpool one day in 1987, when, out of office after the Westland affair, he was just beginning his long-running leadership campaign which he would never say was a leadership campaign, which was why he never became leader. He went to the Albert Dock, his great regeneration achievement, set in train after the Toxteth riots of 1981, a rare example of Liverpool following prevailing urban fashions in Bristol, Brixton and elsewhere. There he was approached by two scallys who engaged him in a lengthy conversation aimed, it emerged afterwards, at discovering if he had any tickets for the Cup final.

Equally whimsical, but in an even more Liverpudlian way, was the ceremony he attended to mark the planting of some splendid new trees along Princes Road, vandalised and damaged during the riots, at which a member of the local community told him, 'We didn't want the fucking Champs Élysées, you know.'

What I am trying to do here is to explain the Liverpool Experience, so that, unlike the unprepared Cambridge lady or Cabinet Minister, you can enjoy the thrill of recognition rather than the shock of the unexpected and even, if you are feeling bold, take part. For example, upon parking your car, it is possible that you will be approached by a younger sibling of the said scallies offering to 'Mind your car, Mister/Missis?' for a fee. You should respond, 'No thanks, there's a dog in the back.' To which he will reply, 'But can it fight fires?'

All this, though, is only the half of it. There is still something more. Eddie Berg is one of the arts entrepreneurs that Liverpool seems regularly to throw up, persuasive purveyors of the new and the abstruse to all. Now artistic director of the BFI's new National Centre for the Moving Image on London's Southbank, Eddie founded another creative mouthful, the Foundation for Art and Creative Technology (Fact), whose headquarters, a £10-million au courant mingling of zinc, glass, concrete, atrium and suspended cinema, are the centrepiece of a regeneration project in the south-east of Liverpool city centre and a big shiny player in the Capital of Culture bid.

Eddie has also been on the board of the Liverpool Biennial, another CC clincher, the festival that promotes Liverpool's contemporary visual arts, livelier than those anywhere else outside London. And, while we're here, can there be an artier city than Liverpool? You know about the music, and the film; and you can say what you like about the hectoring lecturing and sentimental certainties of the Scouse writers, Bleasdale, Russell and McGovern; but can any other city, including London, match them? I can also tell you that the numbers of installation artists in Liverpool have created such a demand for burnt-out cars that, the last time I checked, the scallies were charging up to £200 for one.

This is what Eddie Berg says about Liverpool: 'One of the experiences that people have when they come to Liverpool for the first time and see it on a Friday or Saturday night is that this city is completely out of control. It feels like that, it feels like there's just been a public announcement that the world will end tomorrow morning. There's a vivid quality to life in Liverpool which for some people, me included from time to time, is just too painful to look at, it's too vivid. This is an example of a working-class city, it's like, whoa, there are real poor people here, but set in this kind of incredible grandeur from the eighteenth and nineteenth centuries.'

I can see what Eddie means. I took a walk over from his building down Bold Street, which lasted until the early '70s as the city's premier shopping street, a match for anywhere in Britain before it tumbled into discount and decline. Now it's caught in the most marvellous flux, with stylish fashion shops and new bars and a gleaming delicatessen set between tattoo parlours, charity and chip shops and amusement arcades. Where else would a hairdressers be called Phairverts?

There is, you see, something dreamlike, something stagey about Liverpool, about as far removed from the straightforward, four-square, plain-speaking image foisted on Lancashire as can be imagined; I wish I could use 'surreal', but everybody else does. It's to do with the grand backdropping architecture, certainly, and the monumental contrast it makes with all the coming and going, all the transience, but there's something more. Where else would you discover, for instance, that a fine piece of allegorical public statuary entitled 'Virtue Thrusting Evil from the Path of Youth' has been stolen? It's impossible not to get caught up with it. Driving through the tunnel to Birkenhead, for example, I used often to wonder what strange impulse had led to the hiring of the toll collector holding out, to take the coins, a deformed hand.

Jung, celebrated Swiss psychologist and dreamer, sensed this strangeness. In his autobiography, *Memories, Dreams and Reflections*, Jung wrote about a dream he had in 1927: 'I found myself in a dirty, sooty city. It was night, and winter, and dark, and raining. I was in Liverpool.' He tells how he walked to a square at the centre of many streets. In the middle of the square was a little island, somehow caught in sunlight, with a magnolia tree on it. It was, for Jung, 'a vision of unearthly beauty'.

Liverpool, it seemed to him, was therefore 'the pool of life'. The dream brought 'a sense of finality. I saw here that the goal had been revealed. One could not go beyond the centre. The centre is the goal and everything is directed towards that centre. Through this dream I understood that the self is the principle and archetype of orientation and meaning.'

Fascinating, I think, although you might think he would have been wiser staying off the cheese late at night. Jung, of course, was the friend of Freud who turned, rejecting the view that the unconscious is the receptacle of the repressed and unbearable. Jung thought it the receptacle of the individual and collective psychic history of humankind. Revelation comes in dreams; fufilment, or if we're really pushing it, happiness, comes in recognising the importance of the unconscious and balancing it with the importance of the conscious. Jung was a soul man. In pursuit of the soul, he delved into every belief he could find, astrology, aliens, alchemy and the rest. Particularly alchemy: the alchemists had resisted the divide, sought the link between spirit and reality, thought and fact, magic and science; so did Jung. He was fascinated by people of alternative civilisations that seemed to major in the unconscious – nomads, bushmen, aborginals. Actually, if you felt like it, you could blame Jung for much of the '60s.

Which brings me back to Liverpool, the unlikely setting for one of Jung's most important dreams, even if he never did get round to visiting consciously. Or perhaps it is not so unlikely: here is Britain's alternative civilisation, other, apart, often operating, as Eddie Berg says, on a different level of consciousness. Liverpool, the Dream City, the Jungian City of our Unconscious, where truth and beauty mingle with complaint and uncertainty.

You don't understand Liverpool? Don't worry, Jung didn't fully understand his dreams either: the pattern and point has yet to be revealed. It's like his other great gift to conversations in the pub, the frequency of coincidence and its hidden significance, pointing the way to larger pictures and truths, which he calls synchronicity, and which can allow any number of people to wonder about any number of things. A charming man used to write to me, for example, at my day job as columnist and chronicler of the seemingly inconsequential and hopefully amusing, about the extraordinary frequency of the occurrence of the number 62. He used to live in Bognor and often pointed out that the fire station there was struck by lightning once on Jung's birthday.

But, Liverpool. I can't claim any credit for spotting the Jung thing. It was first brought to wider attention while I was working there in the early '70s by an earlier Eddie Berg archetype (Jung word!), Peter Halligan, a former merchant seaman turned alternative entrepreneur, who had opened an alternative kind of shop in Mathew Street, home of the Cavern Club. Then, declaring, after Jung, that Liverpool was the pool of life, he opened the Liverpool School of Dream, Language and

Pun on the floors above. There had been annual Jung Festivals; during one of them a man jumped from one of the first-floor windows into a skip full of custard. Exactly why, I can't remember. I should like to tell you that I immersed myself in the culture of the Liverpool School of Dream, Language and Pun, that I was a frequent patron of the café upstairs from whose window the man leapt into the custard, that there I mingled with the interesting people of Liverpool, like Ken Campbell, who was putting on his crazed sci-fi extravaganza, *Illuminatus*, a remarkable combination of Jules Verne, Aleister Crowley and Robert Crumb at least, designed by Bill Drummond, later of the KLF, pop guerrillas and counter-culture terrorists.

Sadly, in both its current senses, I was too busy trying to become a proper hack, interviewing bingo winners and covering inquests for the *Liverpool Echo*. Even so, I was not entirely immune to the magic of Liverpool. I did get to meet Che Guevara's sister, who was visiting, although I can't remember why; and I almost contrived to kill Mr Sulu from *Star Trek*, who was at one of the Trekkie conventions and looked the wrong way when I asked him to cross over Lime Street for a photograph. What an end to boldly going that would have been! And I do remember that our canteen manager became a major figure in the field of exploring reincarnation through hypnosis and regression. Then there was Eddie Barford, me and Joan Collins in the bedroom at the Adelphi Hotel, but I'll tell you about that later.

First, I had to find Peter Halligan. Perhaps you would care to come along and judge for yourself what I mean about the City of Dreams. According to report, Halligan was either long gone or just back, which turned into definitely back but not sure where. Hoping for some creative synchronicity, I went to his one-time favourite pub; he wasn't there, but he had been. And I did have some fun going through the dog gag with my car minder.

There was a Biennial going on at the time, and I combined my quest for Halligan with a look at some of its attractions and installations around the city. The festival had a theme of which Carl Gustav would surely have approved, the human desire for control and its frustration. The idea was that the exhibition, reflecting its host, should be ever so slightly out of control. I made straight for Tate Liverpool, down at the Albert Dock, to see The Liver Pool, an installation by the Californian artist Jason Rhoades, inspired by Jung and featuring two large liver-shaped, purple-coloured plastic paddling pools slightly filled with Rhoades' own building material, PeaRoeFoam, made of hard green peas from his family farm, virgin white foam beads and salmon eggs stuck together with white glue, surrounded by 30 wooden pallets bearing identical loads of yellow wellies and other building stuff.

I quite liked The Liver Pool, which was constantly and noisily inflating and deflating, although I would have liked it even more if Jason had been doing the inflating himself, lying on the floor, struggling with the valve, blowing. I asked the woman next to me what she thought of it. 'Well,' she said, 'I wouldn't have it in *my* front room.'

Across the road, away from the water, stood a large yellow submarine. This turned out not to be a Biennial installation, but a piece of work rescued from the International Garden Festival, another of Michael Heseltine's revitalising wheezes in the '80s. It was made by a group of apprentices at Cammell Laird, the famous shipbuilding yard in Birkenhead; one of the last things built there, as it happens, although a return to the clanging days of the *Mauretania* and the *Ark Royal* is always a leading Scouse dream. The yellow submarine was being considered by three tourists, who turned out to be Mexican Beatles fans. I told them the way to Mathew Street and thought no more of it; only later did it occur to me that, as representatives of the continent of magic realism and the mysteries of death, they would be ideal to ask about the Pool of Life. So I hurried to Mathew Street, where, of course, there was no sign of them.

It's still got something, Mathew Street. We do not talk the modern and plastic Carnaby Street here. Why is another mystery. You will probably know that, for reasons never satisfactorily explained, the warehouse which had the Cavern Club in its basement was demolished in 1973 and the club filled in. Now it has been re-excavated, and rebuilt to the same dimensions, using some of the same bricks, but it's not the same. At either end of the street, in the middle of the road, there are pillars that rise and fall to allow only accredited access, with a mechanical voice intoning over and over, 'Warning, Pillar in Motion', which sounds a bit like a Motown title.

Opposite the Cavern, there is a sculpture of the Beatles as babies being cradled by Mother Liverpool. It's the work of the late Arthur Dooley, the inspired Catholic–Communist Cammell Laird welder who received his vocation while doing the cleaning at an art school. Dooley later added a plaque mourning John Lennon, inscribed with the Lamentations of Jeremiah: 'How lonely is she now, the once crowded city, widowed she who was mistress over nations . . .' Splendidly and Liverpudlianly over the top; but you don't have to look far for the equally typical bit of puncturing bathos, another plaque bearing the roll of the city's gold-disc chart-toppers which begins with Lita Roza's 'How Much Is that Doggie in the Window?'. And how Liverpool is it to call your airport Liverpool John Lennon? Lennon, of course, in fate and character and contradictions, also had nearly all of Liverpool about him, needing only the addition of the fates, characters and contradictions of McCartney, Harrison, Starr and Epstein to make it complete.

The Cavern Wall of Fame, inscribed with the names of most of the bands who performed there between 1957 and 1973, is a marvel, too. What crushed hopes are commemorated here; what proof of the indomitability of the human spirit is evident from brave youths who thought that a band called The Rocking Vicars would storm the world. Honourable mentions, too, must go to St James Infirmary, Jackie Martin and the Dominators, Greasy Bear, The Plebs, The Verbs, A.N. Other and The Rest, Scapa Flow, Reception Almost and Hiroshima. What testimony, too, to the compelling, undeniable need to make music that so distinguishes Liverpool and the rest of Lancashire from the tone-strugglers elsewhere. Consider this invincible list of merely the most recently classically inclined: William Walton, Thomas Beecham, Kathleen Ferrier, Peter Maxwell Davies, Harrison Birtwistle, Simon Rattle. Astounding, you'll agree, and something to mull over while you weep to Gracie's incomparable 'Ave Maria'.

I passed down the street to the former buildings of the Liverpool School of Dream, Language and Pun. It's the premises of Flanagan's Apple now, 'The Original Irish Pub, Established 1983', but a bust of Jung, sculpted by Jonathan Drabkin, is there, in a niche on the outside wall, above the stone slab inscribed, 'Liverpool is the pool of life – C.G. Jung, 1927'. The slab was brought by Halligan from Switzerland. It was taken from the same place in the quarry as Jung's stone, the one in his garden inscribed with alchemical quotes, the psychologist's stone. The bust is a replacement for the original, which was, of course, vandalised. Ah, Liverpool.

I went into the pub and asked the barman about the plaque. 'No idea. I just work here,' he said, with that familiar Irish blarney. I approached some veteran drinkers. 'Oh, dat's right,' said one. 'Dat's Jung. He lived round here for a few years, and really liked it.' A less scrupulous reporter would have followed this up with, 'He must have had a few in here, then.' I didn't think of it, which I'm quite glad about, really, as they were charming and courteous and full of hopes for the Capital of Culture.

I was still not having much luck finding Peter Halligan,

although it was said he was living in Canning Street, a fine Georgian terrace up beyond the Anglican cathedral. On my way there, I popped into the Golden Hot Takeaway, setting for an exhibit in the Biennial Independent, or fringe, entitled 'The World on a Plate'. The Golden Hot was certainly a takeaway, but it wasn't immediately clear exactly what type of cuisine it offered, although a frieze featuring the Acropolis on the wall tiles offered a clue. Up there, too, was a map of the world constructed of food smears from the napkins of customers. The owner, a smiling man with little English, seemed to find the exhibit completely unremarkable. I asked him if he had installed the splendid Acropolis tiles. 'Yes,' he said, smiling. Was he Greek? 'No,' he said, smiling. Where was he from, then? 'I can't tell you. You put it in the newspaper and nobody come,' he said, still smiling, before revealing he was, as it happened, an Afghan. This was unsettling. In that Liverpool way, it disturbs your certainties when Greeks are Afghans. I asked him if the Action Man on the counter, naked except for a couple of red paper roses, was part of the exhibit, too. He smiled and said, 'No.' I had a chicken nugget and left my smear. Later, it occurred to me that I hadn't paid for the nugget, so here, by way of compensation, is my recommendation: 'The Golden Hot: one of the country's more remarkable takeaways' – Charles Nevin.

I asked a few people up on Canning Street about Halligan, but no one could help. I moved on, bound for Upper Stanhope Street. There is a list of Liverpool's claims to fame on the City of Culture website: two of the oldest Muslim and Chinese communities in Britain, two of the largest Somali and Yemeni communities, first city to appoint a medical officer of health (1847), first circulating library in the world, biggest bonded warehouse in the world, silver medal won by the Liverpool police tug-of-war team at the London Olympic Games in 1908. But here though, for once, it seems to me, Liverpool is letting itself down, missing an opportunity for another defining swipe of the old anarchic mischief: there doesn't seem to be any mention of Adolf Hitler's stay with his aunt, Bridget Hitler, in the winter of 1912–13, at 102 Upper Stanhope Street.

Where else? You might have heard about it. Beryl Bainbridge wrote a very Bainbridge novel, *Young Adolf,* featuring the stay and some splendid explanations for several Hitlerian attributes, including his shirt. I knew about it because one of my former bosses at the *Daily Post*, Mike Unger, the sort of journalist who gets sent interesting papers old chums come across in the New York Public Library, was sent some interesting papers an old chum had come across in the New York Public Library purporting to be Bridget's memoirs, entitled *My Brother-in-Law Adolf.* Believe me.

In them, Bridget, who married Adolf's half-brother Alois Hitler after they met when he was working as a waiter at the Shelbourne Hotel in Dublin, tells of Adolf's arrival at Lime Street to become an 'unwanted and disagreeable guest' in Upper Stanhope Street, where he loafed about, refused to get a job or learn English, spent a lot of time studying his horoscope, which had been drawn up by Bridget's friend, a Mrs Prentice, and certainly never helped with the washing-up. Eventually, Alois bought him a ticket back to Germany. And, no, frustratingly, Bridget doesn't reveal what Mrs Prentice saw, no 'Hmm. Such a lot of travel, Poland, Czechoslovakia, France, the Low Countries, Norway, Crete, Russia . . .' Why did Hitler never mention this English sojourn, which included trips to London? Simple: he was avoiding military service in the Austrian Army at the time, not something he cared to advertise later.

And there is no firm alternative evidence of his activities that winter. Nevertheless, Lord Dacre doubted the authenticity of the memoirs, which is a pity, but not something we should take as final, particularly given, how shall we put this, the great historian's record elsewhere in the field. Still, we do know that

Bridget Hitler definitely existed: even though Alois left her in 1914 (and went on to contract a bigamous marriage in Hamburg), she kept the name Mrs Hitler and later had a boarding house in Highgate.

Hitler even paid her an allowance through the German Embassy; Dacre knew the officers in the British Secret Service who kept an eye on Bridget, noting her demand to the Embassy for an increase in the allowance because 'How the divil are ye thinking that I can get a job with a name like that?'

This vigorous vernacular is a little at odds with the style of the memoirs. This is Bridget, for example, reflecting on Adolf's spell with her:

> At this point, I pause to ask myself a question. Should I have been more sympathetic to Adolf? Would it have made any difference in the course of events, when Adolf was in Liverpool? I was young and thoughtless. Certainly I didn't concern myself with his future. If I had exerted my influence over him, it is quite possible he might have remained in England. At this time the country was full of Germans. Barbers, hairdressers, carpenters, all varieties of skilled workmen came looking for work. Many of these visitors settled comfortably in England, never to return to the Continent. If I had insisted that Adolf learn English, instead of practising German on him, he might have shared their obscurity.

Indeed. I can see him as a barber, can't you? Mike Unger thinks Bridget had 'some sort of professional guidance' with the writing. Whatever, the details I like best are that it was Bridget who persuaded Adolf to trim his moustache, even if she did think he went a bit far, and that later, when she visited Berchtesgaden, the scatter cushions were decorated with little swastikas.

Anyway, all this is why I came to be in Upper Stanhope Street, asking people, 'Excuse me, but did Adolf Hitler live round here?' 'Oh, yes,' said a charming man outside the newsagents. 'He used to live round here all right.' His nephew, Ahmad, the newsagent, said, 'That's right, he used to come in here for a patty.' Ahmad's 11-year-old son, Nader, looked up from his *Beano*. 'Who's Hitler?' he asked, lucky child.

Ahmad was a Yemeni, with a sense of humour and an eye for things, like the extraordinary concentration of places of worship that would have surrounded young Adolf, including, inevitably, a synagogue on Princes Road, within yards of what had been No. 102 and was now a derelict site. No, I'm not sure what to make of that, either. A teenage girl came into the shop. 'Hitler? I've seen a picture of him dead on the Internet, with Elvis and Marilyn Monroe.'

The derelict No. 102 was not the only sign that Liverpool's regeneration hadn't quite washed up as far as Upper Stanhope Street yet, but Ahmad was enthusiastic. He was thirty-eight and had come here when he was four. 'You know the postcode here? L8 1UN, United Nations. Everybody gets on with everybody round here.' He had been a Liverpool supporter, he said, since he was a kid. So why was he wearing an Everton fleece? 'Whatever keeps me warm, I put it on . . . I'm happy anyway. Happiness is if your kids are healthy and fed, that's the main thing. What is life all about, eh? All these luxuries, they're no good if you haven't got time . . . You're thinking about the future, and you don't know who's going to live till tomorrow.' Advice Adolf really should have taken.

Mike Unger told me that No. 102 had been destroyed in the last German bombing raid on Liverpool, which rather beats the lightning and Bognor fire station, in my view. I was also told that, for many years, a pair of ice skates hung in one of the display windows of the old Liverpool ice rink beneath a sign reading 'Hitler's Ice Skates', which seems an unimproveable example of Liverpool humour and something that might even afford Alan Bennett one of his wry smiles. Alan would not be with Ahmad, though: he once said that his happiness was nearly all retrospective, and that he had been happy at the time on, I think, only three occasions. I can see what he means, but it's still taking Yorkshireness far too seriously.

So, Hitler and Liverpool. How much more evidence do you need that this is indeed a City of Dreams? I do have more, though. Much of it was explained to me in Yates's Wine Lodge by Gabriel Muies. Gabriel, who met me at Lime Street Station, looks like a mole, but in the nicest possible way, which may be another piece of synchronicity, as he is very interested in tunnels, or rather in one particular set of tunnels, excavated under the Edge Hill district of Liverpool in the early nineteenth century.

This being Liverpool, nobody is quite sure how many tunnels there are, for how long they run, or why exactly they were built. It is all quite complicated and some European money is involved, and Roy Rogers and Trigger. Anyway, I was in Yates's with Gabriel, who had with him a worn plastic shopping bag packed with documents, always a warning sign to a journalist. Gabriel explained, in detail, how he became involved in the tunnels, in a manner that suggested, dangerously, destiny. In the '80s, he had become very concerned about the school in Edge Hill intended for his son, as it seemed to be falling down. The cracks prompted a memory in him of his days as a lad in the area, of playing near the railway, stories of old disused tunnels. He made inquiries, asked around, went to the library. He found out a lot about the tunnels, including that they weren't responsible for the cracks in the school; but that didn't matter, because Gabriel had met his passion, the filling for his plastic bag.

Gabriel had discovered the curious Joseph Williamson (1769–1840), a Liverpool tobacco merchant who took early retirement and spent it paying men to dig holes. These were not just any holes – they were solid, brick and sandstone tunnels,

77

inside and on top of each other; a huge chamber, measuring 50 feet high by 50 feet deep by 200 feet long, and goodness knows what else. Williamson seems to have made no plans or maps of his network, and certainly none has been discovered so far.

What was all this for? A hobby? He had married, not to any evident pleasure, the boss's daughter, announcing the event to general surprise, going straight off to hunt after the ceremony and leaving the bride to get dinner ready. There were no children. It may have been the male escape, the garden-shed complex, taken to new heights, or depths. Who knows? There are only a few sources, and they are unsatisfactory. No record has survived even of what the tunnellers thought they were doing. Williamson invited no one down to look.

Gabriel, in Yates's, was for the theory that Williamson had come up with one of the country's first job creation schemes, if you discount Stonehenge and Hadrian's Wall. There were lots of unemployed people in Liverpool in the aftermath of the Napoleonic Wars; Williamson was of humble origin himself. Gabriel recounted, with feeling, the moment when destiny took over: George Stephenson, great creator of the *Rocket*, unstoppable engineer of yet another Lancashire claim to fame, the Liverpool–Manchester line, the world's first passenger railway, was building the tunnel in the 1830s that would take the railway from its then terminus in Edge Hill into the centre of Liverpool; his navvies swing their picks and suddenly find they have broken into another, strange tunnel – it is one of Williamson's. Stephenson has a look and is so impressed that he immediately hires all Williamson's men. 'If the railway hadn't come, Liverpool would have been on stilts now, the way he was going,' said Gabriel.

How much of it is true? Does it matter? Whatever, Williamson and his tunnels have almost every aspect of Liverpool in them, too. Especially now that the seemingly esoteric efforts of Gabriel and his fellow enthusiasts have resulted in £3 million more of that European money being spent on re-excavating the tunnels and turning them into a tourist attraction, so that 200 years later the same tunnels are being dug again in another job creation scheme. The three entrances to them are controlled by two different branches of enthusiasts and a slightly bemused City Council. Gabriel seems to constitute a branch of enthusiast all of his own. The main attraction at one entrance is, for some reason, a swanky bar.

What else? Well, I like it that Williamson, the great philanthropist, was a dealer in the death that is tobacco, and that he used to keep wheelbarrows in his bedroom. I like this, too, a cutting from the *Liverpool Echo*, produced by Gabriel from his bag, about Williamson's last resting place, left behind when its accompanying church was demolished: 'The grave of one of Liverpool's most famous sons is being parked on for 60 pence a time by city shoppers.' (Gabriel has now managed to persuade the Duke of Westminster to put up a plaque as part of his new shopping scheme.) But what spoke most to me about Liverpool in all of this fantastic story was that Gabriel had been unemployed throughout it.

Sorry? Roy Rogers and Trigger? Oh, yes: one of the entrances to the tunnels is at the old municipal stables, where, Gabriel showed me, delving into the bag again, Roy stabled Trigger when he was on at the Empire in the '50s. I was able to tell Gabriel that Trigger's big Hollywood break had been playing Maid Marian's mount in Errol Flynn's *The Adventures of Robin Hood*, but I didn't feel he was that impressed.

I decided to have one last try for Halligan and was making my way to Canning Street when my phone rang. It was, of course, Halligan, who agreed to meet me at the flat of a friend. He was wearing a dark blue jacket, a dark blue shirt, dark blue waterproof leggings tucked into boots and a blue tie with a badge in the shape of a dolphin pinned to it. He had a plastic bag, too, from Tesco. Inside was the manuscript of his memoirs, detailing, among much else, his journey after Jung into physics to try to rediscover the link between mind and matter, lost when alchemy was discredited by our simpler, mechanistic tradition, which sneers at such things and is proving so successful in the attainment of universal happiness, harmony and understanding.

A most interesting man, Halligan, although my glossary and introduction status in the Jungian world, combined with O-level physics, prevented me from fully comprehending all that he said. But we did get somewhere, I think, on the great dream. The centre from which the city was arranged radially was, it turned out, the premises of the School of Dream, Language and Pun at 18 Mathew Street. The pun part came from Joyce, who famously remarked that the Catholic Church was based on a joke, the Latin pun on Peter, Petra, also meaning rock, as in, 'Thou art Peter, and upon this rock I will found my church', which, as it happens, is in Matthew 18.

There certainly seems to have been a whole lot of synchronicity going on. Halligan was told about Jung's dream, for example, by a cousin also called Halligan. No sooner had he launched his Jung events than he was surrounded by any number of Swiss professors living in Liverpool. And he had lived in a house in America with a magnolia tree just outside, even if he hadn't realised it until spring, when it flowered.

As for the rest of the dream, 'the significance has yet to be revealed utterly and completely'. It was like the moment, he said, when Galileo watched the sanctuary lamp swinging in Pisa Cathedral, a moment that would lead, eventually, to the re-ordering of the universe. 'This is a provincial town, but it is the pool of life,' said Halligan, moving on to the scarab, a key element in Jung's dreams, a symbol of rebirth and the overcoming of rationality. And, of course, said Halligan, a scarab is a beetle, thus the Beatles . . .

I was still puzzled by the dolphin on his tie, why he sometimes seemed to be called O'Halligan, and the man jumping into the custard. The dolphin, he showed me, was covering the Queen's Award to Industry emblem on the tie because he wasn't entitled to wear it. He called himself O'Halligan when he was writing poetry, as a poet needed all the vowels he could get. And the jump into the custard had been to celebrate the first import of bananas into this country, at Liverpool, by Sir Arthur Lewis Jones. There had been 1,000 gallons of custard in the skip, together with a large number of bananas, donated by Fyffes; the custard had been warm, boiled up in the skip earlier. There had also been four beautiful girls in leotards inviting people to slip up and see them sometime. Marvellous.

Walking back down towards the centre of the city after my meeting with Halligan, and, as you might imagine, fairly pensive, I reached Hope Street, with its cathedrals, Catholic and Anglican, at either end. Ah, yes, Hope Street: two cathedrals, as the churchmen always intone, in that *Thought For The Day* voice, 'joined by a street named Hope'. If I was allowed an intonation opportunity, I should say that my hope for Liverpool is that 2008 will succeed triumphantly in capturing and showing this city in all its strange and vivid specialness, its combination of whimsy and dreams spiced by the inspired appliance of a sharp and peculiar wit; in short, what the Beatles had together but never apart.

It's shaping up pretty well. Already there has been the espousal, adoption and abandonment of Will Alsop's Cloud – the striking free-form edifice that was to have been the Fourth Grace – amid the usual Liverpool controversy and complaint; already there are the usual Liverpool worries and rumours about everything being ready in time, and anybody turning up, including top artistes; already there are the usual Liverpool concerns about a lack of proper Scousers in charge. And it looks as if there might not be a landing stage ready for the return of the liners. And, already, the new museum, the X-shaped one, the replacement for the Cloud, is known as the Fourth Wheelie Bin.

The World Discovery Centre is highly promising as well. You are right to be suspicious of any £40-million public-private partnership project containing the words 'the', 'world' and 'centre', let alone 'discovery', but bear with this: a scheme to commemorate, utilise and play on Liverpool's past as the gateway to the New World, no less than the digitisation of millions of archives, including birth certificates, parish records and details of people who emigrated from the city, all to be available on the Internet, the world's first online centre for tracing roots, together with displays and exhibitions in a remodelled Central Library. When was the last time you were excited by a grand cultural public project? Exactly!

I like, too, the permanent exhibition dedicated to another one-time, suitably mystical and possibly still present king, Elvis. And I like the plan for a spectacular staging of *Emilia di Liverpool. Emilia di Liverpool?* The opera by Donizetti, shamefully ignored and performed even in Liverpool only a handful of times since the great Italian composer wrote it in 1824. It is set in the Lancashire mountains just outside Liverpool, which seems to be quite near London, and features Liverpudlian mountaineers. Emilia, seduced and now in a convent in the mountains, is finally married to her lover, Federico, who overcomes the opposition of her tyrannical father, Claudio of Liverpool. A happy ending, when you would have thought that you could at least rely on an opera to give you a woman from Lancashire who dies of love. Ah, well.

All, as I say, very promising. But what really has the authentic Scouse mark, the sort of thing that makes you shake your head vigorously in an attempt to clear it as you wonder whether you heard right, is the plan for a 180-foot-high naked statue of Neptune reclining in the Mersey, just off New Brighton, complete with trident and holding a globe. The statue would be hollow, with viewing galleries and an exhibition space in the globe. It would be a transatlantic partner for the Statue of

Liberty, visible from the Pier Head, from all around, with the tide lapping about it and crashing against it.

It's the dream of Tom Murphy and is another splendidly Liverpudlian kind of thing. Tom is the son of a bus conductor, a self-taught sculptor, successor to Arthur Dooley. He is a former seaman, special-needs teacher and biscuit salesman with no fewer than 18 statues on public display around Liverpool, including the unbeatably iconic trio of Bill Shankly, Dixie Dean and John Lennon. Being a Liverpool sculptor, he naturally quite often wears a suit and tie.

Tom conceived the idea of the statue for the other side of the Mersey, but New Brighton, a seaside resort on life support, decided it might be just the thing to help its regeneration. There are problems, though, over funding and feasibility – Tom thinks it might cost as much as 50 million, 'a few yards of motorway' – and it might never be built. His wife is fed up with with him talking about it, and now he is sitting in his studio on the front at New Brighton, dreaming out loud about how it will look in storm and sun and at night and how he can light it inside with sun and solar-powered fibre optics and how it will stand for reconciliation and peace and universal themes like that, and an impertinent journalist with unforgivably bad taste is asking how big its penis will be, as it does look pretty impressive.

Forty feet. Well, I thought it was interesting. While we're in this area, I'd better, as promised, tell you about Eddie Barford, Joan Collins and me in the bedroom at the Adelphi. Joan was in her fallow period, before she bounced and swung and ecstatically shuddered back in *The Stud* and *The Bitch* and *Dynasty* and all that, and was, I think, trying to flog some book or other. Eddie was, and is, a fine photographer with the *Liverpool Daily Post* and the *Liverpool Echo*. Eddie was taking photographs while I was asking Joan my usual penetrating questions about why she liked Liverpool so much (the local angle is important; when Anthony Eden died, I remember, our obituary began, 'Lord Avon's visits to Liverpool were comparatively rare.' My all-time favourite *Daily Post* headline is 'No News From Nepal', during the conquest of Everest; the best *Echo* misprint, meanwhile, chose to refer to Violet Kray, the mother of the twins, as Mrs Violent Kray).

Joan, although remaining consummately professional, was clearly a little unsure about what Eddie was trying to achieve with his various instructions and angles, as indeed was I, until he explained afterwards that he'd been trying to get Joan next to a reflection in the bedroom mirror of 'Liverpool Resurgent', the Epstein statue across the street in front of Lewis's, the department store. It's a rather splendidly endowed naked male figure standing proud in the prow of a ship which seems to be bursting out of Soft Furnishings or whatever; the 'exceedingly bare' statue, in fact, which partners the 'cathedral to spare' in the city's famous anthem 'In My Liverpool Home'. Unfortunately, this piece of advance synchronicity with Joan's future career had not come off. Journalism has its disappointments as well as its triumphs.

Liverpool Resurgent. I crossed over Hope Street and took a turn into the graveyard just below Giles Gilbert Scott's Anglican cathedral, the biggest in Britain, exceeded in all of Europe only by Seville, Milan and St Peter's, a splendour in sandstone, but far too conventional for Liverpool, much better suited by the leaky, cartoonish Catholic cathedral at the other end of Hope Street, Paddy's wigwam, hiding Lutyen's original crypt, base for a building that was going to beat St Peter's. Such dreams, you see. Such dreams. Scouse dreams. Where else, do you think, might a stonemason have concealed a socialist address (wrapped between copies of *The Clarion* and the *Labour Leader*) in the foundation stone of a cathedral?

Down in the graveyard, there was a fine tomb erected to perpetuate the memory of another mason, who had ascended to 'the Grand Lodge above' in 1901. Splashed in white paint on the side was the legend, 'PS. I'm dead.' Ah, Liverpool.

Chapter Four

Clint Eastwood: Son of Stan

Lost Lancs and the Sons of the Desert

Lost Lancashire lies over the bay, beyond the sands. Windermere, Coniston, the Langdales, Ambleside, the Crake and the Leven; steep fells and sheer valleys, still and sparkling waters. The Lancashire Elysium, gone, taken, cruelly ripped, but over there yet, tantalising on a clear day, when you can make out its beginnings, Humphrey Head, Piel and Walney. For what grievous crime, what broken covenant, was this the punishment? All right, all right, this is Morecambe Bay, and you can see Heysham power station, too; but even so, it does seem a bit thick. Lost Lancashire was a fine piece of whimsy, part of the very essence of the place, part of it only when the tide was out but otherwise unattainable, unless you went through Westmorland.

A trial and struggle to reach: that's the point about elysiums. But such things spoke not to the Local Government Act of 1972, one of those thrusting Wilson–Benn, Heath–Walker white-hot reforms of the '60s and '70s, that brief, heady period between Empire and Irony, when Britain, or rather the UK, was

85

to be swiftly transformed into an efficient, rational, modern nation state, more serious than Sweden, more sensible than Switzerland.

The past was but encumbering baggage. The talk was of local superauthorities which would drive the engine of economic improvement and dynamic change. Partition arrived in 1974. Hundreds of thousands found themselves on the move overnight from Lancashire into Merseyside, or Greater Manchester, or Cheshire, or Cumbria. There was a complete tin ear for the brass of the past or the sensitive little harmonies of the present. The likes of Bolton, Rochdale and Oldham moving into Greater Manchester was bad enough; but Wigan, the very image of Lancashire?

And that was as nothing to the wailing over the doilies and the spluttering in the nineteenth as Widnes and Warrington were imposed upon that posh lost Home County, Cheshire, and the Wirral taken away; as Southport was put into Merseyside and Stretford yoked with Altrincham, Urmston with Sale. The forced secession of Lancashire Over The Sands, now part of Cumbria, was rather lost in this outrage further south. The compensation was a bit of a bureaucrat's egg, too: Lancashire was given the rest of Bowland, previously part of both the Yorkshire West Riding and the Duchy of Lancaster. Still, it did include Dunsop Bridge, which allowed me to make that boast about Lancashire being the centre of the British Isles. Well, yes, but then I've never really seen the point of having a cake and not eating it, have you?

It didn't last long, either. Just 12 years later, Merseyside and Greater Manchester were gone, taken out and shot by Margaret Thatcher, convicted of being a bureaucratic layer and guilty by association with the detested Greater London Council. Their principal legacy seems to be one of those fine confusions that tend to distinguish the British from the Swedes and the Swiss, like the unwritten constitution, the rules to 'Mornington Crescent' and the right way to pronounce Featherstonehaugh.

The point about Merseyside and Greater Manchester now I've read about them, and if I've got this right, is that they were intended to be administrative entities only; the traditional county boundaries were meant to be unchanged by the legislation. At any rate, a subsequent Conservative local-government minister, a Mr Portillo, certainly seemed pretty clear: 'I can confirm that the local-authority areas and boundaries introduced in April 1974 do not alter the boundaries of counties. The 1974 boundaries are entirely administrative and need not affect long-standing loyalties and affinities.'

So St Helens, if you like, was in Merseyside administratively and Lancashire geographically. Unfortunately, the Post Office chose to use the administrative addresses while at the same time employing an entirely different basis for its postcodes, so that, in this instance, St Helens is in the Warrington area, which explains why its postcodes begin 'WA'. And Warrington, you will recall, was supposed to be in Cheshire administratively and Lancashire geographically. Where are they now? I rang up the offices of the Metropolitan Borough of St Helens and asked, so they put me through to the Reference Library, where they were clear that St Helens was still a metropolitan borough of Merseyside, although Merseyside no longer existed. Warrington Borough Council put me on to their tourist division, who were equally clear that Warrington is in Cheshire for all and every purpose; and this even though George Formby himself lies buried there, with his father, George Formby Senior, even bigger than George Junior in his day, and in a rather fine tomb, as it happens.

Clear? Good, although I should perhaps enter a couple of qualifications here. Even though the metropolitan counties were abolished in 1986, they still exist legally, and although most of their powers have devolved to their metropolitan boroughs, which are now in effect unitary authorities, some functions, such as emergency services, public transport and civil defence, are still run on a metropolitan county-wide basis. Similarly, in 1998,

Warrington ceased to be partly administered by Cheshire County Council and became a unitary authority, as did Widnes, which now forms the unitary authority of Halton together with Runcorn, which had always been in Cheshire. Excellent. And then, of course, there was to be one of Mr Prescott's referendums, which proposed a North West Assembly and yet another reorganisation of local councils which could have rescued some of famous old Lancashire from Cumbria and out from under the lingering shadow of Greater Manchester and Merseyside and put it into new unitary authorities. So Wigan, Southport, Barrow and Ulverston, Coniston and Windermere would have moved, but not St Helens, Bolton, Rochdale, Oldham, Warrington or Widnes. But only if there was a Yes vote for the new assembly. And only if, as it turned out, the North-east voted Yes first. Which, of course, it decisively and derisively didn't. So now, after a barely decent period of mourning, they're off again, planning another radical reform, or a bit of a tinker, or nothing, depending on such things as political expediency, who's Prime Minister, and when you're reading this.

All of which, entirely fittingly, leaves Lancashire as the national centre for not knowing where you are from one government to the next. It is, if you like, the mainland setting for the famous Irish response to a request for directions, 'Well, I wouldn't be starting from here if I were you.' And, at the very least, you have to concede the strength of whimsy in a place when it invades something as dry and unpromising as administrative reform.

Stan would have liked it. Stan Laurel, the one who was always getting Oliver Hardy into another fine mess, was born in Lost Lancashire, in Ulverston. Stan would have appreciated it being in Cumbria but not in Cumbria. Stanley and Oliver loved confusion; it was what they did. People with tidy minds which move in a sensible, ordered way run screaming from the kinds of confusion Stan and Ollie created. Most of it was created by Stan.

Ollie preferred to play golf, but Stan never stopped imagining confusion; he was still writing sketches in his head for Ollie long after his big, round and gentle friend was dead.

Ulverston, though. The Friends of Real Lancashire, who stoutly promote the old county wherever they can, claim that a sign has now been erected there bearing the legend 'Ulverston, Lancashire'. Everything I saw proclaimed Ulverston part of Cumbria, but the odd sign saying something completely different wouldn't surprise me. Ulverston is that kind of town. A Stan kind of town. Pole vaulting began in Ulverston, you know, or so I seem to keep reading, although I am having difficulty finding anybody who knows anything about it. But it wouldn't surprise me. Ulverston is like that. You might wonder, for example, why it's dominated by something looking remarkably like the Eddystone Lighthouse. It is, in fact, not a lighthouse at all, but rather a monument to the town's other famous son, Sir John Barrow, Secretary to the Admiralty, patron of the doomed Franklin who was frozen alive in the attempt to find the North-west Passage. The town paid for it, eventually, having failed in a whimsical bid to persuade the Government in the 1850s that it might conceivably, at a push, be used as a lighthouse. But why the Eddystone? I'm working on that, too, along with the pole vaulting.

Meanwhile, let's go into the covered market, where, in one corner, you will find the South Pacific stall, purveying all manner of goods from Polynesia and beyond, carved and otherwise. Your eye may be caught by the sign on the wall just below the market's bright-red hose reel, part of its fire-fighting equipment, which reads 'Balinese Hose Reel, £175'. Or the note quoting the late Mahatma Gandhi on the customer: 'We are not doing him a favour by serving him . . . He is not an interruption of our work, he is the purpose of it,' which is near another note inviting customers wanting service to ask at the fruit stall. For John. John is not there but his mum, Joyce, is. She explains that John's having a day off from serving or scouring the Pacific for bargains. She also explains about the hose reel, telling me there have been certain official objections to John hanging his *objets* too close to it, and that his sign has not been that well received, officially. 'No sense of humour, some people,' says Joyce.

Which is rare, in Ulverston. I said it was a Stan kind of town, and I think it's got something to do with being next to Morecambe Bay, which is a strange place, believe me, sometimes one thing, sometimes the other: sea, sand, land, water, depending on the tide, depending on the moon. And this was the way from Lancaster to Lost Lancashire until the railways came. I first saw it on an August day which must have been very similar to the one on which Anne Radcliffe crossed in 1794:

> We took the early part of the tide and entered these vast and desolate plains before the sea had entirely left them, or the morning mists were sufficiently dissipated to allow a view of distant objects; but the grand sweep of the coast could be faintly traced, on the left, and a vast waste of sand stretching far below it . . . The tide was ebbing fast from our wheels, and its low murmur was interrupted, first, only by the shrill small cry of sea-gulls, unseen . . . and then by the hoarser croaking of sea-geese . . . . The wide desolation of the sands, on the left, was animated only by some horsemen riding towards Lancaster, along the winding edge of the water, and by a mussel fisher in his cart trying to ford the channel we were approaching . . .

Just so. And there, too, with the image of the mussel-fisher, a haunting reminder of how lethal the bay can still be, of the dreadful, slow deaths of more than 20 Chinese cockle-pickers in early 2004, when all modern technology could afford them was the opportunity to make last, desperate and impotent calls on their mobile phones.

This is the great Victorian Lancashire writer Edwin Waugh:

> Before the railway was made, the old way of crossing the sands from Lancaster to Ulverston must have been very striking, both from the character of the scenery around and a sense of danger, which cannot but have given something of the piquancy of adventure to the journey. The channels are constantly shifting, particularly after heavy rains, when they are perilously uncertain. For many centuries past, two guides have conducted travellers over them . . . The office of guide has been so long held by a family of the name of Carter that the country people have given that name to the office itself. A gentleman, crossing from Lancaster, once asked the guide if Carters were never lost on the sands. 'I never knew any lost,' said the guide. 'There's one or two drowned now and then, but they're generally found somewhere i'th bed when th'tide goes out.'

Thank you, Les Carter. Very funny. Not too surprising, then, that Ulverston should have a slightly giddy air to it. This, after all, is the place where they ducked George Fox, the rumbustious founder of the gentle and pacific Quakers. George was not impressed. 'The people of Ulverston are liars, drunkards, whoremongers and thieves and follow filthy pleasures,' he said. And they still seem pretty busy today, too: how many towns do you know that have Easter morris dancing and egg-rolling, a May Flag and Banner Festival, a Comedy Festival in June, a carnival in July, a Rose Festival in August, a Beer Festival and a Charter Festival with Lantern Procession in September, and a Dickens Festival in November? Actually, how many towns do you know that have a Complementary Medicine Festival in any month, let alone every June? I rather like the sound of the Charter Longbow Tournament, too: 'Longbows only, medieval dress preferred'. Dickens? I have that down with the pole vaulting and Eddystone.

But now, having plumped for an Indian chicken tandoori sandwich over the chicken fajitas and the oriental tropical sandwich, all £1.95 at Laurel's International Bistro, next to the two large dummies of Stan and his partner knocked up in Colne by a mate of the energetic and ambitious young proprietor, Mr Kay, it is time for me to visit Ulverston's legendary Laurel and Hardy Museum.

There is a school of journalism which holds that you can never do too much preliminary research into your subject. An admirable modus operandi and one which would no doubt surprise those many people who do not hold our trade in the high regard it enjoys elsewhere, in rather more enlightened lands. Some of us, though, believe that a little too much preparation can get in the way of that first, vivid impression which complete ignorance of the subject affords. 'There is,' we are heard to say, 'nothing like a fresh mind.' A kindred doctrine later in the journalistic process involves the avoidance of 'making that one call too many' in case you learn something which will muddy the clarity of your vision. See also, 'When in doubt, print the legend.'

Anyway, I was expecting the Laurel and Hardy Museum to be just another of those museums that you get all over the place these days, the ones with the interactive exhibits and the carefully colour-coded routes, those wand thingies that play tapes to you and are very good if you can only start in the right place, and the embarrassing people dressed up in fitting fashion who come up and engage you in arch conversation that requires you to suspend things like time and critical faculties and the will to live.

The Laurel and Hardy Museum in Ulverston is not like that.

It is a joyous jumble, a heady hymn to clutter and benign disorder. In short, it is exactly like Stan and Ollie themselves, another fine mess, and you can either exit swiftly for air or you can succumb to their conspiracy against the givens of joined-up, grown-up Life and stand dazed among the cases and shelves, the two life-sized dummies, and every sort of connected memorabilia, including the mass of newspaper clippings and photographs pasted and posted over every inch of these two small, low rooms, ceilings included.

And dazed as you are, you might notice, even if no one else does, that the hat on the Stan dummy has just shot up off his head and back down again, which is when you also notice an elaborate arrangement with hooks and fishing wire reeling off somewhere. And it is then that you find yourself weakening and feeling a bit wistful for the arrows and the colour codes and the talking wand thingy, or at least a guide.

But the guide, like Señor Fat and Señor Thin, as they are known in Mexico, is no longer with us. This was his collection. He was Bill Cubin, sometime Mayor of Ulverston, electrical retailer, café proprietor, and all-time biggest L&H fan. These were the storerooms to his shop, and where his daughter did the washing. You can see Bill on video, over in that corner, talking about Stan, and still feel the energy and the enthusiasm of the true obsessive. His daughter Marion runs the museum now, with a smile and a sudden sweet peal of a laugh, especially when you ask her if the collection has ever been collated, categorised and indexed.

Also difficult to collate, categorise and index: the looks on the faces of those people over there, watching the video, when they finally notice that hat going up and down again right next to them. Difficult to categorise the especial atmosphere, the ambience lent this afternoon by that man wandering around with the can of lager, and the rather precise lady with the South African accent who has somehow decided I work there and wants to know if these two particular Stan and Ollie dolls were made in Lanzarote, because she saw two very like them there. Then the hat goes off again, operated, I can now see, by Marion's assistant, Alan, a droll man who keeps wandering in from the front desk to do it, and confides, in response to my inquiry about Clint Eastwood, 'No one today, but it's not over yet.'

Clint Eastwood? Ah, yes, Clint. I will tell you, but have a look at this first: it's a slice of yellow velvet curtain, and it's one of the prizes of the collection, being a piece of curtain from Stan's house in Beverly Hills. It's lined with a heavy black material, because Stan was very worried about air raids during the Second World War. In Beverly Hills. I was also taken with the donors of the slice of curtain: Woody and Martha Tolkien, who had bought Stan's house after he moved to Santa Monica. Tolkien? 'Woody was his nephew,' explains Marion. Woody Tolkien? Can such things be? Something else I'd better check on, although I think we're getting pretty much into that one call too many territory. I can tell you though, while we're here, that J.R.R. Tolkien served in the Lancashire Fusiliers in the First World War, and that his experience of Lancashire soldiers coloured his books. Sam Gamgee in *The Lord of the Rings*, he later said, 'is indeed a reflection of the English soldier, of the privates and batmen I knew in the 1914 war, and recognised as so far superior to myself'. There you are: ubiquitous Lancashire, even in Middle Earth.

But back to Clint. You must have heard. There is this rather wonderful urban legend that Clint is Stan's illegitimate son. Clint, Son of Stan (I must mention here, incidentally, the American tattooist who was sued by a biker when he missed out the first 'A' in 'Son of Satan'). But, Laurel and Eastwood. Look at them and you can see why there's a rumour. And not only that: there's some excellent circumstantial evidence which would more than satisfy the averagely exacting conspiracy theorist or ufologist.

Clint's listing in *Who's Who in America*, for example, makes no mention of his parents. He is also secretive about his year of birth, although it is generally agreed to be 1930. Clint's birthday is in May; it is recorded that in May 1930, Stan and his wife Lois had a son about whom equally little is known. It is the sort of story that you would like to be true. Bill Cubin, when asked if Stan was the man, generally replied, 'Well, he had a bike.' This is a gnomic Lancastrian turn of phrase indicating a man who gets around, puts himself about, goes to call, and leaves the bike propped up round the back, if you follow me.

And Stan certainly did get around, after a fashion all of his own. He got married rather a lot, often to the same woman, for one thing. He doesn't seem to have been legally married to his first wife, even though she claimed he was, which proved a bit of an embarrassment when she arrived while Stan was in the process of getting divorced from his second wife. He then married his third wife before that divorce was finalised, so had to marry her again to make it legal.

When he married his fourth wife, a Russian called Vera Shuvalova (I promise you), the third wife interrupted the ceremony claiming she was still his wife. She then started reporting that Stan's house was on fire, and, on one occasion, sent an undertaker and hearse round to ask for his body. You probably wouldn't be terribly surprised to learn that, after he divorced the Russian (she got upset when he started digging a hole in the garden and indicated it was for her), Stan remarried the third wife before divorcing her again and marrying another Russian, an opera singer who had previously been married to Raphael, 'The World's Greatest Concertina Virtuoso'. The first Russian, meanwhile, was in New York, badgering theatrical agents with her rendition of 'When Irish Eyes Are Smiling'.

Oliver, by contrast, was a model of restraint when it came to wives, making do with just the three. I told you: absolute bloody bedlam. And they liked a drink.

Clint, though: back in Ulverston, Bill Cubin's daughter, Marion, is telling me that when Clint was Mayor of Carmel, one of the local policemen, a big fan of Stan and Ollie, got to sit next to him at an official dinner and asked him the Big Question. Personally, on the one call too many basis, I would have strongly advised against it. Clint, though, just looked at him, and then, with the same straight face that has accompanied the rubbing out of punks and the sticky, perforated end of any number of evil hombres, placed his hand on that strangely reminiscent coiffure and did the Stan thing with the scrabbling fingers. Splendid. Why should I ruin everything and tell you that it's all complete nonsense and that, sadly, Stan's little son died after a few days? Precisely.

Besides, behind Marion, I have just noticed this sign on the door into the second room, reading 'The Nico Mourits Extension'. Naturally enough, Nico is a Dutch L&H fan who paid for the room to be set up with his winnings from a television quiz show. Then there's that other little room over there, the one in the dark, the one where Marion used to have her washing machine, where people in anoraks who I thought had only come in out of the rain, and probably had, are now sitting through endless black-and-white one-reelers of The Boys, as they are known to the cognoscenti. They are sitting on what look like contemporary cinema seats, and are, of course, from 1927, picked up by Bill Cubin as a job lot.

What do you make of Stan and Ollie? I wish I found them rather funnier than I do, as they have some fine admirers, including Kurt Vonnegut, Barry Humphries, Peter Sellers, David Hockney, Winston Churchill and Franklin Roosevelt. And, rather more predictably, Ronald Reagan. Stalin and Tito were very keen on them as well. To make a dictator laugh: that is a thing. I wonder what Stalin liked about them. The biddable stupidity of the proletariat they so amiably personified? Or perhaps he just liked the violent bits.

What I do like is their gentleness and whimsy. Ollie met his last wife on the set of *The Flying Deuces*, a Foreign Legion sort of a thing The Boys made in 1939, which I can take or leave apart from one scene, completely foisted upon the plot, where, for no reason at all, Ollie starts singing 'Shine On Harvest Moon' and then joins Stan in a dance.

The combination of Ollie's unique kind of tenor and Stan's delicate, sad-faced, deliberate hoof and shuffle, straight to camera, is so direct and appealing that it almost makes you believe that the music hall couldn't have been that bad after all. When Ollie joins in the dance with a grace that shouldn't belong to a fat man, you have to steady yourself not to succumb to some flight of fancy about minstrels and loss of innocence and that curious magic which makes you nostalgic for some thing or place you're too young to remember or have only visited in movies, in black and white. And it makes me want to cry.

For there is about them, for all Ollie's bluster, an essentially gentle quality that you wouldn't have expected from one who had come up on the halls in Britain and then spent years struggling to make it in the States while watching his old chum, room-mate and role model, Charles Chaplin, grow ever bigger; nor from the other, the teased and fatherless fat boy from Georgia. It's a gentleness you don't find much in other comedy acts, and a gentleness that fitted them privately, amid all the domestic mayhem, as well as out there in public.

I noted down a letter on display in the museum, written by Stan in 1957 to a couple he kept up a correspondence with for 12 years, which was the sort of thing he did, trying to answer anything anybody sent to him. He thanks them for their latest letter and continues:

> I'm sorry that Mr Hardy is unable to see it, on account of his illness – as you know, he has had a stroke, and his right side is paralysed. Also his speech is affected (unable

to talk). The poor fellow is in bad shape, and still confined to bed (seven months now). It's certainly distressing. I too had a slight stroke two years ago which paralysed my left side but fortunately I made a wonderful recovery, thank God, and am able to get around quite well again. However, I doubt if I shall ever be in shape to work again. Strange that this should happen to us both, isn't it?

Near to this was a copy of an article from *The Oldie* magazine, written by George Macdonald Fraser, author of the Flashman books, in which he recalls going backstage as a boy to meet Ollie at Her Majesty's, Carlisle, when Laurel and Hardy were touring Britain in 1954. Ollie, 62 by then and obviously exhausted after the show, had been charm itself. As Fraser was leaving the dressing-room, Ollie called him back. The boy turned round and saw Hardy doing his famous thing with his tie, wobbling it up and down, the counterpoint to Stan and his hair.

This was the third British tour. The first had been in 1947. Their film career had fallen victim to changing fashion and studios, and there were no more flag-waving wartime concert tours of the sort that had seen Groucho Marx lost in admiration for their way with a whisky. Bernard Delfont, Michael Grade's uncle, with the usual family shrewdness, knew they would be a terrific draw on stage in a Britain starved of most things, including entertainment, and so they were: 8 months, 26 dates, London, Birmingham, Blackpool, Margate, Dudley, Bolton, Swindon, Boscombe, Margate, Butlin's Skegness, where they judged the knobbly knees contest, and even the Glasgow Empire, legendary graveyard of unaboriginal comedians. When Max Miller was asked to go there, he said, 'Listen, I'm a comic not a missionary.' Mike Winters opened there to complete silence, broken only by a lone voice when Bernie appeared: 'Christ, there's two of them.' But they loved The Boys.

It couldn't last, of course. By the second tour, in 1952, after a desperate interlude spent making what turned out to be their final, disastrous film, *Atoll K*, in Paris (really), there were the signs that Stan's career was ending on the boards where it had started, and Ollie's with it. The dates were less full, less starry, less London, the reviewsless kind, and both of them were ill.

But they were caught in the unforgiving, unquestionable going-on of the show, and so were back the next year. George Macdonald Fraser in Carlisle was lucky. Hardy was more and more tired, increasingly on the Scotch. Stan, ever gracious, apologised to a journalist for not being funny in the morning in Sheffield. In the week of 29 March to 5 April, they were appearing at the Palace, Grimsby, before moving on to weeks in Leeds and Edinburgh and then Carlisle. For the Grimsby date, they stayed in Cleethorpes. 'What,' said Ollie one night, staring out of his hotel window, 'are we doing in a goddamn place like this?' The Captain Scott of comedy.

A month later, they were at the Palace Theatre, Plymouth. After the first night, Ollie, suffering from a temperature, flu and what turned out to be a mild heart attack, couldn't go on. Derek Rosaire and Tony the Wonder Horse, Betty Kaye's Pekinese and the other acts had to fend for themselves, although Stan came along to lend moral support. He wouldn't go on alone: 'I would not attempt it. I know it would have been disappointing. I am completely lost without Hardy.' They never made their final date at the Empire, Swansea. It was over.

Ollie had his major stroke in 1956, and was robbed of speech and movement. Stan used to visit him and, victims of an irony that underlines the Great Scriptwriter's occasionally dubious taste, they were forced to try to communicate only by gesture and expression. Silent stars indeed. Ollie died in 1957. Stan stayed on, in a small apartment by the sea in Santa Monica, until 1965, still answering letters, still writing the sketches they would never play.

Not unusually, I had by now run out of space in my notebook and was writing the details of Stan's letter around the edges of a leaflet I'd found on the front desk of the museum which, when I looked at it more closely, turned out to be advertising the Ninth Annual Laurel And HarDay at the Beer Engine in Wigan, organised by the Bacon Grabbers tent of the Sons of the Desert, the Laurel and Hardy appreciation society, and featuring Ronnie Hazlehurst, composer of many popular television themes, including the one for *Last of the Summer Wine*, with his reformed orchestra, performing music from the Laurel and Hardy films. Who should resist?

There is another rule of journalism: never quote a taxi driver. It is held to give too much of an impression of recent arrival and insufficient research. 'Do not indulge him in this tired cliché,' was the message I once saw attached by a *Daily Telegraph* foreign editor to a report from one of his correspondents featuring the wisdom of some far-flung cabbie or other. I tend to get round this by not mentioning that the person quoted is, in fact, a taxi driver; more scrupulous foreign correspondents rely on many taxi drivers having another day or night job.

I'm telling you this for your information and by way of an apology for quoting the taxi driver who picked me up to take me to the Beer Engine in Wigan. 'Could you,' I said to him, 'take me to the Beer Engine?' 'If I must,' he replied, in that Wigan way, the one that while not exactly inviting further conversation, doesn't exactly close the door on it, either. I decided to press on. 'What's wrong with the Beer Engine, then?' I asked him. He looked at me in his rear-view mirror. 'It's personal,' he said. Splendid.

I told him why I was going there. And, no word of a lie, and this is why I have to tell you about him, he then said: 'Is Clint Eastwood really Stan Laurel's son?' I took a non-committal line. Then, for some reason which now eludes me, I asked him if he had any children. 'No, I've got dogs,' he said. Frankly, I can't think why I didn't ask him where he'd heard about Clint and Stan, but there you are.

We were now at the Beer Engine, which is in the Poolstock area of the town, last visited by me, you might remember, in search of The Once and Future King's old haunts. You should imagine a Labour club of the old style, because that's what it used to be. There was a bowling green to one side, a 'newly refurbished function room' to accompany the best Lancastrian social-club mock-Tudor, big carpets and a sign which read 'Licensed for singing and dancing of a like kind'. The Sons of the Desert were easily recognisable on account of their dress, which featured white T-shirts and red fezzes, not a regular sight in Wigan, even in September.

The Sons were conceived after the imaginary fraternal order – lodges, sashes, fezzes, that sort of thing – which featured in probably the pair's best film, *Sons of the Desert* (1935). It was the idea of their biographer, John McCabe, and sanctioned by Stan not long before he died. The fans, or, they would prefer, buffs, are divided into tents, under the nominal charge of a Grand Sheik, and, under him, a Vice-Sheik, or 'sheik in charge of vice'. Each tent is named after a Laurel and Hardy film. Stan himself devised their motto, 'Two minds without a single thought'. Article Five of the constitution reads, 'The officers and board-members-at-large shall have absolutely no authority whatsoever.' There must have been 50 of them assembled at the Beer Engine.

Now, I know what you're thinking. But listen. I've written pieces about quite a few groups of enthusiasts, from potholers to village cricketers to croquet players to ballroom dancers to scrabble players to the people who wait in the hope of an autograph from someone who was in a *Carry On* film just the once. I liked the Sons of the Desert, or at least the ones in the Beer Engine. They seemed to have that Stan and Ollie trick of being in on the joke at exactly the right calibration. The beer probably helped, too. The master of ceremonies was called Ian, a big man with a slow smile and that calm appraisal of the essential ridiculousness of existence which may well be the mark of the true Lancastrian, although I've noticed that West Africans are pretty big on it, too, unlike, say, Yorkshire people, or Londoners.

Ian was a police sergeant. The Grand Sheik of our host tent, the Bacon Grabbers (the title of one of the last Laurel and Hardy silent shorts), was called Chris and he was a tax inspector in Manchester, which is why they'd decided on the name. I must say I was rather taken with the idea of policemen and tax inspectors being fans of confusion and chaos and innocence; splendid to think that, given the right circumstances, Lancashire policemen might start running round and round at a tremendous speed, possibly chasing tax inspectors.

Ian took me to a room round the back of the Beer Engine, next to the bowling green. The Sons were in a preliminary meeting, which, as far as I could gather, was in some earnest, and concerned attempts by the Sons in America to exert rather more control over the Sons in Europe than those Sons deemed seemly. Three options had been proposed and voted on across Europe. The Finnish response seemed to have been particularly amusing. I was pondering on how all this tied in with not having any rules. Ian said, 'You can be certain of one thing: a decision will never be made. And if it is, it will be changed.'

So we stood at the back, chatting. Ian said he liked absurd humour, especially old absurd humour. George Formby, of course, and Ealing comedy; *Carry On* films, before they got too smutty. His ambition was to have a big south-facing garden with a fish pond and a shed, where he would keep his film collection. No serious films and no colour ones, with the exception of Kenneth Branagh's *Henry V*.

Not that he took it too seriously; there was one bloke here who had made a study of the number of appearances of the same wall in the L&H output, which Ian thought was going a bit far.

But they did like to organise a good day. Three years before, the Laurel & HarDay had coincided with Diana's funeral. It was also the 50th anniversary of the day The Boys visited Wigan: 8,000 had packed into the speedway stadium at Poolstock just to watch them being driven round. Ian had planned a mini-parade there from the Beer Engine, but worried that it might be 'inappropriate', given the funeral and everything. In the end, they settled for a 'solemn walk' there. What a marvellous and somehow fitting touch, I thought, on that very strange day: the Sons of the Desert slow-marching through Wigan.

The debate concluded without conclusion. A Son came over to Ian. 'Now then,' he said, 'where's your DJ?' Ian usually dressed up in evening suit for his MC duties. But it was being altered, and his tailor had gone off to Tenerife. So he was in shorts today. What did his wife make of The Boys? 'I don't think she likes humour, really,' said Ian, in that Lancashire way.

There were quite a few women there, including Marion, Bill Cubin's daughter, from the museum in Ulverston. This being a Stan and Ollie thing, girls can, of course, be Sons. The event's first international visitor, Hans, from Holland, had brought his wife, Marike, with him. She was not a fan, but she had been ill, and Hans thought some walking in the Lake District combined with Wigan might cheer her up. Marike looked a little bemused, but not unhappy. Stood near her was a man dressed up as Stan. He was called Gary, he was from Liverpool, and he did a lot of work with his friend Jim as Laurel and Hardy lookalikes. Sadly, Jim had not been able to make it that day.

According to my notes, Gary had been doing a bit of juggling and unicycling, too, but he had met this Clint Eastwood lookalike on a job at the Leeds Hilton who had advised him to concentrate on the Stan thing. Perhaps I'd better check that. But I'm pretty certain that Gary and Jim had been put up in luxury and paid to spend three weeks walking around a new shopping mall in Dubai. Sons of the Desert, indeed.

Ronnie Hazlehurst seemed a bit gruff, but that might have been because he was one of the few there not visiting the bar. Ronnie was clearly a pro, right down to his light-entertainment leisure wear. He had been a fan since he was four. 'It's funny,' he said, 'I wouldn't cross the road to watch Charlie Chaplin, but I've always loved them. I don't know whether it's because Stan was from Ulverston and I'm from Dukinfield, and it's a kind of Lancashire thing.'

Ronnie's band was good, very tight, professional. Ian announced that Ronnie's CDs were on sale at the back. Somebody said it was all right, he had just filmed one with his video camera. This seemed to go down very well with everyone but Ronnie. Ronnie and the band played some fine incidental music. He then suggested that some of the Sons might care to join in. He started on 'Shine On Harvest Moon'. After some hesitation and much encouragement, Ian went up, seized the microphone and had a go. 'You're in the wrong key,' shouted Ronnie. Ian retreated. Ronnie, clearly, had his standards, in every way.

But Ronnie was a Barker rather than a Biter: he relented as the afternoon went on, and soon there were groups of Sons cheerfully assassinating 'Honolulu Baby' with appropriate Hawaiian movements, and much more besides, including, of course, a rousing assault on 'Sons of the Desert': 'Marching along, two thousand strong . . .'

Happy Harry Ingle was sat watching. Harry, 86, from Ulverston, was small and wiry and, as with many octogenarians, wore his trousers up to his neck. He had almost met Stan during the war, when his ship docked at San Diego and he telephoned Stan up the road in Hollywood. Stan had wanted to meet him, but there wasn't time. Stan always did keep his name in the phone book, even when he was living at Fort Laurel, the mansion with the high walls to keep former wives out. I liked the idea of Harry just ringing him up; it reminded me of the story of George Formby appearing on stage in a big theatre in Canada and spotting an old friend from Wigan about 15 rows back: 'Eee, Walter, is that you?'

Harry had managed to meet Stan when The Boys visited Ulverston on the 1947 tour, and Stan was presented with a copy of his birth certificate and visited the house where he was born, where his grandparents, the Metcalfes, had lived, and where Stan stayed in his earlier years while his theatrical father, Arthur Jefferson, and mother, Madge, were on the move. (Stan started out on the halls as Stan Jefferson; why he later chose Laurel is not entirely clear, like much of what was going on inside that head.)

He had always been a fan, had Harry, but he really got keen on the Sons after his marriage broke up, when he was 71. He'd been everywhere with them, to conventions in Valley Forge, Los Angeles, Nashville, Detroit. They'd paid for the one he went on for his 80th birthday. Now he was a kind of mascot and he had certainly had his share of luck. An eventful war, they had said. 'No, very quiet,' he said. 'I happened to be sunk five times, but we don't mention the war.'

And he's one of the few to have shaken the hand, touched the cloak. The Bacon Grabbers always tried to get a good attraction for the day, some connection with The Boys, hence Ronnie. They had been hopeful of getting a child star from one of the films, but unfortunately he was down with a dodgy prostate. A child star with a dodgy prostate; can there be a more poignant illustration of this mortal coil?

I asked Harry if there was anything special about Ulverston. 'We take anybody in. We do.' They had taken Stan in, he said, and George Fox. And there were Buddhists now, at Conishead Priory, up above the bay. People were always coming around to talk about the Bible, too. 'I had one the other day. He said to me, "Brother, can you give me a pound for God?" I said, "How old are you?" He said, "I'm 26." So I said, "Well, I'm 86, so you'd better give me the money, because I'll be seeing Him before you.'" Very good, Harry.

And so it went. David Wyatt, the man who knew about the wall, turned out to be a brick and happily abandoned his projected talk on 'Laurel and Hardy and the Will Hay Connection' when it ran into equally happy and clearly traditional barracking. Sons everywhere were cracking up at shouted lines that only Sons understood: 'You're all nuts!'; 'I ordered a room with a southern explosion!'. England were about to play Germany in that World Cup qualifier, and I thought I might take a look at it in the Beer Engine's bar. 'Where are you going?' said Ian. 'You can't leave now! It's time for the Earsy, Kneesy, Nosey World Championships!'

And so it was that, while England were going one down and the boy Owen was bringing them back in one of most celebrated matches the national game has known, a large audience in the function room were entirely oblivious, preferring to concentrate on a row of seated Sons competing in one of Stan's finest inventions, in which the trick is to touch the ears, slap the knees and pull the nose in strict sequence. I can't remember who won – I rather think it was Hans – but I must say it made me proud to be a Lancastrian.

Back in Ulverston, I went to see the Buddhists at Conishead Priory, as I was rather taken with Happy Harry's theory of Ulverston's rich and hostly embrace (despite his initial welcome, George Fox had later lived just outside the town). It also occurred to me that the Buddhists might have some interesting views on whether or not Lancashire was the county where women die of love.

Conishead began as a leper hospital, run by Augustinian Black Canons. Out in the bay, which was in mist mood this day, is Chapel Island, where the monks prayed for the safety of travellers. The ruined chapel there is a fake, a folly, built by the

Braddyll family in Victorian times, to go with the mock-Gothic extravaganza they built on the site of the priory, ruining themselves in the process. The house became a hydropathic hotel in 1878, so luxuriously appointed that it became known as the Paradise of Furness. And now, since 1976, the Paradise has become the Nirvana, a Manjushri Mayahana Buddhist Centre, following the Kadampa Buddhism tradition as interpreted by the renowned teacher Geshe Kelsang Gyatso promoting wisdom, a good heart and a peaceful state of mind.

Clearly, Geshe-la, as he is known for short, would be the ideal man to ask about Lancashire and love, as he had chosen Conishead to build his first temple in the West, to be followed by one outside New York and then near every major city in the world. Sadly, a note in the office said he was resting and unavailable after a big international meeting. I had also arrived on a day when there were no guided tours, but a charming girl who was studying there offered to show me round. As we made our tour, ending up outside at the Temple, she tried to explain Buddhism to me. I don't know about you, but I can never quite get a grasp on the more subtle Eastern religions; listening to her was remarkably similar to listening to the Sons of the Desert exchanging their more arcane Laurel and Hardy punchlines.

The Temple was a sight, though: built in traditional design, low and calm, and creating a magnificent clash with the crazed gothic style of the Priory. Inside were shrine cabinets containing bronzes of the Buddha and his disciples, and a superbly detailed model of a palace meant to embody the pure world of enlightenment. Placed at each corner of the cabinet was a 500-gram jar of Marmite. Elsewhere were bottles of gherkins and a packet of pasta. Offerings, the girl explained. 'Every single person that visits the temple will receive some good mental imprints,' I read. 'Every being, even pigeons, insects, and flies.'

On the way back, I told the girl I was trying to write a book about Lancashire being the county where women die of love.

107

'I'm dying of love,' she said. 'I'm in love with a Buddhist monk.' This, I think, was a Buddhist joke. Another girl came up, in tears. Her dog had just been put down, she said. I should probably have said something positive about reincarnation, but I didn't really like to intrude.

Stan Laurel believed in reincarnation. In *The Flying Deuces*, Ollie, killed in a plane crash, comes back as a horse, with, of course, a little moustache. Earlier, they had been discussing coming back. 'I'd come back as myself,' says Stan. 'I always got along swell with me.' And here's a funny thing. Dick Van Dyke gave the eulogy at Stan's funeral. Dick was a friend and a fan. Read this bit:

> There were some strange places that Stan and Ollie went
> . . . once they took a tourist vacation and went to China.
> They were in the deepest, deepest part of the interior of
> China, and, as tourists, they visited a Buddhist temple
> there. They were invited to come in and look at the altar,
> and there on the table was a tremendous blow-up in
> colour of Ollie and Stan.

Well. Deep waters. I bought a copy of *Transform Your Life*, by Geshe-la. There was quite a lot in it, but nothing I could see about women dying of love. He did have this to say, though: 'If our love for others diminishes as soon as they cause us problems or fail to appreciate us, this indicates that our love is not pure.' He was obviously on the right track, so I wrote to him, asking why he had chosen Ulverston and what he thought about women dying of love.

While I was waiting for the guru's reply, I thought I would check up on some of those things, as promised, like the pole vaulting, for example, and Dickens; I was lucky enough to find Jennifer Snell, who is not so much a mine of information on Ulverston as a bubbling beck, as they call streams round here.

Jennifer works at the local newspaper, the *North-West Evening Mail*, takes guided tours round Ulverston, serves on the Dickens Festival committee and raises money to get Ulverston's last Morecambe Bay trawler sailing again by organising the annual Shetland Pony Grand National, run in conjunction with, naturally, the world's first Pantomime Horse Grand National. So: pole vaulting. Yes, indeed, said Jennifer, it originated here in the early nineteenth century from the trusted method of clearing the local becks with a pole, although it's not entirely clear why they needed to go up as well as across, except that, being Ulverstonians, they probably felt the need of a bit of a flourish. Edwin Woodburn of Ulverston was both Champion Pole Leaper of England and World Champion, 1874.

Why is the Barrow Monument based on the Eddystone lighthouse? 'I haven't the foggiest.' Thank you, Jennifer, very good, please continue. 'All lighthouses look the same, though, don't they, tall and thin with a light on the top.' What is the Dickens connection? 'None at all, really. Allegedly he passed through on his way elsewhere.' I took the opportunity to ask Jennifer if she was aware of the custom in the area of naming children after Ferdinando, the Earl of Derby in the reign of Elizabeth, Shakespeare's patron. Well, she said, there had been a Ferdinando Hodgson, a local character who had been a regular at the Commercial Inn, run by Theodore Cuthbert Clarke, who claimed to be the son of the King of Corsica. Bramwell Brontë was always popping in, too, apparently. Ah, Ulverston!

I had a reply from the guru's secretary, which was pleasant and helpful, but didn't tackle dying of love. Ah, well. Meanwhile, there's one other thing. About the only fact I had managed to glean about the Laurel and Hardy Museum before I went was that it had the loo seat from Stan's house in Ulverston. I couldn't find it anywhere, though. In Wigan, I asked Marion where it had been. 'On the loo,' she said, with that laugh.

Chapter Five

The Greatest Game

In which Obsession sells a dummy to Detachment and
narrowly beats Disillusionment to go over in the corner

St Helens. Can a beautiful place have an ugly name? Can an ugly
place have a beautiful name? The Bard, famously, had a rosy view
of this. I wonder if he had ever been to St Helens. He could have
stopped by, on his Lancashire excursion, on the way up to
Hoghton Tower for his service with the Hoghtons. Perhaps he
said a quick prayer in St Helen's Chapel, which was all there was
then. Nothing to give him pause, yet; no glass, no smells, no
chemicals, no waste, no coal, no strange glowing dusks, no
steaming waters.

Poor St Helens. It never had a chance, really. Heaven might
have been above, but there was sand to the north, salt to the
south, sea to the west and seams below. The Revolution stops
here, and stays, powered by the Pilkingtons and the Beechams
and collieries and chemicals and Britain's first canal and a hungry
host of Irish off the Liverpool boats. By the middle of the
nineteenth century, there were 15 glassworks, 11 chemical works

and 35 mines: all this and copper smelting, too. Red glare at night, industrialist's delight. 'Its population doubled to 11,000 between 1830 and 1845,' writes Alan Crosby in his *History of Lancashire*, 'as insanitary streets of tiny houses were hastily thrown up . . . the squalid and unsewered streets and the noxious pollution from the copper and chemical works made it a peculiarly unhealthy place.'

That name, though. Wigan, Widnes, Warrington: hard towns with names that announce it. St Helens suggests something else. Even the names of its districts, the old submerged and swallowed villages, have a poetry: Thatto Heath, Pocket Nook, Toll Bar, Finger Post, Peasley Cross. Or maybe it's just me. I do like a bit of romance, and it is my home town. I used to believe that it was called St Helens because Helen, the British mother of the great Constantine, daughter of Old King Cole, had stopped to have a look there in her quest for the True Cross. Sadly, despite my best efforts, it turns out that she was, in fact, an innkeeper's daughter from Bithynia who quite sensibly concentrated her search on the Holy Land.

So, not romantic. A certain indefinable quality only in so far as the eastward expansion of Liverpool has muddied its identity as an independent Lancashire township. It was made part of Merseyside when there was a Merseyside, and, as I have pointed out with appropriate wonder elsewhere, remains a metropolitan borough of Merseyside even though Merseyside no longer exists.

Not that Liverpudlians are too impressed. They call citizens of St Helens 'woollybacks', a description which, with its combination of city condescension and completely inappropriate rural imagery, sums up the Scouse sense of humour almost as well as the story I told you about Cilla earlier. The chief practical effect of the link is that the accent in St Helens is a head-on collision between Scouse and Lancs, achieving a unique high-pitched effect heard to best advantage in that most famous son of the town, Johnny Vegas.

Me? I don't have a St Helens accent. I don't have any sort of accent, really. As I said in my introduction, my mother was hit so hard by her introduction to the place just after the War that she struck back in any way she could, including a permanent veto on the use of hard vowels by any of her children at any time. My way with an 'a' gave everybody a good laugh when I arrived in the preparatory class of the local grammar school, especially when combined with my first name. Still, it could have been Sue, and I have always been grateful for this early introduction to the nuances of the English social system, as it takes a long time to work out, and I'm not there yet. Why, for example, does no one expect my middle-class acquaintances from Essex and Berkshire and Worcestershire to speak with a mouthful of burrs and glottals and truncated terminals? And yet people always say to me, accusingly, when I tell them where I'm from, 'Well, you don't sound like it.' Why? What is that all about? The Indivisibility of the Northerner? It makes me feel like some sort of imposter.

Which I would be if I tried to make too much of my link to St Helens. The fact is that, from the age of ten, I spent most of my time somewhere else, being educated in a minor public school by the Jesuits; when I was fourteen, my mother persuaded my father to move out to the somewhat more rural environs of Ormskirk, eleven miles north. And when we were in St Helens, it was, as befits a relatively successful grocer, at the relatively posh end, a good mile or two up from the glass heart of 'Pilks' – Pilkington's – and the rest of it, still glowing and belching and steaming, though not as badly as a century before. We backed onto the golf course, near the park, next door to one of the town's leading solicitors.

My family's struggles were done; my father's father had fought his way up and over the counter. None of that for me. (Socially, though, we clearly still had a little way to go. The solicitor was overheard by my father discussing him at the annual charity ball: 'He's in trade.') After school, it was Oxford, and then London, Fleet Street and such, where my struggle has been mostly with the fantastically irritating way that English refuses to do what it's told, and a slight but lingering uncertainty under the ever-watchful eyes of the upper middle classes when there's more than one knife and fork.

There were no cobbles; cruelly, too, we had a Labrador, not a whippet. But that doesn't mean I haven't been able to conjure up my own little bit of Northernness, my own useful but entirely safe piece of outsider status, about as dangerous as being a Catholic, my little bit of evidence that I'm not conforming like mad to what I suppose to be metropolitan middle-class sophistication. I like rugby league.

I do. I love it. I loved it before I laid on it all that angsty, exiled, displaced emotional claptrap; I loved it from the moment I first saw it, at the age of nine, when I went down the road from the grammar school with a couple of schoolmates who had agreed to overlook my aforesaid social shortcomings (the vowel thing, the first name) to stand in the Boys' Pen and watch St Helens play the touring Australians.

Why do you fall in love? What is it in particular about this particular particular? I don't remember much about the Australians, except that Saints, as, inevitably, they are called, beat them, less remarkable then than it would be now; I don't remember much about Saints, either, except for the wingers, both South African, Jan Prinsloo and Tom Van Vollenhoven. Australians, South Africans: it all seemed awesomely exotic and exciting for St Helens. And this Vollenhoven, he was a star, with a blond crew cut, aloof on his wing, waiting, his pace and grace ready to explode at an instant, but hidden beneath the poise. And, if you were fat, nine and bespectacled, this was something truly to behold.

Those are the good years to be a fan, from then to sixteen, when hero-worship is fine and uncomplicated, when it's natural to entrust your immediate happiness to the efforts of people over whom you have no control because that's what you do all the time anyway, and when you can still have dreams that you might be able to do it yourself, which, however unlikely, is still more likely than if you're fifty.

You've got your team, your favourites, and you don't worry about there being two different types of rugby, the one you play at school and this one, the one they don't seem to play anywhere else. Just another mystery of life to add to the list, along with girls and logarithms and why my armpits had suddenly started smelling. But this mystery had a magic that was marvellous to be caught up in, with the sudden changes of tempo on the pitch and the gusting moods of the crowd, all bantering solos one minute, united excitement the next. My dad didn't go, but his friends did, and took me up to the back row of the stand, where they sat, the St Helens middle class, at ease in a satisfied and comforting fug of tobacco, lunch and position, but ready for brisk and forthright upbraidings of misguided referees or ungentlemanly opponents. They were mostly self-made, these men, or from family firms, and you don't seem to get them so much in English towns any more, now that it's all chains and Gap and groups and Currys and franchises, and the wholesalers and the gents' outfitters have all gone. A lost hierarchy, and not such a bad thing on the whole, perhaps.

But the game was what it was all about – and Vollenhoven. The year after my epiphany, 1961, St Helens reached the Challenge Cup final at Wembley, playing their rival of rivals, Wigan. You could see the great man was in the mood. Perhaps it was the hot day in May that did it, reminding him of home. He almost got away a couple of times in the first half, those moments when the roar starts and is as quickly stifled, leaving the expectation up a new notch. Another hero, Alex Murphy, the St Helens scrum-half, had skittered his way over for a typical try, all jink and cheek, in the first half, but it didn't look to be

114

enough, particularly when Billy Boston, Wigan's great winger, as black and bullocking as Vollenhoven was white and racing, went over our line with three men clinging on, only to be called back for a foot out in touch.

The game was moving towards Wigan; you could feel it, everyone knew it. Then, a dropped ball in the St Helens 25 and the St Helens centre is away. He draws one man and then passes to Vollenhoven, who draws another and passes it back, to receive it once more in return and accelerate beyond Wigan's floundering full-back and surge to the line and round under the posts. What a try! Almost the length of the pitch and plenty of chances for it to be checked and thwarted; time and reason enough for a mighty roar, catharsis and climax, as good as it gets, Wembley, against Wigan, against the run of play, the killer blow.

What a try, I said to my Uncle Frank. To which he replied that it wasn't as good as the one Tom had scored against Hunslet in the Championship final at Odsal in 1959. 'Now that was a try,' said Uncle Frank, who had a laugh like a happy bark that he used a lot, especially in my grandmother's kitchen, where he wisely chose to spend family parties, serving drink and taking some on himself. He travelled a lot, late in life, on business, and enjoyed going abroad; but he saved his faraway look for talking about the old Saints, the Saints that had gone before, a holy roll of names like Carlton and Honey and Gullick and Llewellyn and Moses. Moses! Glyn, a fine Welsh full-back, as it happens.

Alex Murphy used to go to our church, smart in a blazer, but I didn't dare speak to him. In 1965, I stood next to Tom Van Vollenhoven at the urinals in the Savoy Cinema, Bridge Street, St Helens. No, of course I didn't look. The next year, St Helens beat Wigan at Wembley again, more convincingly but not as entertainingly; soon after that, Vollenhoven retired back to South Africa, and Murphy left to be player-coach at Leigh. I stayed with the Saints.

What can I tell you? I could tell you about Saints until your eyes were as glazed as anything from Pilks. I could tell you about the exhilaration that soars at the sight of a big prop forward charging clear before slipping it to a lung-pumping second-row forward at full tilt and then finding the scrum-half, who suddenly cuts inside, wrong-footing the desperate defence before feeding his winger to race in at the corner, leaving you laughing at the sudden, common, uncomplicated joy of it.

I could tell you about the drawn-out, common, uncomplicated despair of sitting in silent misery at one end of Wembley while Wiganers are singing and waving and generally going mad at the other as your side succumbs 27–0. I could tell you that the dull passages of play are there to provide the necessary contrast to the excitement, for enjoying the crowd and its humours, and for cheerfully abusing the referee, or any of your players deemed to be not quite up to it, as in, 'Lumbey, you're no bloody use, you!', or, if a player has reached the veteran stage, 'Come up here with us, Tunstall, you bloody useless old pillock!' Most satisfying.

And there's more. I've done some thinking about it over the years, especially during those dull bits I mentioned, and at half-time. Rugby league isn't just a game, you know. No. It is, in fact, the Epic of the North, its finest symbol and metaphor, perhaps the only example of full cross-border Lancashire–Yorkshire cooperation. And it certainly yields to none as the illustration par excellence of the North–South divide, the most satisfying clash imaginable between chippy Northern chauvinism and smug, uncomprehending Southern condescension.

The Great Divide, or Secession from the South, came on Thursday, 29 August 1895, when, at a meeting in the George Hotel, Huddersfield, 21 clubs from Lancashire and Yorkshire voted to leave the Rugby Football Union. The overt cause was the payment of compensation to Northern players for time off from mill or mine. Surrounding it was as marvellous a mix of snobbery, class envy and attitude as England has ever served up, which, you will agree, is no small claim. But then sport does something to the English: for them, it is the continuation of everything by other means.

If, for example, you were middle class, from south of the Trent, and something of an enthusiast, you might hazard that rugby was invented at Rugby School in 1823 when, during a game of football, William Webb Ellis suddenly picked up the ball and ran with it (Ellis: 'Was it a goal, sir?'; 'No, Ellis, but it was a good try.'). You might then trace rugby's rise through the public schools, which recognised the value of organised violence in creating the muscular Christians who were to guard the Empire against any of that effete sewery sort of stuff that had done for the Greeks and the Romans.

And so on to the formation of famous clubs like Harlequins and Wasps, Twickenham, the Calcutta Cup, the Five Nations, Prince Obolensky, Richard Sharp, Will Carling, the advent of professionalism, inevitable, really, England win the World Cup, Jonny Wilkinson, splendid, All Blacks always dangerous, though. And you might just, as an aside, mention rugby league, a curious heresy confined to the North and satellite television that only hangs on because of that resentful perversity they specialise in up there; but it has provided one or two good players, especially Jason Robinson, who really came on.

If you were working class, from north of the Trent, and something of an enthusiast, the first thing you would point out is that rugby is the original people's game, played for hundreds of years in a loose and riotous way around towns on high days and holidays, for rewards and prizes; a game that was subverted by the upper classes, who grafted on to it their ridiculous idea of playing the game for the game's sake, which is all very well when you can afford it. You would then go on to name the great day at the George when those clubs took a stand for a fair reward for the honest effort of the working man and, rejecting the arrogant toff hegemony, established their own Northern Union, later the

Rugby League. You would tell how rugby union had kept the game down ever since while stealing all its best ideas, until, in the ultimate act, turning the thieved coat, it had gone professional too and started stealing all your best players, like Jason Robinson. And wasn't this exactly how the Establishment has always treated the North? And hadn't we got at least five as good as that bloody Jonny Wilkinson? And who scored the only tries in that over-hyped so-called World Cup final? Two former league boys, that's who, Jason for England, Tuqiri for Australia.

Well. Let me tell you how a half-Northerner, half-Southerner, middle-class, public school-educated, rugby union-playing (second row, non-jumping) rugby league supporter sees it. You, Mr Chippy, must grant the spread of the game to the toffs. You can't deny that they condescended to allow a few working men in the North to start playing with them. You, on the other hand, Mr Softy, must allow that the toffs couldn't bear it when the workers proved to be rather better at it, and couldn't give a toss for the tosh about the game being the thing. You must concede, too, that the toffs allowed themselves handsome expenses, but seemed to have problems when, in that direct Northern way, the workers wanted money rather than the occasional leg of mutton, and in the hand rather than in the boot.

Then the three of us could have a highly satisfying (for us) trip around the old arguments, about how union is just, in one of those relishable Northern sneers, 'kick and clap'; about how league is all big forwards rumbling forward, getting tackled, and then playing it back for the next big forward to rumble forward and get tackled. We could talk about how league used to steal all the best union players but it's now the other way round, and why, if league is such a great game, it has never managed to travel much beyond two counties in Britain and two states in Australia. And then we would be in for all the stuff about how league expansion was strangled by union, how it wasn't allowed in the Services, before we moved on to all these places where league is played, like Moldova, Morocco and the Lebanon; well, all right, not the Lebanon, because, although they have a team, they are all Lebanese Australians who've been to Bondi but have never been to Beirut.

And while Mr Softy had taken his superior expression off to the Gents while I got the next round in, Mr Chippy would have a go about league selling its soul to Mr Rupert Murdoch's satellite channels, whither it is almost exclusively contracted and out of sight of all but the committed. The switch (at Mr Murdoch's behest) to summer rugby has changed the game's very essence, he'd say, and it's being smothered by this and by incompetent administrators and directors who are more interested in their seat and their lounge and their sandwiches at half-time sliced diagonally with the crusts cut off.

Well, I did warn you. But I will just press on to say that although union has improved since it turned professional to the point where, at its best moments, it might almost be league, it's still a fair few points behind The Greatest Game, as we like to call ours, with that usual transtrentine droll bravado.

And the reason why ours is The Greatest Game is because it's folk art, the art of the people, a piece of theatre that uses its hard skies, dark brick and dour backdrops to emphasise its skill and grace and drama. It is a triumph of adversity, drawing on a rich, local and sustaining history of hard graft, hard laughs, creative resentment and beauty in unexpected places. It's the baseball of the North, full of myth and legend, without them only a game. Its heroes are successes against the odds, small men, fat men, bald men, black men, touched by wit and a dash of whimsy, booted by hard drive. The nonpareil would be Brian Bevan, a bald, frail, toothless, bandaged winger who woke up early to chain smoke and looked an unlikely bet even to get from one side of the pitch to the other. He arrived off the boat from Australia, where he had been disregarded, and was turned down after one look by Leeds. So Warrington took him on, and he proceeded to score a record 796 tries; and died, in best heroic fashion, an almost forgotten recluse.

There is, too, the appeal of the shared secret. We all smiled when Jason Robinson made his debut for the British Lions union side against Australia and he got the ball 20 yards out on the right and the big Australian full-back came confidently across to nail him, because we knew what he was about to find out, because for a marvellous moment we knew the future, and it was sudden acceleration meeting desperate, lunging, too-late realisation, what we call a T-R-Y, no danger, thank you, five points.

Another cameo. Central Park, Wigan. It is Good Friday, the traditional date, along with Boxing Day, for matches between Wigan and St Helens. Central Park is a big, sprawling ground, a bit of a mess of earth and shale paths round the back of tatty stands and steep concrete terracing which allow views of the old mills and chimneys beyond. The weather is traditional: cold, a sky of watery ink. I am way up in a stand, and down there, pale face anxiously upturned, the St Helens full-back waits under a high, high kick as the Wigan forwards thunder ever nearer; he is caught in a moment, frozen against the stands and shale, the mills and the chimneys. And then he catches it, and the game goes on. A few minutes later, the ground, with around 24,000 inside, falls silent as the St Helens prop forward, a legendary veteran of the game, with a face like a threat and a strange grace in his ruthless force, goes down and doesn't get up. The stretcher comes out and he is carried off, on his side, his bulk forcing the canvas of the stretcher almost to the ground. We know it's a leg and that he will never play again. And he doesn't. And the game goes on.

Central Park didn't. It's a Tesco now. Wigan play in that fancy new purpose-built ground I told you about earlier, the JJB Stadium, all concrete and car parks, shared with the Premiership new boys Wigan Athletic, known in St Helens as the Pie Dome.

Saints themselves, meanwhile, in typical style, are going to a new ground one minute, the next staying at the old one, Knowsley Road, home for over a century.

I, of course, hope they stay, mostly because I've gone. I'm a romantic, and Knowsley Road was the romance I found in St Helens. I loved how Saints used to play, the unfathomably whimsical approach of the club to the game. Players would be bought and sold to no apparent pattern; good young ones would be offloaded, old mediocre ones would hang on for ever, veterans would appear from elsewhere, Welshmen from rugby union would arrive, some terrific, some really awful. I suppose it was all a matter of how much was in the till.

On the pitch, it was the same: sometimes they were dire, occasionally they were brilliant, mostly they were a mixture of the two. The defence was generally a joke and there seemed to be no game plan other than to fling the ball about a bit and hope for the best.

No Yorkshire club would play like that, and not many Lancashire clubs, either, although Swinton and Salford had their moments. It's the same way Lancashire play cricket, as currently displayed by the great Andrew 'Freddie' Flintoff, and perhaps best shown by the Cup-winning side of the '70s, with those inspired bits-and-pieces players like Jack Bond and Flat Jack Simmons and David Hughes crashing sixes in the last-over gloom, and about as big a contrast imaginable with that dour, bickering, introverted lot to the east. Can you imagine a Yorkshireman writing 'As the run-stealers flicker to and fro, to and fro/Oh my Boycott and my Close long ago'? Of course not. There is a wistfulness to Francis Thompson's lines about the great Lancashire openers, Hornby and Barlow, that only a Lancastrian could write. Was there ever a Lancastrian more wistful and gifted than Thompson, mystical fleer from 'The Hound of Heaven'? But even with him, Lancs wit and mockery will out. Try this parody of Omar Khayyam:

Wake! for the ruddy ball has taken flight
That scatters the slow Wicket of the Night;
And the swift Batsman of the Dawn has driven
Against the Star-spiked rails a fiery smite.

Marvellous. He saw a few dawns, sleeping rough after selling matches, stranded in London among 'the southron folk', before he was rescued from the bad for verse. Dick Barlow, by the way, was, by all accounts, a sweet man, even if Hornby seems to have been a bit of a Boycott.

Lancs soccer clubs all used to play the way Saints did, too: Everton, Preston, Bolton, Blackburn, Blackpool, Burnley, Manchester City, Liverpool and, of course, Manchester United, all flair and ball players – Stanley Matthews, Denis Law, Tom Finney, Alex Young, Jimmy McIlroy, Albert Quixall, Roy Vernon, Bobby Charlton, Bryan Douglas, Mike Summerbee, Francis Lee, Eric Cantona, George Best. But now the beautiful game takes its oversold self far too seriously for anything like that, or them, and will doubtless squander and mar that marvellous young throwback Wayne Rooney, too.

Our way, the old way, sometimes made for deep despair, occasionally deep joy, but mostly a mixture of the two. Ideal for the true fan, a morose romantic, a gloomy optimist who lives in hope of that wonderfully unpredictable moment when the general unspeakable unfairness of Life is gloriously, meaninglessly relieved and, for once, we actually manage to beat Wigan just like we used to, long ago, for that brief, heady period in the Decade of Love. And, meanwhile, we will just nod with grim satisfaction at the road sign on the M6 reading 'Wigan 16 St Helens 12', or when Lumbey drops it again, or Tunstall falls over. It is all of a piece with the early legend of the club, when, before the Great Split, the gentlemen founders (one of whom, spendidly, had been a German glassmaker) played two games against some young lads, lost both times, decided to hang up their boots and handed the whole thing over there and then to the youngsters.

Well, yes, of course, I did dream of turning out for them, taking to the pitch as the loudspeakers blared 'The Entry of The Gladiators', and imagined that roar rising for me; until, that is, one Saturday, when the great Dick Huddart, a mighty-hewn Cumbrian second row, arrived to change and passed close by me, aged 12; I have never seen anything as frightening in my life, and he was on our side. I played union at school. I was a forward, but I wasn't big enough, quick enough or, most crucially, brave enough. My finest hour was at university, in the semi-finals of Cuppers, the inter-college cup. Cuppers! I can see Huddart's face now. Anyway, the scores were level and there wasn't long to go when a gap suddenly opened, like the Red Sea, the sort of gap which only you can see, and which I saw only two or three times in thirty years, and I was off, and then through, with just the full-back between me and glory. I could even hear the rising roar.

So, should I beat him on the left, or the right, or just chip over his head and hope? Yes, a Lancashire dither, which he solved by tackling me. We lost. Ah, well. My friend James was standing next to the Master of our college, Lord Redcliffe Maude. 'What a great run, James!' said the Master. 'Who is that chap?' Ah, well. And he was the man who wrote the government report that led to the Lancs partition, too.

Saints. I bought a bottle of champagne before our Cup semi-final against unfancied Wakefield in 1979 in happy anticipation of a return to Wembley that would erase the unhappy memory of the year before against Leeds, when that centre of ours who I still cannot bear to name dropped the ball with the line at his mercy, and the winning score a formality. (Please note the easy, expert use of 'erase the memory', 'line at his mercy' and 'formality'.) Wakefield won with an interception try with three minutes to go. I gave the bottle to a friend to keep for the next year.

It took eight, and then we lost to Halifax by one point after our star centre had two tries disallowed. Still, I was proud to weep a little when the lads came down to our end to salute us, even though none of them had thought about dropping a goal to level the scores despite all my frank and robust encouragement. I hadn't wept over them since they lost that crucial match against Leeds by one point in 1961 and I found out by looking up the score in the *Liverpool Echo* and confronted the inexplicable, implacable and unspeakable unfairness of Life head-on for the first time. My friend, by the way, drank the bottle of champagne shortly after I gave it to him.

Two years later it was that 27–0 defeat by Wigan that I was telling you about earlier. We got back to Wembley to be beaten again by Wigan in 1991. By 1996, fond as I was of the North's cock-snooking, mickey-taking, good-humoured and utterly useless proselytising day out in London, I was hoping to confine my tears to the beginning and the unfailing Hovis–Pavlovian effect on the exiled, amateur, part-time Northerner of 'Abide With Me'.

Imagine, then, my feelings as we started against Bradford in best manic mode and shot into a two-try lead and then fell away into worst depressive mode and fell away and then came back and then fell away again, so badly that we were 26–12 down halfway through the second half; imagine my feelings as Bobbie Goulding, a scrum-half in finest Saints bonzo-gonzo tradition, hoisted a succession of up and unders that somehow ended up as tries for us, mostly due to the fumblings of the poor Bradford full-back. Imagine, finally, how I felt as the huge and delightfully named Samoan, Apollo Perelini (born in the year of the moon landing), crashed over for the clincher, allowing me to scream 'PER-E-LI-NI!' as he did so. Can it get any better than a match-winner with four syllables? (Vollenhoven: count them.)

We beat them again, more convincingly, the next year, and then, in a decision splendidly in keeping with the club's philosophy and tradition, sacked the coach. His replacement stood out even in a long line of crazed and marvellous mavericks and mercurials, including a Scottish PE teacher who had never actually played the game and the great Alex Murphy, who could conjure a victory for us at Central Park against all conceivable odds and then fail to get the message through about that drop-kick at Wembley I was weeping about earlier. Ellery Hanley had been a peerless player, mostly for Wigan, of course. He had very little experience as a coach but did have bracing self-belief and real talent as a controversialist. Think, say, a mixture of Sir Alex Ferguson, the Rev. Ian Paisley and Chris Eubank, remember that he was a Yorkshireman, and you're almost there. It was fantastic fun, with rows, resignations, strike threats, a surprise Championship and a dreadful drubbing by the Australian champions all in just over a season. And, of course, we sacked him.

For a time, it was just not the same. Ellery's successor turned out to be rather good. St Helens became consistently successful. They still chucked the ball about, but they defended, too. They beat the Australian champions. They signed top-class, reliable players and developed a sensible youth policy. They beat Wigan, though not as often as one would like.

And then, suddenly, deliriously, the old Saints were back. The new man, Ian Millward, a small, smart and lippy Australian with the promising nickname of Basil, started to show increasing signs of having caught the traditional eccentricity, particularly when he decided to field a team of reserves against one of our major rivals, setting off the old wacky chaos, which ended with two of our top players being suspended for placing a bet against their own weakened side. I especially relished the reaction from one of them, Sean Long, another great gonzo scrum-half: 'It does look a bit dodgy, doesn't it?'

Even better was to come. First, despite all that, we managed to win the Cup, in style, against Wigan, with Long, of course, man of the match. And then, of course, they sacked the coach. For swearing. 'For swearing!' wrote a commentator in the New Statesman. 'In professional sport!' He continued:

> How's that for a bit of counter-intuitive, old-fashioned St Helens madness! The club's anguished claims that it's a bit more than that have been lost in a whirl of amazement, admiration and gaping disbelief, much of the last from the fans, who have mounted a seethingly angry protest and see in Millward a true Saint: a crazed genius at odds with the small minds and straight suits running the club (the poor sods).
>
> What happens next? Frankly, anything. By the time you read this, Millward may be back as Dictator for Life after a putsch and defenestration. For you should not make the mistake of thinking that the people of St Helens are dour and grim-up-northerners; they live where Lancashire whimsy meets Liverpudlian wit, and they like their life and their rugby the same.

Excellent stuff; you might even recognise the style. Yes, I was that commentator, and, with the usual regard for my perception, a new, delightfully dull coach was soon installed to general acclaim and the Saints went marching on, although not without a couple of further trademark twist and turns, which began with, inevitably, Wigan snapping up Millward. A certain chill up on the moral high ground was then gloriously gusted away by the scoreline on his first return to Knowsley Road: St Helens 75, Wigan 0. Chuffed? I have the souvenir mug in front of me as I write. Excuse me a second, I think I'll just do that again. St Helens 75, Wigan 0.

The *New Statesman* piece on Saints was not my first. No. I once wrote a big feature about them for the *Sunday Correspondent*, a brave new but doomed newspaper clearly attracted to another minority interest. Certainly, the full board of St Helens, before whom I had to appear to secure approval for the piece, didn't seem that impressed, but I got the nod on the strength of my dad, who had an advertising hoarding in one corner of the ground which read 'Nevins – The Great Home Supporters', a slogan, as it happens, suggested by Oliver Pritchett, the newspaper columnist and son of V.S. Pritchett, which just goes to show that not only Wigan can boast of its literary associations, thank you.

Anyway, it was the season after the aforesaid Wembley fiasco against Halifax and Alex Murphy was still in charge, though not for much longer, even though the then chairman had announced on securing his coaching services a couple of seasons before that 'the Messiah has returned'. But he was still excellent copy. Murphy was the cheeky chappie, prime purveyor of the strong music-hall element that invades any activity in Lancashire, no matter how serious, even rugby league; one of the great St Helens moments, for example, was in the Challenge Cup semi-final against Dewsbury in 1966, when the excellently named Minnie Cotton took her small self and umbrella onto the pitch and began belabouring a Dewsbury player who had been a little over-robust with her lodger, one of our enormous, mean Welsh second-row forwards.

Eddie Waring, the famous BBC commentator of the '60s and '70s, was strong on this side of it, too, much to the disgust of many fans, who thought he should have kept the laughs private, not broadcast them for the passing amusement of Southerners on sofas on Saturday afternoons. It reminds me of an article I once wrote about Irish cricket. Just as the secretary of the Irish Cricket Association was urging me not to play up the Irishness aspect of it, one of the umpires was laid out cold, cartoon-fashion, by a misplaced piece of fielding. I liked Eddie, though; it was just a pity that he lacked that Lancashire lightness of touch, also being from Dewsbury.

127

The essential Murphy story, though, dates from when he was playing with Vollenhoven. In many ways, Murphy was a better player than Vollenhoven: extraordinary speed of thought and just as quick off the mark, and, at scrum-half, more closely engaged than a winger. A cameo in parenthesis: Knowsley Road, a sunny day. The visitors, one of those big-forward Yorkshire teams, Hull, or maybe Halifax, are defending in their own 25. One big forward has his arms out to the left, having just passed; another big forward has his arms out to the right, waiting for the ball; 20 yards behind them, Murphy is touching the ball down, one-handed, behind the posts.

Still, Vollenhoven was paid more than Murphy and, crucially, he was paid all the year round, unlike the rest of the team, who were paid by the game, the amount depending on a win or a loss. You should forget, if you have remembered, that rugby league is now a summer game; it was then strictly autumn, winter and a touch of spring. Murphy went to the board and asked for the same deal as Vollenhoven. The chairman said to him, 'But you're not as good a player as Vollenhoven.' Murphy replied, 'I am in't bloody summer!'

I went with Murphy and the team to Widnes and was allowed into the dressing-room. As the players got changed, Murphy was carefully combing his hair in the mirror. From the adjacent loos came the sound of a big second-rower throwing up. Murphy didn't pause in his combwork. 'Does it before every bloody match,' he said. 'It's absolutely tremendous for morale.' I then watched in amazement as the lads drank tots of Harvey's Bristol Cream prior to taking the pitch. 'Very good for the tubes,' said Murphy. But they did pretty well in the first half, which was slightly disappointing, as I had been hoping for one of Murphy's half-time pep talks, famed for their robust encouragement. Turning up late for a reserve match when he was coaching at Leigh, he apparently got the impression that his side was losing and gave them the most terrific dressing down at half-time.

When someone protested that they were winning, Alex didn't miss a beat. 'I know. Just think what I would have been like if you were losing.'

The Widnes coach was Dougie Laughton, another former Saint. Widnes are now, in the fashion for fancy new nicknames, the Widnes Vikings; then, they were always known as The Chemics, an accurate reflection of the town's main industry, but not romantic. Making conversation, I mentioned to Dougie the great height of the factory chimneys surrounding the ground. Dougie gave me another of those looks I used to get at the grammar school, and said, 'That's because they're kicking out shit.' Nothing more to be said, really. But he did relent to tell me about his tour down under to Australia. 'Everybody kept telling me that Big Artie, Artie Beetson, the prop, was going to get me. "Big Artie's going to get you," they said. I went pretty well in the First Test. Then, after about 20 minutes, I found myself on the ground coming round. "What happened?" I asked. "Big Artie got you," they said.'

Hardness, in the giving and the taking, has always been a large part of the legend. In 1958, Alan Prescott, the St Helens prop, played all but three minutes of the Second Test in Brisbane with a broken arm. Never show you're hurt is the philosophy, even if, once again, it has a limited appeal. But let's not get carried away by all this grit; the music-hall element is pretty strong here, too. Most teams carry a player who, rather in the manner of pantomime, or wrestling, is a villain. And when home villain meets away villain, there usually results the brief all-out mayhem known as 'a bit of biff'.

Kevin Ashcroft, who hooked for Murphy at Leigh, was asked by the referee what was wrong with the figure revealed prone on the ground after a scrum had broken up: 'Sunstroke, sir.' St Helens, in the '50s, had the fearsome Duggie Greenall, five foot eight and eleven stone, but possessor of a unique crash tackle known, for reasons far too complicated to explain, as 'the Mammy'. 'We used to shout, "Give him the Mammy, Duggie,"' said Uncle Frank, 'and by God he did.' After several visiting Australians had been given the Mammy in an eventful match at Knowsley Road, the young Murphy, of an inquiring mind even then, asked Greenall, 'Why, Duggie?' 'I'm a pro, Spud,' came the reply. 'If I was marking my own mother, she'd have to go.'

I enjoyed writing the *Correspondent* piece; shadowing the team had, though, brought out rather more of the fawning fan in me than I felt easy with. I was reminded rather too much of the creepy old man who latches on to Richard Harris in the Lindsay Anderson film of David Storey's *This Sporting Life* – you must remember him. It got much worse when St Helens celebrated the centenary of Knowsley Road in 1990. Vollenhoven came back. I met him. And, of course, he wasn't spare, rangy and silent. He was stocky, chirpy, very South African and balding, with a bit of a drape. Such was the trauma that I can't remember if he really said that the number of cigarettes he smoked back then depended on how many drinks he'd had the night before or whether it was the other way round, or whether he even said it at all.

But I do remember that as we were talking, a hand sneaked out from the crowd and tried to steal his centenary souvenir tie from the table in front of us, and Tom was still quick enough to grab it back. His souvenir tie! We were in one of those lounges that rugby clubs, union and league, are warrened with, all graded in exclusivity up to the directors' lounge. This wasn't the directors' lounge, but, even so, I didn't think we'd be in for that sort of thing. Then another great and former player, a renowned gentleman of the game, came out of the directors' lounge with his wife, and I heard him mutter to her, through his smile, 'Keep moving and keep your mouth shut.'

I withdrew to the marquee put up for the past players. The lights weren't working. Vollenhoven and Murphy were laughing in one corner in the gloom. I went up to Ray French, former St Helens player and successor as BBC commentator to Eddie Waring, and asked him an anorak question about whether union and league would ever come together. He told me he was more interested in talking to his old teammates than talking about that, again. I slunk away. Don't get too close: your past will be trampled. Stay with the roar, on this side of the greasepaint. Well, liniment, I suppose, really.

And I still love it. I loved it when I had to stand to one side of the pool table, having to get out of the way when they needed to play a shot over there, watching it on the satellite telly with the volume turned down in a south London pub. I love it now I have paid the Skygeld and watch it at home on the video, after the rest of an uncomprehending family has gone to bed, except when I muck up the video, my most sharp modern encounter with the inexplicable, implacable and unspeakable unfairness of Life.

I could go on. I could tell you about 'Cockney' Cliff Watson, the London-born prop who answered a newspaper advertisement to join Saints and used to prepare for a game with a four-course meal and extra chips an hour before kick-off; Dave Chisnall, another prop, possessor of an improbably graceful sidestep and a belly which would go one way as he stepped the other; Frank Wilson, a blissfully unpredictable winger who once or twice a season could almost make you forgive him for the rest of it; Mal Meninga, the incomparably gifted 16-stone Australian Test centre, just the one season, but what a season, what a player – skill, speed, strength and that aloofness, the calm confidence that I had first seen in Vollenhoven; but I never saw Vollenhoven make a full-back fall over backwards ten yards in front on the strength of a threatening shimmy, and I never saw Vollenhoven time a pass like the pass Meninga timed that sent Roy Haggerty careering over the Wigan line without a finger laid on him, clinching our first win against them in what seemed for ever. Ah,

Roy Haggerty: when they asked him on tour in Australia where he was from, he replied, 'Top of Elephant Lane.'

The business with the video has reminded me. Tom Van Vollenhoven's try against Hunslet in the 1959 Championship final, the one that Uncle Frank really rated, the one named the Try of the Century in that series *The Guardian* ran in the '90s. Well, all right, I did write the entry, and, yes, I know I hadn't seen it, but Uncle Frank was a good enough judge for me. Then I saw an advert for a video of the history of St Helens, including footage of the 1959 final. Marvellous. Only a pity that I wouldn't be able to tell Uncle Frank.

The match began. Black and white, obviously, but not that bad quality, with Eddie Waring doing the commentary. Hunslet had taken the lead, Saints were rattled, Voll's moment was at hand. I was getting really quite excited. It was at this point that Eddie suddenly went uncharacteristically quiet and was replaced by a solemn, slightly prissy, almost Southern, voice-over: 'Probably the most unforgettable try of all time was scored during the championship final at Odsal Stadium when Tom Van Vollenhoven beat several opponents during a 75-yard dash to the line. Unfortunately, the cameraman didn't capture the moment.' So. There you are. Do you know, I think that just about sums up Saints, and me. And rugby league, probably, too, when I think about it, not to mention Life and the unspeakable unfairness thing.

Shortly after that, I went to Edinburgh to watch St Helens play Wigan at Murrayfield in what was then known as the Kelloggs Nutri-Grain Challenge Cup. We were hot favourites – so hot that, quite understandably, a lot of Wigan supporters didn't make the trip, as the presence of Atomic Kitten and the Minister of Sport wouldn't really compensate for sitting in that silent communal misery I was talking about earlier.

It didn't work out like that, of course. Wigan won. Our boys never fired properly. Goals weren't kicked, tries wouldn't come. It reminded me somewhat of the Battle of Jutland, that rather expensive score draw in the First World War, when Admiral Beatty expressed similar frustration to mine, as the hot favourites, the British Fleet, failed to pull it off: 'There's something wrong with our bloody ships today.'

With a few minutes to go, it was clear we had blown it. Near me, a man sat silent, chewing miserably on his complimentary Kelloggs Nutri-Grain bar. Further along the back row, a small band, with trumpet, drum, cymbals, was still trying to rally the team with another defiant, ragged version of 'When The Saints Go Marching In'; I imagine it was a little like that on the wrong side at Bosworth Field. At the final whistle, a small boy filed out, weeping. I knew exactly what he was going through, but I didn't cry. I might next time, though.

Chapter Six

The Southport of the South

. . . and its really quite possible inspiration

To the casual observer, unversed and uninitiated in the ways of Lancashire whimsy, Southport must be a bit of a puzzle. Actually, I'm not too sure how even a smart casual observer would get on with Southport. Its southerliness is not crashingly obvious, and it's not a port. There's not much sign of the sea, either: it tends to stay way out there, over the sands, well beyond the pier, about a mile off.

I never thought much about this, probably because Southport was familiar from childhood, somewhere we visited that was just there, near. So near that we didn't really bother to ask questions about it. Children are thought always to be asking questions; actually, they don't ask enough. Besides, the proper seaside was exciting and different and a long way away, and only supposed to exist in the summer. Southport wasn't like that.

Yes, there is the pier, but Southport doesn't face the sea in the way a good resort should. It's as if all that sand were a little too much. There's a promenade, and, beyond that, another one, called the Marine Drive, but Southport's point is Lord Street, back behind them, a broad straight sweep of arrestingly unexpected elegance. Shops parade behind glass and wrought-iron canopies and wide pavements on one side; a line of fine barbered and arboured gardens flatters grand frontages on the other.

You might say, crikey, what's going on here, then? But I hadn't really noticed. This is just Lord Street, with the Bold Hotel at the one end, where my grandmother, my father's mother, used to go sometimes for morning coffee, and the Prince of Wales Hotel at the other, very posh, where my grandfather, my mother's father, was wearing this blue suit he'd had for 40 years, put on to impress everyone, and the waiter spilled tomato soup down the back of it at lunch, and where they had these splendid marbled loos where my father slipped that time at the Charity Ball.

In the middle, there, is the Scarisbrick Hotel, where Laurence Isherwood – a local artist who had gained some fame by painting, from imagination, various celebrities, including Barbara Castle, in the nude – drank and blustered, and I played the odd game of pool during my brief tenure on the *Southport Visiter*, my start in journalism, on a graduate trainee course run by its owners, the *Liverpool Daily Post & Echo*. On my first day, the piece of paper in my typewriter read 'NO GRADS HERE', but they were all very tolerant, really. I especially enjoyed the chief reporter, a man in a black leather jacket of the nervously energetic journalistic type, given to saying things like, when the phone rang, 'Answer that, it might be the phone!'; and the news editor, playing the traditional weary sardonics of the role for all he was worth; and the veteran photographer, who would arrive at a job already shooting and shouting, '*Southport Visiter!*', which certainly seemed to give his subjects an animated look. As it happens, my father bought a couple of Isherwoods that were hanging up at his local; he said they would be a good investment. I've got them, but nobody's naked, and the Isherwood revival is not yet here.

But, you're right, Southport does seem an odd place for Lord Street to be. And there is something about Lord Street, some echo of somewhere else, isn't there? As I say, though, it was all too close to me, and, in any case, during my few weeks on the *Visiter*, I was too busy trying to ingratiate myself as a non-stuck-up, local-boy kind of a graduate to dare ask any obvious questions about Southport.

It is, though, for the most part, quite a standard English seaside town story. Most of our resorts were, until quite recently, yellow-sand or grey-pebble sites. Southport got started at the end of the eighteenth century when miners from Wigan started coming down the nearby Leeds–Liverpool canal to the village of Churchtown for its August Fair, which, with the fashion for a healthy dip in the sea, came to be known as Big Bathing Sunday. Big Bathing Sunday! South Hawes, a couple of miles away in that direction, was a better spot for swimming; William Sutton, a Churchtown innkeeper known as 'The Duke', built a small hotel there, first nicknamed The Duke's Folly, then, more archly, the South Port Hotel. So Southport is a joke.

But jokes are fated to be taken seriously. Sutton might have ended up in Lancaster Gaol for debt; Southport caught on, took off. It's usual to think of Blackpool as the popular resort and Southport as the posh one, but that's not quite true, even leaving aside the Wigan miners. True, it was, like other posh resorts, started by aristocrats, in this case the Heskeths and the Scarisbricks, and it was also heavily populated by Lancashire's retired and recently rich in their big and heavy red-brick mansions in stately grids; but Southport was a popular Wakes Week destination when the railways came, and stayed so, until an ever-brasher Blackpool and the curse of the Costas killed off most of that trade, leaving the resort to subside into a familiar slumbering decline, relieved by daytrippers from Liverpool and by the fairground, still raucous with rides, jumping and popping and queueing. Meanwhile the gentler pleasures of the Marine Lake, the pier, the formal gardens, the bowling green, the miniature golf, railway and village, the delights of earlier generations, simpler escapes from harder lives, faded and frayed, as if nobody was quite sure what they were for, or who would want to use them. Have you tried explaining to a child what a disused bowling green is all about?

Now, though, equally familiarly, revival and reinvention are here. There are plans for Southport to become the centre of the Golf Coast, playing on its position between Birkdale and Lytham. The pier, very nearly dismantled, has been restored and reopened; there is a new bridge, one of those big modern steel-and-hawser confidence statements, onto the Marine Parade, leading to what the regenerators call modern mixed retail and leisure developments. Only a melancholy romantic old churl would find himself missing the old fade and fray. Thank you.

So, it's not quite what it was, Southport; less distinct, more like everywhere else. Except Lord Street. The shops may not be so grand now in their offerings and aspirations, but they can't take away the style and sweep, the product of the aristocratic beginnings not long after the miners, when the new town became briefly fashionable, subsequently sustained by all that new money, or brass, as I suppose we should call it.

Yes, there's definitely something about Lord Street, and, of course, despite all the excuses so affectingly rehearsed earlier, I felt pretty foolish not having realised exactly what it was until I read *The Times* of Tuesday, 25 April 2000: 'Napoleon III was inspired to build the *grands boulevards* of Paris after a jolly holiday in Southport, research suggests.' Of course! There was more:

An architectural historian has claimed that the dramatic reconstruction of the French capital during the Second

Empire (1852–70) owes much to the genteel Merseyside seaside resort. Quentin Hughes, a former professor of architecture, believes that the Emperor was so taken by the sweeping panorama of Lord Street, Southport's tree-lined boulevard, laid out in the first quarter of the nineteenth century, that he wanted to recreate it in Paris.

He has discovered that the young, exiled Louis Napoleon took a flat off Lord Street for a season, long before he rose to power in a Bonapartist coup d'état and ordered his architect, Georges Eugène Haussmann, to rebuild the capital. Southport is often called the 'Paris of the North', because of its tree-lined central avenues, arcades and pavement cafés. Mr Hughes suggests that Paris should really be called the 'Southport of the South' . . . [He] said: 'Lord Street has trees down the centre and shops along the sides with covered arcades just like Paris. When Napoleon III got back to Paris, he must have thought, Let's build Southport here, only bigger.'

Eh bien. First Balzac, now this. Quelle county! And yet more evidence, if it be needed, of the sympathies and sophistication and tastes that Lancs shares with its larger sister over the channel, a shared sympathy and sophistication that has escaped the less finely attuned sensitivities of its nearer neighbours, who need to be told.

And this Professor Hughes, he was clearly a man to help me. I was, though, a little concerned to read that he was in his eighties. I worried less when I got in touch and found he was giving a lecture in Italy, and stopped altogether when I met him. His house was in Liverpool, and situated exactly where that of a professor of architecture in his eighties should be. It was a split-level, sixties-style conversion of an old stable in an early Victorian gated estate near Otterspool Promenade, full of enormous houses, one with a glass turret built for its shipowning owner to look up the Mersey for his ships coming in.

Professor Hughes was in regulation patched tweed and fine form. One of the joys of journalism is meeting enthusiasts. I'm quite keen on obsessives, too, but Prof. Hughes had far too many enthusiasms for any of that single-issue nonsense. Architectural history, for one thing, yes, but a wide spread, moving from Liverpool to Malta with ease. He'd taught in both places and fought in one, during the Siege. He was a gunner, very keen on guns. He'd also been in the SAS during the War and had blown himself and several German spotter planes up on a raid behind lines in Italy, thus, if he said so himself, allowing the Anzio landings to proceed in a rather less challenged way than they might have. The story appears in his autobiography, typically, I soon gathered, entitled *Who Cares Who Wins?*

The Prof had published it himself and also written his own blurb, which contained this:

> He [the Prof] was a much-loved and respected teacher, and many a callow undergraduate will remember with affection his early-morning appearances in the lecture hall dressed in battle fatigues (well before such garb became de rigueur on the fashion scene!) sporting a 9mm captured Luger modified as a cigarette lighter.

Only a very few can get away with this sort of thing: the Prof was one of them. Perhaps being over eighty helped, but it was more to do, I think, with his energy and enthusiasm, and the speed with which he moved from one thing to another.

Before we got down to Southport and Paris, for example, the Prof was eager to offer another theory, this one to do with Napoleon basing the landscaping of the Bois de Boulogne and the Parc de Vincennes on Princes Park in Liverpool. It was clear to the Prof that the parc's kidney-shaped lakes and meandering, curving paths, creating the illusion of more space, had all been borrowed from Joseph Paxton, the designer of Princes Park and, of course, the Crystal Palace. This, it seemed entirely likely to the Prof, was based on the prefabricated cast-iron construction of St Michael in the Hamlet, Aigburth, also in Liverpool. Nor, said the Prof, making coffee at the same time, should we be neglecting the similarities between Napoleon's methods of financing the reconstruction of Paris by selling off plots in advance and what Liverpool had done with the houses flanking Princes Park. Napoleon had, after all, visited Liverpool several times during his stays in Britain.

This was terrific stuff, and we hadn't even got started on Southport yet. The Prof flurried off to his photocopier and came back documented up. We got into the car and set off for Southport and lunch in the Prince of Wales.

A good time to bring you up to speed. Prince Louis Napoleon, later Napoleon III, born in 1804, was a nephew of the great Bonaparte. At this point, you will have just started wondering, idly, about Napoleon II. You can't place him because he reigned only in the eyes of dedicated Bonapartists: Napoleon's only legitimate son, François, the Duc de Reichstadt, died of consumption at the age of 21. Napoleon III became France's second emperor in 1852 after a coup d'état, four years as an elected president, two previous failed coups and six years in prison. He visited England for three months in 1831, again between 1838 and 1840, and 1846 and 1848, finally dying here in 1873, in exile, three years after the fiasco of the Franco–Prussian war. His time in Southport came during the second spell, when he was being entertained in Britain, hunting in Berkshire, shooting in Scotland and fishing in Wales.

Even so, Prince Louis (his title then) was not entirely accepted in the highest circles, being what is now known in Southport and surrounds as 'a bit of a lad'. Well, more than a bit of a lad, really; more a man for whom the exercise of his manhood was always a most pressing concern. Allow me to give you a flavour; he spent a lot of time with the Comte d'Orsay, another exiled

Bonapartist, and his lover, Lady Blessington. 'Lady Blessington,' writes John Bierman in *Napoleon III and his Carnival Empire*,

> a widowed Irish beauty now past her prime, was the author of several somewhat trashy novels, which fact – together with the fortune inherited from her husband and the lavishness of her table – had helped establish her as the centre of a notorious literary and artistic circle. D'Orsay, sometimes called 'the last of the dandies', was a man of considerable sexual versatility, having been simultaneously her lover and that of her late husband. He also happened to be his mistress's stepson-in-law, Lord Blessington having forced his innocent daughter into marriage with D'Orsay to provide a cover for his own relationship with the Frenchman.

Rather more Blackpool than Southport, you might say.

Whatever, there was certainly something uncannily Lancastrian about Louis, La Gloire as interpreted by Laurel or Formby, the dreamer undone, an unhappy potential for humour in the mismatch between the man and the myth he was supposed to continue. 'From time to time men are created into whose hands the fate of their country is entrusted. I am such a man.' That was what he said, and what he believed; and, indeed, what he achieved, for a time, until it was all punctured by Prussian iron, steel and efficiency.

But there was always that bathos and pathos. People clearly had difficulty in seeing him as a commanding figure, even when he was Emperor. 'How long are you in Paris?' he asked Lady Blessington in an attempted rapprochement of the long froideur that had existed since their London friendship. 'How long are you in Paris?' replied her ladyship. In England, in exile, he was forever issuing invitations to dine with him one day at the Royal palace in Paris, the Tuileries. 'What on earth was that all about?'

141

asked the wonderfully named Honourable Frederick 'Poodle' Byng after one such offer.

His first two attempts at a coup have the inescapable feel of silent comedy about them. At Strasbourg, in 1836, he donned his uncle's famous tricorn hat; a sympathetic veteran colonel in the garrison threw his regiment behind him. They seized the garrison commander but guarded only the front of his house, allowing an officer to escape out the back and raise the alarm. Louis' attempts to address another regiment at its barracks were met with cries of 'Shut up!' Someone had shut the barrack gates, leaving all Louis' troops outside. The commanding officer then knocked off the hat and arrested him.

The second attempt, in 1840, after exile in America, Southport and London, was even better. Louis hired a paddle steamer called the *Edinburgh Castle* in London and sailed for Boulogne from Ramsgate, telling the skipper it was a pleasure cruise. The majority of the 56 men on board were French, Italian and Polish waiters hired in Soho for 40 francs a head. Tethered to the mast was a tame vulture, which the invaders hoped would look like an Imperial eagle from a distance. Needless to say, the attempt failed miserably. This time, Louis attempted to escape in a rowing boat back to the *Edinburgh Castle*. He was, though, the man who the year before had managed to strand another one, containing no less than Mr and Mrs Benjamin Disraeli, on a mud bank in the Thames, and true to form, at Boulogne the boat overturned, leaving Louis to swim for a buoy and cling on until he was arrested. Eleven of Louis' waiters were arrested by one bather. The fate of the vulture is unknown.

'This morning's papers,' wrote Disraeli,

> publish two editions, and Louis Napoleon, who last year at Bulwer's nearly drowned us by his bad rowing, has now upset himself at Boulogne. Never was anything so rash and crude to all appearances as this 'invasion', for he

was joined by no one. A fine house in Carlton Gardens,
his Arabian horse, and excellent cook were hardly worse
than his present situation.

Quite. Yet this was the man the French elected President and
then Emperor, whose period in power saw France embark on a
successful Industrial Revolution, who rebuilt Paris, and whose
foreign policy, often barmy though it was, particularly in his
promotion of the doomed Habsburg Mexican Emperor,
Maximilian, would have been accounted a success, too, but for
Bismarck.

This was also the man who, one afternoon in Dorchester, for
a joke, thrust his walking stick between the legs of a man walking
in front of him. Louis had thought it was a friend; it wasn't, of
course, and before you could say *vive la France*, the angry
stranger had his coat off and his dukes up. 'The Prince
immediately apologised,' writes Ivor Guest in his *Napoleon III
in England*, 'and finally managed to calm the irate gentleman, to
the great relief of the nervous ladies crowded near with their
prayer books and bibles, and the disappointment of the boys and
less genteel of the townsmen.' Silent movie classic.

Try, too, Louis on the train to Manchester, with his current
mistress and his cousin, Prince Napoleon, a bumptious fellow,
tolerated beyond any measure of reason or worth, known to all
by his childhood nickname, Plon-Plon. Louis snoozed off and
woke to find the other two in flagrante. He pretended not to
have seen anything, and resumed his slumber. But he has the
revenge of history. 'Papa, what is the difference between an
accident and a misfortune?' asked his son, the Prince Imperial,
later to be killed, not by Prussians but by Zulus, while serving
with the British Army. (His party was surprised; all got away
except the Prince, who was undone when the stirrup snapped on
his horse, called, I promise you, Fate.) 'Well, Louis,' replied the
Emperor, 'if our cousin Napoleon were to fall into the Seine, it

would be an accident. If someone pulled him out, it would be a misfortune.' Brilliant. That's the Lancashire comic bit of him. And surely this is a Stan Laurel line, in the middle of some crucial negotiations: 'Well, you can tell the Spanish that you're giving them Portugal, and the Portuguese that you're giving them Spain.'

So, there you have it, the answer to the enigma that has puzzled many great historians: Napoleon III was a Lancastrian manqué, 'a dreamer, entertaining vast, nebulous schemes, but vacillating, confused . . .' as Lewis Namier put it. You will not be surprised when I tell you he also had a fantastically formidable wife (whose trials with trapped wind were the talk of Europe, or at least of that gossipy double act, Marx and Engels).

Two more stories: in his last exile, after he was deposed, Napoleon used to watch cricket at the West Kent ground across from his house in Chislehurst. After a spectacular catch at long-on, a member of the Imperial suite delivered a message from the Emperor asking if it could be done again. Marvellous. An equally spectacular piece of entirely useless, and therefore pure, information is that they named the old Chislehurst and Bickley telephone exchange after him: Imperial, it was called. And it was the Imperial Hotel in Torquay, too, where he sent his compliments to the chef, saying that he hadn't tasted such good food since he'd left Paris. The chef then told him this was probably because, up until the recent rearrangements, he'd been his chef.

The Prof, meanwhile, had moved on to Hitler, another figure from history who, as we've seen, spent a little-known period during his formative years in the North-west. And Freud, too. He stayed with his relations in Manchester, and visited Blackpool, twice. The second time he sent a postcard with the Tower on it; make of that what you will. But you should also know that in his great work, *The Interpretation of Dreams*, he mentions a dream of being back on the beach in Blackpool. So,

144

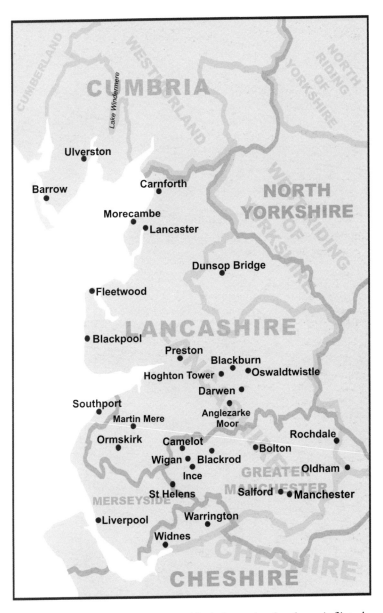

A fine depiction of the cartographical chaos that has been inflicted upon Lancs: the true county lies beneath. (© Andy Laycock)

How the brave new Blackpool might look.
(Reproduced with the permission of Leisure Parcs Limited)

Scouse dream: Tom
Murphy's mighty
Mersey god.
(© Tom Murphy)

Lost Lancs: Lake Windermere,
jewel of the Lancashire Elysium. (Courtesy of
www.britainonview.com)

Lost Boys: Stan and Oliver outside
Stan's birthplace in Ulverston, 1947.
(Courtesy of the *North West Evening Mail*)

The Golden Springbok: Tom Van Vollenhoven scoring again, with just the two trailing. (Courtesy of the Alex Service collection)

El Inglés: Frank Evans at Benalmadena, with mural.
(© Tom Pilston)

LORD STREET, SOUTHPORT

4077. PARIS — Boulevard Montmartre
Montmartre Boulevard

Uncannily similar: the Paris of the North and the Southport of the South in the early 1900s. (Paris © Corbis; Lord Street courtesy of the Brian Farris collection)

Prophet and charmer: Mr Gandhi in Lancashire. (© Corbis)

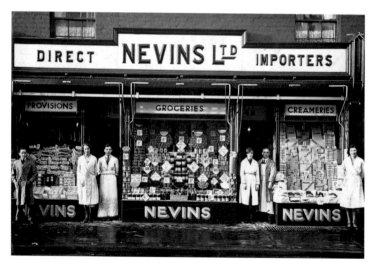

A bagful of bargains: one of the original Nevins
shops in St Helens. (Author's collection)

Towering inspiration: Shakespeare and Dickens
were both here, you know. (Courtesy of Lancashire Tourism)

Brief Encounter: Celia, Trevor and a rather fine station.
(© BFI/Carlton)

Debts to Lancs: just three exotics with county connections: Butch Cassidy, Dan Leno, and Napoleon III (with family). (Cassidy © Corbis; Leno and Napoleon © Hulton Getty)

Freud and Jung: Lancashire dreamers. I must say that surprises even me.

Anyway, Hitler: the Prof said he had wanted to put a plaque on the house, but it had been pulled down. He was now thinking of one of those tourist signs, 'Liverpool, Home of John, Paul, George, Ringo and Adolf'. 'I've never been very serious, as you can see,' he said. He did like a theory, though, he said; he was, for instance, convinced that a painting he had once owned was not really by Christopher Wood, but Picasso.

We arrived in Southport. 'I know very little about Southport,' said the Prof. But he had stayed at the Prince of Wales for a week over a Christmas before the War, when the whole family had been put up by his grandfather, a wealthy Liverpool builder. We had a look round before lunch. The Prince of Wales had not weathered quite as well as the Prof. The ballroom was occupied by a meeting of the Arriva Trains Northern RMT Conductors' Strike Committee, complete with backdrop banner.

There was no chance of a waiter spilling soup on the Prof's suit, as lunch had succumbed to the curse of the carvery, £5 up front and serve yourself. The waiters were all in boxy ventless suits, like daylighting bouncers. One of them said the grand old dining room wasn't in use at the moment, as it was too big. We decided that two halves of bitter might be the thing. Another waiter brought us them. They were lager. 'It is bitter,' said the waiter, in a middle-European accent, 'lager bitter.' Do you ever get the feeling that you're in a comedy sketch?

The Prof didn't mind. 'I wouldn't say it's declined. It's different,' he said. I don't suppose these things are quite so important when you've survived the Malta Run, the Malta Siege, parachuted behind enemy lines, blown yourself up, lost the sight in one eye, been sentenced to be shot as a spy, escaped by hurling yourself off a train, joined the Italian partisans and finally got yourself back to your own lines by taking a small, leaking boat highly likely to be shot up by the RAF. I asked him how he ever settled down to normal life after that. Did it all seem unreal now? 'My whole life seems unreal,' said the Prof, briefly serious, and I could see what he meant.

I told him a little about this book and, in particular, about my persuasive contentions for the early history of the county, with especial reference to the pervasive Gallic influences which had clearly spoken so loudly to Louis Napoleon. The Prof was greatly impressed with my theory that the Parisi, the original Parisians, had decamped over to the west coast to get away from Hull. 'That's even more far-fetched than mine!' he declared admiringly, before telling me about a Welsh fellow officer who had found that many Welsh words had an obvious derivation from Phoenician.

I suppose, eventually, we will have to examine the Prof's evidence for the Paris–Southport theory. Key quotes to bear in mind here are, 'Just because it is a myth doesn't necessarily mean it's not true,' and, 'Obviously, there are a lot of suppositions here, but if you put them together, they make a clear picture, even if it may be the wrong one.'

I think we can say with some certainty that Napoleon III probably visited Southport. His Uncle Joseph, formerly King of Spain, later a farmer in New Jersey (yes, indeed), later still resident in London as head of the family, wrote a letter in 1833 in which he mentioned that his nephew had been to Liverpool. Louis was friendly with Sir John Gerard, of Garswood Hall, near Wigan. The Prof had come across Francis Bailey's *History of Southport*, published in 1956, which contains this:

> The sole tangible evidence for [Napoleon's] visit, however, is an old but undated manuscript, in a feminine hand, preserved among the papers of the former Southport historian C.H. Brown (died 1915), which reads: 'Napoleon at Southport. About 1838 Prince Napoleon was staying with Sir John Gerard and came to Southport. He took a house, South Lawn, Lord Street,

for some years occupied by the late Dr McNicol and now made into shops. He paid rent for the house but did not live in it. It is said he hunted and shot in the neighbourhood with the Gerards.

There is also a pamphlet written in 1898 which has Napoleon visiting Sir John again at Garswood in 1847. And that seems to be about it, apart from one more tantalising detail: Napoleon's favourite horse when Emperor was given to him by Sir John Gerard, and its name was . . . well, I wish I could say it was Lord Street, or even Southport; as it is, Phillips doesn't help us all that much.

The Prof had a map of Lord Street, 1834. It showed one house called Green Lawn in Lord Street, one called South Lodge across on the other side of the Nile, but none called South Lawn. The Nile? Well, no one really knows for sure how this now-vanished brook got to be called that – a tribute to Nelson's great victory in 1898, perhaps, or, more likely, another little Southport joke involving a droll comparison between their tiny sandy inlet and Egypt's mighty irrigator.

The Prof and I went to look where the house might have been; it's a Safeway now. There was little to inspire us, although I did find out later that somewhere under its car park is the lost Southport Scroll of Honour, listing 28 of Southport's famous sons and daughters, a suitably whimsical and eclectic collection which includes Jean Alexander – Hilda Ogden in *Coronation Street* – Red Rum and Frank Hampson, creator of Dan Dare. Bit of a cock-up during the redevelopment, apparently.

It was time to take the Prof home. He had remained triumphantly vimfull throughout, and concluded our meeting by selling me his autobiography; there's obviously a lot to be said for surviving the Malta Run, the Malta Siege, parachuting behind enemy lines, blowing yourself up, losing the sight in one eye, being sentenced to be shot as a spy, escaping by hurling yourself off a train, joining the Italian partisans and finally getting yourself back to your own lines by taking a small, leaking boat highly likely to be shot up by the RAF.

The following Saturday, I engaged in a little light research of my own. We have already, you may or may not remember, covered the important journalistic concept of avoiding making that one call too many, the one that can wreak havoc with the elegant simplicity and persuasive narrative drive of what we tend to call 'a bloody good tale'. You will also have gathered, despite my best efforts, that the Prof wasn't presenting his entertaining theory as anything approaching incontestable fact; and I haven't mentioned the possibly later provenance of the ironwork that gives Lord Street so much of its Parisian feel. It was, then, probably a mistake to go to the reference library and talk to Southport's local history librarian, Andrew Farthing, whose key quote was, 'I think it's a great story and I'd love to find something to substantiate it.'

Magnificently undeterred, I embarked on a search through the rent books listing the landlords and tenants in Lord Street for the relevant period. There were no clear leads, but I have studied at the school of Von Daniken and I know the lessons: do not be overawed by the obvious explanation and never neglect the fascinating one just because it is extremely unlikely to be true. It is in the extremes that great theories are born, history is made and books shifted by the ottakars.

So it was that I fell upon two names in the rent books. Mrs France, you will concede, is the sort of joke that is absolutely typical of Louis, combining as it does levity with a serious point: that he is married to his country. And then there was Monsieur Barralier. It seemed to me that the handwriting here would allow an alternative spelling: Monsieur Barralieu. Barralieu! Of course! *Barre-lieu*: barred from his rightful place, Emperor of the French!

True scholars are cautious, so I decided I wouldn't mention these bombshells to Mr Farthing just yet. If ever. Besides, I wanted to know what he made of the curious structure in the 1850s engraving of Lord Street on the frontispiece of Francis Bailey's history of the town, what looked to me like a tall, iron, pyramid-shaped tower at the northern end: clearly previous researchers had overlooked the huge significance of this, vis-à-vis both Paris and Blackpool. Mr Farthing looked at it. 'That's a church spire,' he said.

Outside the library, back in Lord Street, I stopped a few people to see if they were familiar with Paris's debt. They were. So familiar that they didn't seem to feel any need to brag about their main street's importance and influence, let alone any sense of a slight incongruity. To them, it was just a matter of fact and so they were matter-of-fact about it. Mostly, too, they added the extra piece of information that Louis had liked the layout of Lord Street because it would afford a clear field of fire in the event of insurrection, something at the forefront of his thinking when he rebuilt his capital.

As it happens, a fusillade on this particular June Saturday would have delivered a blow from which Lancashire clog dancing might never have recovered, as it was the Argarmeles Day of Dance, and clog dancers from all over the North-west were in town, including the Milltown Cloggies, Fidlers Fancy, the Fylde Coast Cloggers and the Singleton Cloggers. The hosts, the Argarmeles Clog Morris Troupe, take their names from the lost village of Argarmeles, swept away by the sea in the 1500s, before the erosion went into reverse. Wonderfully French sound, Argarmeles, hasn't it? *Eh bien*, let's talk about clogs. I had wanted to keep away from clogs, but it's a bit difficult when there are clog dancers as far as the eye can see. That Bill Tidy – a resident of Southport, as it happens – has a lot to answer for, even if *The Cloggies* was a terrific strip, and I still relish the one with Neville, the 'hard' Cloggie, at last orders, lying horizontal across the top of a three-deep queue at the bar, shouting, '96 pints and get your finger out!'. It is also true that Lancashire clogs are made with square toes so as to enable the wearer to get closer to the bar.

This all gives the impression that clog dancing is merely another perverse provincial private practice. Whereas I could tell you, for example, that Bernard of Italy, grandson of Charlemagne, and a man not unversed in the art of the dance, used to wear clogs of red leather. Never forget, either, that, according to no less an authority than the *Encyclopaedia Britannica*, 'Clog dancing, after being introduced into the USA, became one of the basic elements in the development of tap dancing.' So there: Lancs fed the feet of Astaire and the soul of Bojangles.

And, indeed, two of the most famous clog dancers weren't Northerners at all: Dan Leno and Charlie Chaplin. Leno was, of course, the first proper stand-up comic, the man who, as Max Beerbohm realised, shifted the balance of the lone performer on stage from song to patter. He was also the successor to the great Grimaldi in pantomime, doing for the dame what Grimaldi had done for the clown. He was just as barmy, too. You might remember the story of the man suffering from depression who is advised to go and see Grimaldi: 'But I am Grimaldi.' In 1903, Dan, in a similar state, began to stalk Constance Collier, Sir Herbert Beerbohm Tree's leading lady, begging for the chance to play Hamlet. He died the next year at the age of 43. 'Ever seen his eyes?' asked Marie Lloyd. 'The saddest eyes in the whole world. That's why we all laughed at Danny. Because if we hadn't laughed, we should have cried ourselves sick. I believe that's what real comedy is, you know. It's almost like crying.'

Later, Dan was to spend a lot of his time advising Peter Sellers, after they had been introduced by Red Cloud, the spirit guide of Sellers' medium. Peter Evans, who wrote Sellers' authorised biography against Leno's wishes, has written about going with Sellers to Leno's old house in Kennington:

Before I could begin to explain the reason for our visit, the psychic pull of Leno became too strong for Sellers, who pushed past the woman and rushed into the tiny hallway. 'Dan. It's me, Pete,' he called out, flinging open doors, rushing from room to room. 'I know you're here. Talk to me, Dan.' 'It's Peter Sellers, the actor,' I explained, keeping it as brief and factual as I could. 'He is a great admirer of a man who once lived here.' The woman said she didn't care who he was, she lived here now, and if he didn't get out at once she'd call the police. Eventually, I persuaded him to leave. But not before Leno had got in another dig at me. 'Dan isn't at all happy with that book of yours,' Sellers told me reproachfully.

But, before all that, Leno was the Champion Clog Dancer of the World. He even had an engraved belt to prove his triumph at the People's Music Hall, Oldham, after a contest lasting six nights, from 14 to 19 May 1883. He was twenty-three and had been on the boards since he was four. Clog dancing, freshly inspired by the rhythm and roar of the mill machines, was tremendously popular in the North. This is Arnold Bennett in *Clayhanger*:

> And thus was rendered back to the people in the charming form of beauty that which the instinct of the artist had taken from the sordid ugliness of the people. The clog, the very emblem of the servitude and the squalor of brutalised populations, was changed on the light feet of their favourite into the medium of grace.

The clog championships were organised by music-hall impresarios to cash in, bringing together all the top Northern dancers. Leno, who had mostly danced in Ireland, surprised everyone by winning the first event, in Leeds (the judges didn't actually watch the

151

contests; they sat under the stage, listening). He lost the next, at Ohmy's Circus, Accrington (Ohmy's Circus!) to a suspiciously home decision; then came the Oldham triumph, which was the last, and left him champion in perpetuity. Even after he became better known as a comic, he still kept his dancing clogs at the side of the stage, ready for a routine if required.

You can't hear Leno dance, but you can hear some of his monologues, which sound no better to our ears than those of any other music-hall comic, especially since the Goons finally buried all that tiresome wordplay which struggled on with the likes of Tommy Handley and Cheerful Charlie Chester into a more sophisticated world. There is a far better flavour of what made him a star in the biography by J.H. Wood, who knew him, and spends a lot of time retelling what are clearly polished Leno anecdotes. The North obviously tickled him, and his stories of the Northern halls have a feel of Les Dawson or Peter Kay. There is, for example, the young clog dancer and his manager, who fixes the dancer's colours to his cap with a large pin: 'We're ready now, I think. How do you feel about it, my lad? Are you all right?' 'Aye, I think I'm all right! The pin's stuck in my head an inch deep. Should it be?'

There's the proprietor who distributes complimentary soup and is forever trying to smuggle his son, an alarmingly bad ventriloquist, onto the stage, often by dint of announcing that an act advertised but never actually booked has regretfully had to cancel at short notice and will be replaced by . . . 'Silence up there! Silence! Or I'll stop the soup!'

Then there's the music for Leno's clog dance – 'a selection of operatic airs . . . all culled from the most high-toned and thoroughly classical composers' – and its effect, when first introduced, on the conductor and his band at 'a small music hall in a manufacturing town in Lancashire', which I paraphrase slightly: 'Good morning, Mr Leno! I don't think we'll have to worry about your music. All th'lads know it very well by now . . . By gum! This is a bit of something extra . . . There's lumps of it . . . Stand by, my lads, I'm sending you something tricky down now. [Result, a wild whirlwind of sound, during which Dan stood petrified and wondered what to do.] If you'll take a fool's advice, Mr Leno, you'll leave this stuff alone and go back to th' good old la-tum-tiddle . . . Very good, off we go again. Cornet, what the blazes are you blowing at? I thowt there was something wrong. Tha's got th'second fiddle copy. [The conductor undertakes to practise further after everyone else has gone home. That night, Dan comes on to the sound of a familiar chord, the old one.] It's no use, Mr Leno, the lads couldn't tackle your job under a matter of three weeks; so unless tha can be content with th'old la-tum-tiddle, tha must dance wi'out any music.'

Give order!

Chaplin was not quite so keen. He joined the Eight Lancashire Lads, even if he was from Kennington, as an eight year old in 1896. The Lads were a clog dancing troupe founded by the splendidly named John Willie Jackson, from near Wigan, with his three sons and his daughter, dressed like a boy, plus four ringers. 'Audiences liked the Eight Lancashire Lads,' Chaplin remembered, 'because, as Mr Jackson said, we were so unlike theatrical children. It was his boast that we never wore grease paint and that our rosy cheeks were natural. If some of us looked a little pale before going on, he would tell us to pinch our cheeks.' The first boy band.

But Chaplin didn't stay long: 'I was not particularly enamoured with being just a clog dancer in a troupe of eight lads.' Stan Laurel was also a Lancashire Lad, but not at the same time. Later Stan was with Chaplin in America, part of a troupe sent over by Fred Karno. They shared rooms; Laurel spent a long time imitating Chaplin and then trying not to imitate Chaplin. But he always admired him. Chaplin mentions him once in his autobiography, in a picture caption. I suppose I could argue that this lack of warmth was a result of being only an ersatz Lancastrian. But it's more about growing up with a drunk father, a mad mother and no money. The section of his autobiography which deals with the Lancashire Lads goes on to deal, in detail, with the number of comedians he'd known who had committed suicide.

Earlier, there had been this, about being on his own, locked out, late at night in Kennington:

> Suddenly there was music. Rapturous! It came from the vestibule of the White Hart corner pub, and resounded brilliantly in the empty square. The tune was 'The Honeysuckle and the Bee', played with radiant virtuosity on a harmonium and clarinet. I had never been conscious of melody before, but this one was beautiful and lyrical, so blithe and gay, so warm and reassuring. I forgot my despair and crossed the road to where the musicians were. The harmonium player was blind, with scarred sockets where the eyes had been; and a besotted, embittered face played the clarinet.

Comics, eh?

In Southport, as it happened, I got talking to a lady clog dancer who turned out to have been the first woman ever to win the Lancashire and Cheshire Clog Dancing Championships. Sue Bousfield was her name, and her white outfit and boater were the only concessions to Tidy. Her mentor had been Sam Sherry, the dancer from Preston who helped to revive clog dancing in the '40s and '50s, finding a home after the halls in folk, along with morris dancers and bearded men who cup their hands to their ears. But the steps he used were the same ones Dan Leno did, Sue told me. She said that Lancashire clog dancing was all toe and no heel, and more inventive than other styles. Mind you, she said, her own husband had been against her taking up clog dancing, man's preserve, that sort of thing, better these days. I asked her if she knew Lancashire was the county where women died of love. Her reply was what I would have described as a snort if she hadn't been a clog dancing champion. 'That's my laugh for today,' she said.

This, though, had all rather got in the way of my main area of current research. It was time for a bold stroke. I resolved to take the Eurostar, to discover what the Southport of the South made of its debt. And it was a bold stroke, as my record in the foreign correspondent game has not been one of startling success. I may have boasted elsewhere about gaining entry to an American base on the Azores by flourishing my *Daily Telegraph* canteen card, but that was a high point. A representative cable from HQ would be the one I got in Baghdad, during the Iran–Iraq war in the '80s: 'Why you not Ahwaz?' I found this a little perplexing, as Ahwaz was in Iran, and several hundred miles away. Still, it was certainly true that the bar had become rather emptier recently. Ah, well.

I also followed the great Max Hastings, later to be my editor, into Port Stanley, but at some distance. If Max was the first man into Port Stanley, I was the last, replacing the *Daily Telegraph* reporter who had done the hard stuff and yomped his way across the islands. I walked into the Upland Goose, the famous hotel, and ordered a drink from mine host, mercurial in the way of all mine hosts, Mr Desmond King. I took a sip of the beer, and said, 'Have you had some trouble round here, then?' Happy days. My principal contribution thereafter was helping the Islands' fire chief nearly drown when he fell between two boats while we were going for a drink. Did you know that Falkland Islanders can't swim? Well, they couldn't then. The Upland Goose was also the place where a Scottish journalist, incensed by the ease with which Sir Max had scooped the war's top honours, went for him with a commando knife, only to be pulled back with the immortal words, 'This is neither the time nor the place to kill Max Hastings.'

Enough old hackery. The pressing concern with the Parisian mission was the miserable state of my French. Do you remember when Ian Botham recreated Hannibal's trip to Italy, complete with circus elephants, for charity? I went along and managed to pull off the rare feat of crashing into an ambulance. Anyway, the BBC man there was so impressed with my accent and way with the French locals – '*Connaissez-vous* Ian Botham?' – that he broadcast it to the nation. Before stalking the *grands boulevards* to test opinion, Southport-wise, I therefore took the precaution of arranging to borrow the services of Emma, the charming assistant of John Lichfield, *The Independent*'s man in Paris, half a Lancastrian himself and entirely persuaded by my arguments for the Lanco–Gallic affinity, if not quite so taken with the Southport angle.

It was springtime in Paris. Do you know the famous story about David Ogilvy, the noted advertising man? He had seen a man in New York begging beside a sign on which was written, 'I am blind', and not doing very well. Ogilvy changed the sign to read, 'It is spring and I am blind'. The money poured in. It was spring in Paris and it was raining. But it was still Paris. Whatever else you might say about Napoleon and his great engineer, Haussmann, the autocratic, German-descended, public-health-obsessed claustrophobe, they knew how to make a city that balances grandeur and intimacy, swagger and softness, stone and leaf, like no other.

What was I expecting, on the Champs Élysées, near the Place de l'Étoile, from where the *grands boulevards* radiate? Well, to be honest, I wasn't expecting anyone to say, '*Mais oui, tout le monde sait que Southport est la mère de Paris!*' I was expecting some of that old and legendary Parisian hauteur and dismissiveness, particularly as John Lichfield was in the middle of writing a column about the appalling rudeness of Parisians, which he was finding particularly rampant just at that moment. In a few days these same streets would be full of angry French persons protesting vehemently against plans to interfere with their pensions; soon Cherbourg would be blockaded by, for some reason, incensed teachers. And here was this ageing

Englishman in a slightly shabby mac bearing a few somewhat curled photocopies of pictures of some place in England he claims inspired Paris. Can you imagine the reverse effect of a Frenchman in Regent Street approaching people to claim that Nash had ripped it all off from Balaruc les Bains? *S'il vous plaît*!

And so, of course, they were charming, patient and open-minded to a man and woman. This could have had something to do with Emma, who was probably saying, 'He's quite mad, please humour him,' but I also approached several people on my own. M. Jean Ripayre, 31, for example, who had obviously benefited from his business course at Camden College. Had he heard of this theory? 'No,' said M. Ripayre, with a wide grin. Had he heard of Southport? 'Not really,' he said, with exquisite politeness. I showed him an early engraving of Southport from before 1848, and a coloured postcard from around the turn of the century. This was a test both for M. Ripayre's English and manners. Eventually he settled for, 'It looks a little like it.' Had he heard of Lancashire? 'Yes.' What did he know of it? 'It has a very nice landscape.' I told him about Balzac. M. Ripayre giggled, but in a nice way. *Quel homme*! He even promised to spread my theory around. So just wait a couple of years, and who knows?

It must be said, though, that M. Ripayre was unusual in having heard of Lancashire. Olivier and Melanie, two students, had heard of Yorkshire, but rescued themselves by confiding that they wouldn't be amazed if Paris was based on Southport. They were from Rouen, however. M. François Beaucaire was a Parisian architect, and not so persuaded. He said the Haussmann reconstruction was the result of many influences and suggested I try a library. There was a Gallic shrug, but it was done most courteously.

By now, Emma was on the case. Daniel, a medical journalist wearing a jacket in the kind of turquoise only a middle-aged Frenchman could get away with, stood patiently with his umbrella. Being a journalist, he was, of course, sceptical about

Southport, but he had heard of Lancashire. '*Mouton*!' he said, turning to me, 'You know, sheeps!', providing a reason why women might die of love that I hadn't so far contemplated. Did he consider the Southport proposal a slur on the honour of the capital? Not if it were done politely, he said. Ah, yes, politesse.

Next up was M. Jacques St Raymond, who, by charming coincidence, turned out to be a high-ranking member of the lorry drivers' union, and thus an expert on streets. M. St Raymond, a smiling 61 year old, far removed from the barricade-building image of the French worker, nevertheless managed to air the wide-boulevard–clear-field-of-fire theory. He thought more than one influence had been at work, but looked at my pictures politely, before murmuring, 'Maybe you're right.' He also promised to go to Southport and have a proper look, as did Annie and Renée, two French ladies *d'un certain âge* and that certain Parisian look, who were each attending to a post-déjeunerial *chocolat*. '*Pourquoi pas?*' was their attitude, which, frankly, fell into an emerging pattern. What we wanted was less of this laissez-faire double-shrugging; what we wanted was someone in a beret and *travails bleus* who would spit and that sort of thing at this insult.

The first man on the Champs Élysées approximately dressed like that turned out to be an advertising executive wearing what was presumably the current *haut ton*. St John Gerard listened to Emma, and then turned to me and said, in English, 'So, what's your problem?' Did he think the Southport thesis likely? 'Maybe, why not?' (Do you know, I've only just noticed the remarkable similarity between M. Gerard and Sir John Gerard, Napoleon's host. How odd is that?)

Another promising prospect, Daniel Lardeaux, a *pâtissier*, gave us an erudite lecture on Haussmann, politely. Rarely had I encountered such unanimity and, let me tell you, I have done quite a bit of this sort of stuff in my time. I think I'm proudest of the one I did for the *Daily Telegraph* at the once mighty

Llanwern steel works in South Wales, late at night, very close to deadline, after management had put forward a new offer to end a strike. I went to the main entrance and spoke to a picket who was firm for staying out. I then drove for miles round to the back exit, where I found one who was a bit wavery. 'Steel workers were divided last night over a return to work,' I wrote. Marvellous. You have to be a bit careful, though: in Liverpool, I interviewed a Scottish football fan who told me he was called 'Big Tadger from Paisley', and so he appeared in the *Liverpool Echo*. I realised why his mates had been laughing so much when a Scottish colleague told me what a tadger was in Paisley.

But this was Paris and I was getting desperate. So desperate that I authorised Emma to approach a taxi driver. Bernard, 57, moustache, bored taxi look, listened and then gave us an erudite lecture on Haussmann, politely. We suggested he should go and have a look at Southport. Bernard gave us a big beaming smile, exposing two missing front teeth. A smiling taxi driver. *Sacre bleu*! I couldn't even get anybody excited by my picture of Blackpool Tower.

Enfin, people were prepared to entertain a theory that the inspiration for the magnificent heart of their city and, indeed, the nation, was a place they had never heard of in an area they had never heard of in a country for which they were supposed to reserve the highest condescension, or, at very best, an ennui-filled dismissal. Can you think of a better illustration of French sophistication? Now, remember that comparably composed acceptance on the streets of Southport? *Voilà*!

We turned into the Rue du Faubourg St Honoré, one of those narrower, quieter, gentler Paris streets that leads up to the Boulevard Haussmann, where, on the corner, Haussmann's childhood home stood; before, of course, he knocked it down to make way for his vision. That Haussmann. So driven, so intense, so unFrench, somehow, even if he did like to live in style and had the obligatory affair with a young dancer from the Opéra before dying ignored and forgotten. Still, he has a statue on his boulevard now.

Halfway up towards the Boulevard Haussmann was an antiquarian book shop, H. Picard & Fils. Ideal for a bit of historical input, I thought, and besides, it was beginning to rain heavily. M. Picard welcomed us. M. Christian Picard. M. Henri Picard was the H. Picard in H. Picard & Fils, the present M. Picard's grandfather, who had opened the shop in 1902. M. Christian's daughter, Christelle, was in the shop, as was his wife, Jeannine. M. Christian was everything you could hope for in an antiquarian bookseller: studious, grey-haired, bespectacled, a little diffident, and distinguished from his British counterparts only by the smartness of his light grey suit.

He considered the Southport theory, looked at my pictures and drawings, and concluded that it was 'possible'. The pictures of Southport at the turn of the century reminded him particularly of those done of Paris at about the same time, by that painter . . . now what was his name? Neither his wife nor daughter could remember, either. His daughter, I felt, was less persuaded by Southport. We discussed Haussmann and his autobiography, just the three volumes. M. Christian had a collected paperback version, for 44 euros, but I felt this would be one book too many. I told him that Southport was known in Britain as the Paris of the North, and aired the Prof's suggestion that perhaps, given this discovery, Paris should now be known as the Southport of the South. M. Christian looked grave, and said this was certainly logical. M. Christian was, I think, enjoying himself, although it is not in the nature of an antiquarian bookseller to be too demonstrative.

Yes, he agreed, perhaps Paris should give thanks, and not only for this. Britain had provided so many influences and innovations. I asked him what he was thinking of particularly. Everyone thought hard for some time, and then M. Christian said: 'Roundabouts.' This was fascinating, as I have, for reasons which need not detain us here, quite an interest in roundabouts, and I happen to know that M. Eugène Hénard, the city architect of Paris at the turn of the nineteenth century, has a fair claim to having invented them, in no less a place than the Place de l'Étoile, which means that, wait for it, the Arc de Triomphe is actually the world's first roundabout. But I didn't mention this to M. Christian, as I didn't want to deliver too many shocks in one day. I told him, too, about Balzac and the famous quotation from *Le Lys dans la vallée*. He wasn't familiar with it. How much would a first edition cost me, I wondered, sentimentally. About 15,000 euros, he said. We settled on a rather later edition for 50 euros. By now he had also found an art book containing the work of the watercolourist who painted Southportish Parisian scenes: Edouard Cortes. I looked and he was right. Also in the book was a rather fine study, painted by Jacotter in 1835, pre-dating Napoleon and Haussmann, showing the wide tree-lined expanse of the Boulevard des Italiens, but everyone, including myself, was too polite to mention it.

I bade farewell to the Picards, and to Emma. John Lichfield agreed to come for a drink in the Brasserie Balzac, at the corner of the Rue Balzac, to submit the theory to its stiffest test: a Parisian waiter. He looked promising as he took our order, but, as John explained Southport and Balzac, the waiter's face, and I hesitate to write this, became sunnier and sunnier, until, finally, there was a broad smile. A taxi driver was one thing, but a waiter, in Paris: this was too cruel! I turned to Cyrille and Charles, two twenty year olds having a drink at the next table, in the hope that a hard day and a couple of *vins ordinaires* might make them turn nasty. *Pas du tout*, although they were less impressed by my pictures of Lord Street than most. 'The buildings are nothing like Paris,' said Cyrille, who was in finance. I told him it was my mission to persuade the people of Paris that it was the Southport of the South. 'I think I'm not sure that you're going to be very lucky,' said Cyrille. Then Charles, who was in the wine trade and

161

had been studying the photos of Southport, said that the buildings reminded him rather of Bordeaux, where both of them came from. Cyrille agreed. It was time to go home: Bordeaux was where Haussmann had worked before Paris. How complicated could all this get?

Besides, we shouldn't get too hung up on this, you know: it's not as if it's Southport's only claim to fame. I've mentioned Hilda Ogden and Red Rum; Hawthorne and Melville might interest you, too. Nathaniel and Herman, that is, mighty American men of letters. Hawthorne lived in Southport while he was American consul in Liverpool; Melville came to visit him. A splendid picture: Hawthorne recalls the two of them sitting in the sandhills smoking cigars, staring out to the sea, or at least where it should have been. (Hawthorne wrote after his second day there: 'In all my experience of Southport, I have not yet seen the sea.')

But you are ahead of me: you are wondering whether Southport beach was the inspiration for *Moby-Dick*. Already written by then, 1856, I am narrowly compelled to reveal. Melville wrote nothing of any consequence after sitting there, and Hawthorne was clearly not impressed either:

> Southport is as stupid a place as ever I lived in; and I cannot but bewail an ill fortune, to have been compelled to spend these many months on these barren sands, when almost every other square yard of England contains something that would have been historically or poetically interesting.

Thanks a lot, Nat. Let me just say that your fellow American, Roy Orbison, visited the town while I was working there, and he seemed quite happy, although it was a little difficult to tell, what with those dark glasses, and those songs.

Nothing French about Nat, although he did note that Charles Scarisbrick, one of the town's founders, was reputed to have kept a gambling house in Paris in his youth. And, as it happens, the second wife of Peter Hesketh Fleetwood, another influential figure, was a Spaniard whom he met in Belgium, which is pretty close. And I haven't even got on to Louis Philippe yet.

First, though, one last literary excursion: Michael Arlen, the exotic Armenian inter-war novelist, spent a lot of his childhood in Southport. Arlen wrote a now almost forgotten but then fantastically fashionable novel, *The Green Hat*, full of decadence and beautiful cars and a heroine of mystery and sophistication, a woman of the type summed up by my father as 'no better than she should have been', who was forever pointing her Hispano Suiza in the direction of Maidenhead from Mayfair. I've often wondered why I was so fond of it; now I have discovered that Arlen returned to Southport to write it. Take that, Nat. I went to interview Anthony Powell once, a rather daunting business, as he was scrupulously polite but completely unforthcoming. As I sat having lunch with Powell and his wife, Lady Violet, at home just outside Frome, with him leaping up with that careful agility of the old to fill my glass with immense civility but not the slightest hint of any enjoyment of his hostly duties, I mentioned, for some reason, probably to show off, that I was very fond of *The Green Hat*. Neither Powell made any comment. Later I read an interview with him in which he claimed it was among his favourite books. Later, too, I read in his diaries an account of our meeting and my bloodied stone of an article: 'Charles Nevin of the *Sunday Telegraph* came to luncheon for interview; gave impression of rather run-of-the-mill journalist.' Ah, well, thanks, Tone.

But, to Louis Philippe, after pointing out that 'the Paris of the North' is not Southport's only Gallic soubriquet. No: according to Mr Bailey's fine history, it was known in the 1820s as 'the Montpellier of England': 'In external appearance, there was of course little or no resemblance between Southport and the ancient French cathedral and university town, which did not even stand on the coast. Montpellier was renowned as a centre for the study of medicine, and the medicinal qualities attributed to the North Meols coast must have prompted the comparison.' Did not even stand on the coast, eh? No, after you.

Mr Bailey notes, without approval, that this proud claim was slightly watered down to 'the Montpellier of the Coast of South Lancashire'. I am reminded of Connaught Avenue, Frinton-on-Sea's *grand boulevard*, which has gone from 'the Bond Street of the East Coast' to 'the Bond Street of Essex' to, now, 'the Bond Street of the Tendring Peninsula', which, you'll agree, doesn't have quite the same ring to it. I've always liked Frinton, though, where we used to go on day trips when we were staying with my mother's parents. It is one of those English shortcuts to a smile, like Des O'Connor records. The reality, fiercely defending itself against ice cream vans and other such debaucheries, is rather better summed up by the old graffito, 'Harwich for the Continent, Frinton for the Incontinent', but I defy you not to grin at Dudley Moore's conceit of the friend who was now 'living with a sailor in Frinton'. Last time I was there, it was early in the season, and, being Frinton, we were advised we would do better for a room in Clacton, where we stayed at the ungrand Grand Hotel and had a marvellous time eating a richly battered seafood selection while a party of pensioners listened to the organ and my five year old danced with a waitress. Sorry, Frinton.

But, to Louis Philippe, the citizen king, the one Louis Napoleon had so conspicuously failed to topple with his two attempted coups before the Paris mob did it for him in 1848. The citizen ex-king fled to England, under the splendid *nom de guerre* of Mr Smith. And, Mr Bailey also tells us, there is, yes, a tradition that long before that, in 1815, while also in exile, Louis Philippe, then rejoicing in the equally striking surname of Égalité, stayed the night in Southport. And who was it that drove the very first *grand boulevard*, the Rue Rambuteau, through from the Marais district to the market at Les Halles? All right, all right, I'll stop now.

Chapter Seven

Old King Cotton

His Heirs, Entailments and Bequests

Weaste is a couple of miles but some way off the centre of Manchester. Weaste doesn't have a lot of the sparkling sheen, all class and glass and gleam, that shocks you about the New Millennial Manchester, especially if the Manchester you remember best was the dull, dusty, dirty, dozing Manchester, the one that hadn't yet been shaken awake into the old energy by the Thatcher recession and the Irish Republican bomb.

No, Weaste is not like that, even if it is pretty hard by two of the very shiniest symbols of this great stirring, the Lowry Centre and the Imperial War Museum of the North. Weaste, over here, in Salford, on the Lowry side, still awaits the steam clean, wash and brush-up of economic regeneration. But it is promised. Meanwhile, the United Reform Church has a big message on its board saying 'Martial Arts classes – all welcome', and behind a wall on the north side of Liverpool Street, two men are fishing.

It's hard to see exactly what they are fishing in. Not a pond;

man-made, certainly. No grassy banks here: concrete, brick, iron railings. Much bigger than a tank, a bit small for a reservoir, surely. But that's what it is: a reservoir that once fed a mill. A very famous mill, as it happens, not that Nigel and his mate know much about it. And why should they? It was a long time ago, and now there are tench and bream and all sorts to be caught, that's the thing.

A cotton mill, of course. Cotton. You won't get a better word association with Lancashire than that. Lancashire, cotton, mill, chimney, steam, coal, Arkwright, spinning jenny, Crompton, mule, weavers, spinners, shawls, clogs, cobbles, hooter, knocker-up, our Gracie, Wakes Weeks, Britain's bread hangs by Lancashire's thread. What happened to all that, what happened to Old King Cotton?

Well, much the same as happened to the other kings and princes, coal, iron, steel, shipbuilding and car manufacturing. They got old and other places grew up, caught up, that sort of thing. They used to call Manchester, over there, 'Cottonopolis'. It was the centre of an industry that, at its peak, just before the First World War, employed half a million people, one in five of Lancashire's total workforce, and imported one billion tons of raw cotton a year. And now? A workforce of about five thousand.

On a busy day, over there, in the Royal Exchange, a satisfied, burgherish neo-classical extravaganza the size of two football pitches, some fifteen thousand cotton lords, their attendants and representatives would gather to buy and sell and shout and murmur.

Not now. Now there's not much more than a whisper. The dealing board from the last day of trading is still up there, but that's all. It survived the IRA bomb in 1996, as did, just about, the Royal Exchange Theatre, the clever and stylishly restored steel module that takes up most of the space inside it now. And the mills and warehouses that survive are luxury lofts.

Should we feel sorry that those days are gone? I don't. The

accounts I've read of what it was like to be a weaver or a spinner, in or out of the mills and factories, are unrelieved in their grim-up-northness, and exceeded only by tales of the mines. But why should it matter what I think? I don't even understand why miners fought till the end for their right and the right of their children to carry on going down there and doing that.

But I am taken by cotton, by the curiousness and quixotry of it. I can see why you mine and farm and make things from various raw materials that happen to be around; the stuff is right there, waiting, ripe for exploitation. But, cotton? The nearest cotton to Lancashire is on the other side of the Mediterranean. Yes, I know, they used to tell us in school about the special humidity in east Lancs, nurtured by the Pennines and Walter Greenwood's warm west wind, which was crucially important, preventing as it did snapping and all that; but can it really be that around 1500, or perhaps a little later, someone sheltering, with collar up against the famous local drizzle, instead of sighing or scuttling quickly for cover, or saying, with a wry smile, 'Lovely weather for ducks', suddenly exclaimed, 'Cotton! That's what would be good here!'?

It's just about possible, I suppose. There had been some local wool manufacture, and linen was being made from flax imported from Ireland and grown in the west of the county. And then, in the late 1500s, Flemish asylum seekers in East Anglia introduced fustian, made from a linen warp and a cotton weft, using cotton from the Levant. The technique moved north and west; who knows, perhaps a Flem did come and shout, 'Cotton!' In which case there ought to be one more famous Belgian.

But I still have doubts that he or she then went on, 'Yes, I can see it now! We could bring the raw cotton from thousands of miles away and then, helped by some clever and rather complicated machinery, we can use it to make thread and yarn and clothing and send it thousands more miles to be sold! That's a really sound and sensible economic basis for what will be

Britain's leading export from 1803 till 1938, bringing in by 1830 just over half of Britain's overseas earnings!'

Curious. Curious, too, that this exotic material should kindle and fire so much ingenuity and effort and spark the world's first Industrial Revolution. But not curious that some would see striking injustice and inequity in its workings at home and abroad, between employers and employees, imperial manufacturers and colonial clients, the developed and the developing.

One of them was the junior partner in the mill at Weaste, Victoria Mill, operated by the firm of Ermen and Engels. Indeed, Friedrich Engels. Victoria Mill, where Nigel and his mate now fish in the post-industrial, post-socialist quiet, was the mill that made the money that Engels gave to Marx that helped him kindle and fire the next revolution, the one where theory and ideals and hope became converted into practice, pragmatism and disillusionment in the most death-ridden and destructive century humanity has yet contrived.

How much should we blame Manchester and Lancashire for all this? Could we say that there was something in the water, something unique in Manchester's mix of crusading radicalism and rampant capitalism which persuaded Engels that the romantic, doomed attempt to impose equality was a real runner?

You can certainly see the attractions and the arguments. Manchester was, in Asa Briggs' phrase, the 'Shock City' of the world in the first half of the nineteenth century. It was a city immersed in steam and smoke, and, yes, muck and brass, humming with wealth and throbbing with poverty, seething with the energy of ideas, aspirations and resentments, a world city, at once cosmopolitan and provincial, the city of Chartism and the Anti-Corn Law League and nonconformity, of the freedoms to trade and vote and worship and be different, whether you were Cobden, Bright or Peel, or, for that matter, the wonderfully named Rev. William Cowherd, pioneer teetotaller and vegetarian. And it was, of course, the city of Peterloo, flashing blades and state cavalry crushing the proletariat and their legitimate demands, the symbol of the British revolution waiting to happen.

Engels arrived in Manchester in 1842 to take up a position with Ermen and Engels. The Engels in Ermen and Engels was his father, third generation of a Rhineland textile-manufacturing family, partner in the newly established Manchester company with the three Ermen brothers, sons of another Rhineland manufacturer. Engels, though, was not like the sons of other Rhineland manufacturers. Engels was batting for the other side. He arrived fresh from anonymous newspaper attacks on German capitalists and a meeting with Marx. His father was anxious that he should be taken away from such influences; Engels was not entirely displeased to be in the Shock City, even if he had to spend a lot of the time on a clerk's stool.

And, in the Shock City, the other side was undoubtedly restive. Chartism was resurgent, fuelled by an economic downturn and wage cuts; a general strike in Manchester that summer had brought out troops, police and special constables, thanked for their efforts after it was over by Ermen and Engels in an advertisement on the front page of the *Manchester Guardian*.

Engels plunged in off his stool, but only outside office hours, a revolutionary on and in his own time. He took Mary Burns, the factory-girl daughter of an Irish immigrant, as his mistress, and she took him round the stews and sinks of Manchester, like Irishtown and Gibraltar. The result was *The Condition of the Working Class in England in 1844*, as fine and indignant a diatribe as any 24 year old has produced in 20 months:

> The view from [Ducie] Bridge, mercifully concealed from mortals of small stature by a parapet as high as a man, is characteristic for the whole district. At the

bottom flows, or rather stagnates, the Irk, a narrow, coal-black, foul-smelling stream, full of debris and refuse, which it deposits on the shallower right bank. In dry weather, a long string of the most disgusting, blackish-green, slime pools are left standing on this bank, from the depths of which bubbles of miasmatic gas constantly arise and give forth a stench unendurable even on the bridge forty or fifty feet above the surface of the stream. But besides this, the steam is checked every few paces by high weirs, behind which slime and refuse accumulate and rot in thick masses.

Above the bridge are tanneries, bone mills, and gas works, from which all drains and refuse find their way into the Irk, which receives further the contents of all the neighbouring sewers and privies. It may be easily imagined, therefore, what sort of residue the stream deposits . . . on the lower right bank . . . the background embraces the pauper burial ground, the station of the Liverpool and Leeds railway, and, in the rear of this, the Workhouse, the 'Poor Law Bastille' of Manchester, which, like a citadel, looks threateningly down from behind its high walls and parapet on the hilltop, upon the working people's quarter below . . .

Such is the Old Town of Manchester, and on re-reading my description, I am forced to admit that instead of being exaggerated, it is far from black enough to convey a true impression of the filth, ruin, and uninhabitableness, the defiance of all considerations of cleanliness, ventilation and health which characterise the construction of this single district, containing at least twenty to thirty thousand inhabitants.

And such a district exists in the heart of the second city of England, the first manufacturing city of the world. If anyone wishes to see in how little space a human being

can move, how little air – and such air! – he can breathe,
how little of civilisation he may share and yet live, it is
only necessary to travel hither. True this is the Old
Town, and the people of Manchester emphasise the fact
whenever any one mentions to them the frightful
condition of this Hell upon Earth; but what does that
prove? Everything which here arouses horror and
indignation is of recent origin, belongs to the industrial
epoch . . .

Tremendous power, you'll agree. But the book wasn't translated
and published in Britain until 1892. And, as Nigel and his mate,
fishing, could tell us, Friedrich's confident prediction that the
revolution of the proletariat would imminently overthrow the
capitalist system in Britain matches anything that Nostradamus,
the Mormons, Jehovah's Witnesses or even the *Today*
programme's racing selections have ever come up with.

He hadn't properly understood Manchester. Which was not
surprising, given the 20 months. He had confused his
radicalisms, failing to see that the Anti-Corn Law League was a
middle-class radicalism whose freedoms to trade and make a
profit also included freedom to exploit and freedom from
Chartist social reforms. But that doesn't entirely explain
Manchester, and why he had to start the revolution without it.

I like the famous story of Engels in conversation with another
businessman about the 'disgraceful unhealthy slums' in the city
and the 'disgusting condition of that part of the town in which
the factory workers lived . . . I declared that I had never seen so
badly built a town in my life. He listened patiently and at the
corner of the street as we parted company he remarked: "And yet
a great deal of money is to be made here. Good morning, sir."'

The authentic voice of the Manchester Cotton Man,
confident, cocky even, but not chippy, because this is
Manchester, where what he thinks today, London thinks

tomorrow and where, for example, if the Liverpool Gentlemen start charging too much in the way of port dues, he will simply move the Atlantic by building a canal 35 miles long, 120 feet wide and 28 feet deep. As A.J.P. Taylor puts it:

> These were the men who gave Manchester its historical character. We think of them in retrospect as radicals, and so they were in lack of respect for traditional authority or in their ruthless destruction of whatever stood in their way . . . They had succeeded by their own energy, and they supposed that the duty of the society was discharged if it gave others the chance to do the same.

But there was something else, too. In 1861, Engels had been back in Manchester for ten years after his brief mounted skirmish with glory in the quickly suppressed rising of the Rhineland against the Prussians, still working for the firm, still waiting for the Lancastrians to do their bit. The American Civil War looked to provide an opportunity. Lincoln and the North were blockading the South, source of most of Lancashire's raw cotton. The mills went on to short time and there was great distress. Revisionists now claim that the cause of the lay-offs was previous over-production, but there was no doubt then where the blame lay.

Despite this, the reaction of large numbers of cotton workers was to express their solidarity with Lincoln, the North and the abolition of slavery. Lincoln called it 'an instance of sublime Christian heroism which has not been surpassed in any age or in any country'. I know I was a bit flip about it in the introduction, but I still reckon it a splendidly idealistic, whimsical, romantic gesture.

But it was not without its hard consequences. The suffering at home – a drop of more than 50 per cent in employment in one year – was affectingly documented by *The Times* in 1862.

> An old woman was visited. On entering the lower room
> of the house the visitors saw there was not a scrap of
> furniture; the woman, ever stricken, sat on an orange
> box below a low fire; and to prevent the fire going out,
> she was pulling her seat to pieces for the fuel, bit by bit.

What is perhaps less appreciated is that Marx and Engels, long discouraged by the English proletariat's wilful refusal to rise, saw the Cotton Famine as a demonstration of exactly the sort of international working-class solidarity they were looking for: it became one of the chief prompts for the founding of the First International in 1864. The rest is Communism.

Whatever the consequences, Lancashire's support for Lincoln was a splendidly idealistic gesture. It is sad that Marx and Engels chose to ignore the inconvenient fact that it was also a demonstration of inter-class solidarity. There were complaints about hard-hearted mill-owners, but there were also firms paying wages for no work. Soup kitchens were set up, clothing distributed, relief funds started. Small shopkeepers gave credit. Rent was suspended. There were large anonymous donations. I find this side of it equally whimsical, uplifting and romantic, not at all gruff and A.J.P. Taylorish, and something that I might argue was not, as Engels might put it, hypocritical bourgeois benevolence, but instead something rather typically Lancastrian. This is Edwin Waugh: 'The people of Lancashire never were remarkable for hawking their troubles much about the world. In the present untoward pass, their deportment as a whole has been worthy of themselves, and their wants have been worthily met by their neighbours.'

I'm not quite sure I'd buy the quiet bit, but I do think that this goes some way to explain why Lancashire never rose red. The rest, I would suggest, is covered by the Lancashire preference for a bit of enlivening drama rather than any more hard slog. This is what fooled Fred: Lancastrians are great talkers and dramatisers, but not so hot on the action. For a fine example of their talent for drama, read Fanny Kemble witnessing the Duke of Wellington coming into Manchester as the *Rocket* opened the Liverpool–Manchester railway in 1830:

> High above the grim and grimy crowd of scowling faces a loom had been erected, at which sat a tattered, starving-looking weaver, evidently set there as a representative man, to protest against the triumphs of machinery and the gain and glory which the wealthy Liverpool and Manchester men were likely to derive from it.

But they were far too whimsical to get on with it. How many, after all, died at this famous Peterloo? Eleven.

Fred was a romantic. How can a revolutionary not be? I like to think that Lancashire got to him, too, although he was certainly always that way inclined. He loved music, carousing and all the fun of the night. He liked to think of himself as the man of action, standing firm before the fusillades of the mighty Prussians in the Rhineland, but he could laugh, as well, at his nickname, 'The General'. He had insatiable curiosity and energy. He 'loved a joke in every language': at the age of 70, he learnt Norwegian so that he could read Ibsen in the original. And he did like a bit of embroidery. Did he really believe, for example, as he wrote in *The Condition*, that mill-owners had the *jus primae noctis* over their employees? Well, I'll go to the foot of their stairs.

Look at his responses in this question-and-answer session with Marx's daughter, Eleanor, in 1869:

> Favourite virtue: Jollity
> Chief characteristic: Knowing everything by halves
> Idea of happiness: Château Margaux 1848

174

Idea of misery: To go to the dentist
The vice you excuse most: Excess of any kind
The vice you detest most: Cant
Your aversion: Affected, stuck-up women
Your favourite occupation: Chaffing and being chaffed
Favourite dish: Cold: salad. Hot: Irish stew
Favourite maxim: Not to have any
Motto: Take it easy

Take it easy! And how splendid that what inspired him most about 1848, the famous year of revolution, his time in the uniform, was the Château Margaux. He loved hunting as well. 'Last Saturday,' he wrote to Marx in 1858, 'I was out hunting – seven hours in the saddle. That sort of thing makes me hellishly excited for a few days; it is the greatest physical pleasure which I know.'

He rode regularly with the Cheshire Hunt, which at the time was embroiled in the 'Cheshire Difficulty' over an improper relationship, imprudently committed to paper, between the Master of the Fox Hounds and a lady not his wife, leading to all sorts of demands for satisfaction, refusals, accusations of rank cowardice and caddishness and the like, and which I mention only because the MFH's name was Captain Mainwaring.

As you might gather, hunting in Cheshire was a lively occupation and not just for the toffs. There were also all manner of Manchester Men and Liverpool Gentlemen, jumpers and climbers and on at least one occasion, in 1858, gloriously recorded in song, 24 chimney sweeps on donkeys. I like to think that might have been the day Marx joined Engels in the chase. Sadly, the day I visited him, Captain Gordon Fergusson, author of a magisterial work on hunting in Cheshire, couldn't track down any more information in the archives in his outhouse outside Tarporley. He was, though, able to tell me about another occasion, when the Empress of Austria was out with the hunt and a Manchester Man over-rode the hounds, taking a fence and landing on top of one of the best bitches, killing it, and prompting the unimpressed Master, Captain E.W. 'Puffles' Park Yates, to tell him in front of the Empress that he deserved to be publicly buggered in Tarporley by six Irish navvies.

All human life was there, then. Of course, hunting was a rather less controversial hobby then than it is today, and fine training for the armed struggle. If you're interested in the inconsistencies and incongruities of Engels, imagine Engels the merchant, moving round the Exchange, inwardly rejoicing at every piece of bad news for the industry that sustained him and Marx, hoping for a revolution. He wrote with glee, for example, that in Liverpool 'people are absolutely cleaned out and have hardly the courage left to go bankrupt', while in Manchester 'the cotton-spinners and manufacturers are paying away in wages and fuel costs all the money they have got for their goods, and when that disappears they must go sky-high too . . . Peter Ermen [his partner] is already shitting his pants when he thinks of it – and that little bullfrog is a good barometer of the state of trade . . .'

All that time he was maintaining two residences: one was that of the cotton lord and polite society gentleman, while the other concealed Mary Burns, his working-class Irish mistress. And what was the vice he detested most? Precisely. Yet, as I say, I can't help feeling fond of Fred, not least because, in old age, he had the grace to hold his hands up and admit that he'd got it wrong about the imminent English uprising and ask to be excused on the grounds of 'youthful ardour'. Calling to mind the grand clamour and destiny-laden phrasemaking of international socialism, it makes me smile that when, according to Engels' wishes, they scattered his ashes at sea, they did it, with the bathos that Lancashire likes, just off Eastbourne. *Vale*, Fred.

But, cotton. Asa Briggs considered it 'an intensely moral commodity'. W.R. Greg, Bury mill manager and essayist, said that had not Providence planted the cotton shrubs, those majestic masses of men which stretch, like a living zone, through our central districts, would have had no existence; and the magic impulse which has been felt during that period in every department of national energy, which has affected more or less our literature, our laws, our social condition, our political institutions, making us almost a new people, would never have been communicated.

Briggs also quotes another cotton lord: 'What a satisfaction it is to every man going from the west to the east, when he clambers up Mount Lebanon, to find one of the ancient Druses clothed in garments with which our industrious countrymen have provided him.' Funnily enough, as it happens, in a mill in Garstang, a substantial part of what little is left of Lancashire cotton production is devoted to satisfying the Middle East's demand for the keffiyeh, the checked Arab headdress.

'Cotton,' wrote A.J.P Taylor,

is a nice industry to spring from and live among. The making and selling of cotton is one of the few human activities which is wholly benificent. It never did anyone harm and it has done mankind much good. Every piece of cotton cloth is going to make someone warmer or cleaner or more comfortable. You don't have to conquer people in order to turn them into your customers, and you suffer no imperialist craving to control your own raw materials.

The cotton trade conspires with the climate to make the inhabitants of Manchester a kindly people, inclined perhaps to rather simple solutions, but gentle and sensible. It is no doubt foolish to believe that cotton cloth contains the secret of human happiness, but it is at any rate less foolish than to believe it of motor-cars or machine guns.

Well, yes. I suppose I could continue like this, but even romantics need a bit of contrast. This is a description of Manchester mill-workers in 1831:

> The children were small, sickly, bare-footed and ill-clad.
> Many appeared to be no older than seven. The men . . .
> were almost as pallid and thin as the children. The
> women were most respectable in appearance, but I saw
> no fresh, or fine-looking individuals among them . . .
> Here I saw, or thought I saw, a degenerate race – human
> beings stunted, enfeebled and depraved – men and
> women that were not to be aged; children that were
> never to be healthy adults. It was a mournful spectacle.

Fourteen-hour days, starting at around 6 a.m., with eight-hour days on Saturdays; an hour for dinner and half an hour for breakfast in some mills. Cotton and dust hanging down in footlengths; little in the way of ventilation; temperatures as high as 80° F. Chris Aspin, in *Lancashire: The First Industrial Society*, tells of factory children marching for the Ten Hours Bill in 1847 carrying an overseer's whip and a thonged strap under a banner which read, simply, 'Behold and Weep'.

I don't want to get too Pythonesque on you, but the handloom weavers, away from the factories, marginalised by the advent of the power looms, had it even worse. In Westhoughton in 1827, half of the five thousand inhabitants were 'totally destitute of bedding and nearly so of clothes', and six per cent were in a state of famine. Aspin records that some manufacturers, appalled by others who were cutting costs and cornering business by paying the weavers starvation money, appealed to the President of the Board of Trade to impose a statutory minimum wage. He replied that this was 'a vain and hazardous attempt to interpose the authority of the law between the labourer and his employer'. His name was William

Huskisson, and you might recall, a touch sardonically, that, for him, progress was to prove fatal when he ran into the *Rocket* on that famous opening run in 1830.

Things did, of course, get better. But then the rest of the world began to wonder whether what was good for Lancashire was necessarily good for them. Indians, in particular, began to ponder if it really made sense for a cotton-producing country to be Lancashire's main export market. They, in particular Gandhi, would have been a little sceptical about Taylor's comfortable assertion about not needing to conquer people in order to turn them into customers, and suffering no imperial cravings to control your own raw materials. Cotton, for Gandhi, was crucial; the spinning wheel was literally the symbol of the independence struggle. Homespun, for him, was the virtue that would provide employment and recapture lost dignity (even if not every member of the Congress Party was entirely enthusiastic at his insistence that they should all spin 200 yards of cotton a month). For once there was some measure of common cause, if not motive, with the Government of India. Gandhi called for a boycott of foreign cotton to protect and stimulate the village weavers, while the Government agreed to demands for tariffs from the Bombay mills. In Lancashire, another type of spinning ensured that all the blame for the effects of this descended on the Mahatma.

And so it was that an unlikely but charming episode took place during Gandhi's visit to Britain in 1931 for the Round Table conference on India's constitutional future: he made a special trip to Lancashire. Blackburn and Darwen at that time were engaged almost exclusively in weaving cotton for Indian export; the *dhoti*, Gandhi's standard dress, had long been a speciality. J.P. Davies, later Lord Darwen, a leading Quaker, owned the Greenfield Mill in Darwen; one of his senior employees, a fellow Quaker, had written to a British friend of

Gandhi, suggesting a visit by the Mahatma to see the effects of the boycott. The invitation, combining as it did a call on the saintly conscience and the saintly eye for a PR coup, proved irresistible.

At 11:10 p.m. on Friday, 2 October 1931, the 6:05 from Euston arrived at Spring Vale railway station, Darwen, carrying Gandhi, a small entourage and about 40 members of the press. Some 2,000 people and a large body of police, led by Mr Askew, the Deputy Chief Constable of Lancashire, were waiting. The crowd cheered as Gandhi was driven in a Rolls-Royce Silver Ghost for about 400 yards to a modest house in the Spring Vale Garden Village, a small development built by the Davies family next to the mill and modelled on that other Quaker enterprise, Bournville. He stayed in the small three-bedroomed 'parlour-type' house of one of the Quaker executives. 'Our Indian visitor,' the *Darwen News* had announced, 'will be received with simple Lancashire hospitality. He will, presumably, use the same kind of dishes and plates as are used in thousands of working-class Lancashire homes, and he will warm himself before a fire of Lancashire coal.' In the event, he chose nuts and cereals and there was some difficulty getting hold of his goat's milk.

The Garden Village was closely guarded by police throughout the night, as there were fears that resentment about the boycott might receive some concrete expression. But, as with Lincoln's blockade, so with Gandhi's boycott: apart from one woman shouting to the cheering crowds, 'What do you want to clap him for? He's the biggest enemy you've got!' and a man yelling, 'Send us some work, please,' politely, at the Silver Ghost, the main reaction was one of intrigued admiration. 'Mr Gandhi does not belie his photograph,' wrote the *Darwen News* man on the spot:

> He has the real Indian tan, the legal eye and the forehead
> – an eye piercing as a rapier – of moderate physique and

slender proportions; he walks with a slight recline forward, and were he not Mr Gandhi he would probably be accepted as one of the many teeming millions of the Indian Empire. He gave me the impression of being rather tired; probably this impression will be common to those of his acquaintance, as it is possibly a characteristic of the Indian race.

The next day, he went walkabout, and, as the *Darwen News* put it, 'there are some people in Darwen who will remember as long as they live that once they touched the hand of Gandhi and that he touched their hands'.

A prophet had arrived in Lancashire, bringing with him hard truths and chastening foretellings. Over that weekend, in talks and meetings with delegations of dignitaries, employers, workers and unions, these were delivered gently but implacably.

This was the Mayor of Darwen, Councillor Walter Knowles, after his meeting with Gandhi:

> He was not by any means an oyster, neither did he seek to draw the deputation and not give away anything himself . . . He did not in any way try to hide his own feelings. At the beginning he invited straight talks and heart to heart questions . . .
>
> He tells us that England must recognise, and Lancashire must recognise, that they can never get back to the quantity of goods they formerly supplied to India. He tells us quite candidly that we, by our excellent organisations in England, and through the people who have gone to India, and from the example we have put before them, have taught them the benefit of organisations, and shown them how it was possible to increase the standard of living of their people, just as we have increased the standard of living of ours . . . He did

181

not give us the slightest hope that there would ever be the quantity of cotton trade done with Lancashire that had been done in the past. It might be a question of Lancashire reshuffling and becoming producers of something other than what had been their staple trade.

Time and again, he repeated that the poverty he had seen in Lancashire distressed him, and further distressed him because of his part in it; but, and this was the essence of the uncomfortable message he brought with him: compared with the poverty and pauperism of the starving millions of India, 'the poverty of Lancashire dwindles into insignificance'.

I'm not sure how well this message would accord with modern PR advice, but there is, of course, a relentlessness in sanctity, and Lancashire had asked for it: 'He then went on to state his view,' the *Advertiser and News* reported,

> that Indian poverty is the result of British policy – through the overthrowing of India's old cotton industry by the machines of Lancashire more than 100 years ago. He argued that the descendants of those who destroyed the supplementary means of livelihood (which supplied the butter to the bread which the peasant earned from the soil) could not now complain if the descendants of the dispossessed tried to rehabilitate themselves . . . He drew an idyllic picture of little children spinning while they were playing and contrasted the life of the villagers who lived on a little bit of rice flung by insolent wealth with their position when the glorious work was done in their own homes. The only solace he could bring to Lancashire was that these teeming millions had no ill-will to Lancashire, and did not know what Lancashire was.

182

Some solace.

Pressed further, he was equally and as distressingly clear on the prospects for the Lancashire cotton industry as any economist, now or then:

> He declared that it was an impossibility to seek to revive the Lancashire trade on its original foundations, and he could not lend a hand in the process . . . Mr Gandhi repeated his argument that the boycott may have been the last straw, but was only a contributory factor in Lancashire's loss of trade. He noted the other causes of Lancashire's decline. He also repeated his suggestion that . . . it is possible to have a contract with Lancashire . . . for taking, on a decreasing scale from year to year, goods from Lancashire. This, he admitted, would simply tide over Lancashire's difficulty for a little time and no more . . . He left his hearers with some final words about Japanese business methods, and urged that it would be better for Lancashire to divert her attention from India and solve her problems in terms of the world crisis in which the Indian contribution was only a speck on the screen.

When he was not delivering his judgements and warnings, the prophet was out taking early-morning walks up on the moors, leaving members of the 'burly Lancashire detective force' gasping along in his wake. On the Sunday afternoon, there was another prophetic exchange, reported by the *Northern Daily Telegraph*:

> He smiled when a Blackburn weaver summed up for him, 'Your attitude is, "Charity begins at home".' It would not be right, he said, for him to tickle the palates of the Lancashire people by telling them untruths and

saying they should come before his own people. He did not want to cause suffering in Lancashire, but what could he do? He could not see his own people idle and starving if he could find them even a little work making their own cloth. 'I feel helpless,' he said, with a gesture of despair. 'That is the only way I can see. If we pray, and God shows us some other way out, that will be good for both, but I cannot see it yet.'

And then he was gone. The only casualty of the visit was Mr Askew, the Deputy Chief Constable, who tripped over a piece of wire in the Garden Village and dislocated his shoulder. Otherwise, everything had been carried off without incident, apart from the imposter dressed in a tablecloth who was escorted to the police station after attempting unsuccessfully to hold a press conference at the Swan and Royal Hotel.

There wasn't, though, much sign that the prophet's words had struck deep; there was no rush to either diversification or repentance. 'Lancashire,' observed the *Darwen News*, 'gave Mr Gandhi a courteous and orderly reception as being the guest of His Majesty's Government; what he may do for the "suffering operatives" will, to our mind, neither start a solitary loom nor sell a single piece of cloth. Mr Gandhi has seen Lancashire, and Lancashire has seen Mr Gandhi, and there is the end of it.' Fifty years later, Gandhi's chauffeur couldn't recall much about him, apart from shaking his hand, but he remembered that the Silver Ghost was lovely to drive, a squat shape, dark blue in colour, with an open top and silver filigree work on the front, and highly polished, needing a lot of work to keep it so.

Fifty years later, it was also clear that the prophet had spoken the truth. Mills were closing everywhere, mill-workers were being thrown out of work, but this time for the last time. Gandhi could see 30 chimneys from the Spring Vale Garden Village; now there is only one of any consequence, the one belonging to

India Mill. But what a chimney! Built in the 1860s by Eccles Shorrock and Co., cotton spinners, the India Mill chimney is 303 feet high, Grade II listed and a pretty fair copy of the Campanile in St Mark's Square, even more so now that it doesn't smoke any more. Peregrine falcons nest at the top and the mill is a business centre, home to various enterprises, including a call centre, the modern multi-hand operation.

They too are under threat now, call centres, from cheaper operations in India. And if they start closing round here, there will be a lot of British Asians thrown out of work. But that is only one, minor irony; the major irony is as imposing and unavoidable as the India Mill chimney. What Gandhi didn't foresee was that large numbers of his fellow south Asians would end up working in the mills of Lancashire and that many of them would be the people thrown out of work when the mills closed. God clearly did have another way, and a typically mysterious one at that.

Nobody in Darwen seemed too sure where the Greenfield Mill might be, which was not that surprising, as it was knocked down some time ago now. But I did find Spring Vale Garden Village, a little hemmed in by later and less distinguished developments, assailed by the curse of the white plastic window and the porch, but still green and still there, unlike the mill.

I knocked at the door of the house where Gandhi had stayed. The woman who answered the door was doubtful. She said I could come in, but I could see she wasn't that keen. There wasn't a lot of interest, she said, but the television people had been round, once. 'Don't get me wrong,' she said. 'I like company, but I like to choose my company.' I'd be better off talking to Kathleen Jebb at No. 15 – she knew all about Gandhi.

Kathleen Jebb was 76 but looked younger, in the way that small, neat people do. She was happy to talk, which she did in the real east Lancs manner, with the 'r' rolled and held, most notably practised now by Jane Horrocks. She'd been five years old when Mr Gandhi – she always called him Mr Gandhi – came. Her mother hadn't let her go and see him, though, because the crowds were too big. Anyway, they lived on Bolton Road then; they had moved to Spring Vale in 1937.

It had been between two mills, Greenfield and Waterfield. She'd always loved the house. 'They were built by the Quakers on Cadbury lines. They felt it fitting that workers should have three bedrooms, a bathroom and a garden. The bath used to be in the kitchen, with a panel to pull down.' Her mother had worked at the mill and Kathleen had worked there too, as a warper. A few years before, an Indian film-maker had come to make a film about Gandhi's visit. He had got some of the women who used to work in the mill together, including Kathleen. One of them had been saying, aye, what happy times they were. And Florence Renshaw replied there weren't so much to be happy about because nobody had owt, and the Indian asked what language they were talking, and everybody laughed.

But Kathleen wasn't so sure things had got better. The Davies family had provided a works canteen at the mill, and a day nursery, sports facilities and a library. Kathleen had got involved in the Workers' Educational Association, and more: she'd ended up secretary of the local Labour Party; she'd marched at Aldermaston. 'What's better today? I would say at this moment not a lot. All the cotton's gone. The steel's gone. The mines are gone. Now what are we doing? Arms, not cotton. And if it's not that, it's all leisure and pleasure now, isn't it? It reminds me of the Romans.'

Kathleen was a widow, with two daughters. She'd been doing yoga for 25 years and in 1998, at the age of 72, she'd been on the *Winston Churchill* with the Sail Training Association, and climbed the rat lines, up the mizzen. She had a partner, but she didn't live with him because she didn't want to go to Blackburn. No, she didn't think much of Lancashire being the county where women died of love. She had, she said, read Jean-Paul Sartre

186

(who would have been surprised at the number and length of the 'r's in his surname), even if it were a bit heavy. Her philosophy was that you should 'give time, because time gives pleasure' and 'do unto others as you would have done to yourself'.

I asked her about cotton's other curious legacy, the Asian population. She was worried about the numbers and this idea that lots of them were living off the state and getting preferential treatment. Blackburn now had a BNP councillor. 'He can't do anything on his own,' said Kathleen, 'but I don't think he'll be on his own much longer.'

There. I can point out any number of whimsicalities and ironies about the Asian presence in Lancs, leaving aside the central oddity of an industry's overseas market suddenly arriving in numbers to work for it. I could note that the majority of the Lancs Asians or their parents or grandparents seem to have arrived accidentally, after working somewhere else in England, Bradford or Bedford, Birmingham or Slough, and speculate on some hidden, mystical pull. I could note that the majority of them or their parents or grandparents are from Kashmir and point out that both places have splendid lake districts.

I could do all that, and more, but I couldn't really pretend that Lancashire has been at all times, in finest tradition, a jolly and indulgent host. Six BNP councillors in Burnley and three days of race riots in Oldham causing £1.4 million worth of damage doesn't exactly suggest that there's a whole lot of come-in-love-and-have-a-cup-of-tea going on.

Amid all the debate about imperial legacies, economic pressures, multiculturalism and positive discrimination, there's little doubt that the first casualty of a riot tends to be whimsicality. (Not absolutely always, though. I was covering the riots in 1981 in Dalston, in London, filing a story from a pay phone, detailing the lootings and depredations of the local youth while three very large representatives stood waiting outside the box. I exited with a nervous smile and was making a swift departure when I heard a shout: 'Hey! Hey, you!' I turned round. The biggest one had something in his hand. 'You forgot your pen,' he said.)

Anyway, I did want to see how Lancashire whimsicality coped with the demands of being a BNP councillor, so I arranged to interview Robin Evans, the party's elected representative on the Blackburn-with-Darwen Council, already declared as Jack Straw's opponent in the next general election. We met at a café in his Mill Hill ward, typical of unregenerate Lancashire, with that feeling of factory fall-out still baked on hard and sense of purpose lost. Robin was dressed like the builder he is. He was wary, in the BNP way, of 'the media', which is to say wary but flattered by the attention. He spoke slowly, without the rolling 'r', probably because he was from Haslingden and had spent only about 15 years in Darwen. 'You have to be in Darwen 20 years before you're accepted as a proper Darwener,' he said. I don't think he appreciated the irony. I didn't until I thought about it later.

He wasn't stupid, though, if not well-schooled. You might describe him as the shrewd peasant type if you didn't mind being thought of as prejudiced. I asked him why he'd got involved in politics, why he'd stood for the council. He said it was because grants and funds weren't being apportioned fairly in Blackburn. For as long as he could remember, council and government funding had all been going to 'so-called deprived areas'. This created a 'discontent in the majority of the people who have paid the rates, paid the taxes, who deserve their fair share of this money that's getting distributed to the minority areas year in, year out'. And this discontent was what he intended to address. People had been moaning about it for too long: it was time to take a stand, time to help the people who were here, not bring in new people from outside.

I am not one of the world's natural cross-examiners. I did

188

read for the Bar, as it happens, and I was called, but my only appearance, instructed by myself, at Acton Magistrates' Court, to answer a charge of parking too close to a zebra crossing, convinced me that hardened criminals were unlikely to sob suddenly that the jig was up in the face of my remorseless questioning; the look, too, on the face of the chief magistrate gave a fair indication of the chances of a Lord of Appeal suddenly exclaiming, 'Bless my soul, I never thought of that!' In fact, it reminded me uncannily of the look on the face of Lord Justice Hoffmann, as he would become, while he considered my refreshingly unorthodox views on promissory estoppel during our challenging tutorials at Oxford.

I mention this because I thought of it, but also to indicate that I was not trying to trick Robin with any clever questions. I was just interested to know his views on things. Who exactly, for example, were these 'new people' coming in? I asked him if the people he wanted to help, those that were already here, included Asians. 'If they need help, they're welcome to come,' he said. 'So', I asked, snappily, 'it's not a racist thing as far as you're concerned? I mean, it's a question of not having any new people in, rather than a question of not wanting people of a particular creed or colour?' Evans hesitated a bit, then said, 'Good question. First and foremost, not having any more people in.' And then? 'I would like to preserve, to do everything in my power to preserve, the indigenous British race. If it's racist preserving a race instead of destroying a race by whatever means, whether it's multiculturalism that blends together and therefore destroys races . . . if that's racist, then you can call me a racist.'

Well. That was interesting. I wanted to hear more about this indigenous race. What, I asked, were the things that were important about the indigenous culture, that he wanted to preserve? I had a sudden vision of thousands of clogs marching with thunderous precision over reinstated cobbles by restored mills, right arms outstretched beneath black flat caps past a raised dais where a doughty figure in a floral housecoat, Gracie or Thora, say, arms folded over bosom, was singing, with feeling, 'Lancashire Belongs To Me'.

Sadly, Robin wasn't ready with anything concrete, or even cobbled. 'It goes back not hundreds, but thousands of years. There's a history behind it. It's in your blood. It's been in my blood since I was born and it's in my son's blood. It's in the majority of the indigenous population of Britain, but it's being stifled by political correctness or fear of being branded a racist . . . I do not want to lose our history and culture. I do not want it to be replaced forcibly, which is being done here. We're not creating a new culture here, we're replacing it with Asian cultures, for example.'

I suppose I could have told Robin about King Arthur being from Lancashire, but I thought that was probably the last thing the old boy deserved, particularly given all the trouble Siegfried got into with the Nazis. In any case, Robin was now talking about labels, calling himself a 'white bloke' and more: 'I'm not frightened to be a white Aryan male,' he said. He shot me one of those cunning peasant looks to see how this had gone down. I did some wishy-washy liberalising about the dangers of a label like that, but I could see that Robin rather enjoyed shocking, in a naughty-boy kind of way. At a recent council meeting, he had been under concerted attack over the BNP's Holocaust-denying tendencies: 'It was good fun, really, to have 50 or 60 of them stand up and call me all sorts.' And the Holocaust? 'I don't admit it, I don't deny it, it was a long time ago, I don't know enough about it.'

And that was that, really. There might be some points to be made about the effects and dangers of the arrival of numbers of people with fixed, firm and different ways of behaving from the people already there, particularly if the people already there are convinced that the newcomers are being treated more favourably in the matter of funds and grants and amenities; but it's difficult to discuss this in a helpful way if you're talking about your son looking forward to a future 'up to his knees in the paddy fields on the hillsides of Blackburn'. Ditto, if you're talking about the isolationist dangers of Faith Schools and then saying that you don't want to mix with Asians because you 'want to preserve the Aryan culture, the British Aryan culture and race'. And I thought Asians were Aryans too.

So I said goodbye to Robin. The last time I asked, he had left his wife and the BNP before starting his own party and going on to a round trouncing in the subsequent council elections. All the same, people had voted for him; people worried by the numbers and what they saw as preferential treatment. And if people like Kathleen Jebb shared those worries, then we should be worried, too.

I was on my way to Oswaldtwistle, a town, I noted in a guidebook, 'whose name has given generations of comedians a source of humour, and countless "Southerners" an exercise in pronunciation'. I had picked up the guidebook in the Textile Time Tunnel at Moscow Mill, along with my school pack and a family tree which informed me that the mill had been run by six generations of the Hargreaves family, cousins of James Hargreaves, also of Oswaldtwistle, inventor of the spinning jenny.

Ah, yes, James Hargreaves. The poor weaver with whom, in a way, it all began. It was his daughter, Jenny, who knocked over her mother's spinning wheel. Hargreaves looked at the wheel, still spinning, and with its spindle now upright, and realised that the wheel could drive lots of spindles at the same time. A bit of a carpenter, he knocked up a prototype that so impressed his fellow toilers that they came round and smashed it up. Too late: the threads were spun, the machines and mills were on their way. This being a particularly instructive story, Hargreaves, redoubtable, moved to Nottingham, built more machines and began to turn a modest profit. But he didn't patent his invention quickly enough and Lancashire copied it for nothing. It used to be said that poor Hargreaves died in poverty. He didn't, but he wasn't nearly as rich as he should have been.

That was 1778. Today, at Moscow Mill, his descendants neither spin nor weave. Now they have their Time Tunnel and weaving shed full of stalls full of knicknacks, all the floss and fluff of modern living: ornamental camels, £44.95, made in China; hand-painted plaster ornamental Beethovens, Buddhas, Shakespeares, Aphrodites, Apollos and Jesuses from £13.99 upwards. Or, if you prefer, two-foot-high renderings of Stan and Ollie for £72; a Pink Panther, leaning on a gramophone in a cream cabinet picked out in strawberry, last of line, £149; a set of three elephant stools, £130; other unusual gifts, such as, at the Serengeti stall, a model of Kali windsurfing, £39.99; cookware, glassware, Mexican and Indian furniture; bespoke pine furniture; fragrances; candles; leather goods; patchwork; lighting; jewellery; towels and bedding. There's a children's play area, the Enchanted Wood, where Santa lies sleeping until next Christmas; Gnomeland, with more gnomes than you could shake a rod at in and around the old mill pool; the biggest pear-drop in the world; a garden centre; and Accrington Stanley's club shop. But no looms clattering now.

Yes, I know I said I didn't feel sorry it was all over, but it's difficult to be always wildly and completely enthusiastic about what's there instead. And there's something sad and somehow reduced and certainly forced about the changed circumstances of these old places, as there is with the enormous number of museums they contain, celebrating and explaining the past principally because the present has no other use for them. Shouldn't we, I wonder in my unoriginal way, be concentrating a bit more on the future? Can you imagine the Victorians setting up all this stuff? 'Leisure and pleasure,' Kathleen Jebb had said, 'Leisure and pleasure.'

But I did find one working loom, in the Time Tunnel. Brian Smith was working it and it was very loud. 'Oh, yes,' he said. '70 or 80 per cent of the workforce was a bit deaf. My mother was deaf. She was a weaver. In every industry there was something to put up with. Like the coal mines, or iron smelting, tremendous noise and heat. The human body was the last thing to be considered.' How long had he been working at the mill? 'All my life.' He'd prepared the warps, done warp-knotting in the weaving shed, then gone into overseeing, ending up as general manager of the mill until he retired at the age of sixty in 1997, four years before it stopped working.

Then Peter Hargreaves, managing director of the mill's parent company, the man behind the move into retail, had asked him to come back and had shown him these looms he'd bought from Skipton for the Time Tunnel. 'They were 110 years old, made by George Hattersley of Keighley. I said to Peter Hargreaves, "What do you want me to do?" And he said, "Get them running." It was like building a meccano set, but I did it, and I got a letter from Peter Hargreaves saying he was amazed. I've kept that letter because it's something I'm proud of.'

I wondered if he felt it was a bit sad, being at the fag end and becoming a museum piece. Well, he said, he was a big fan of museums and it was important to show what the industry had done, what it had been like. I made my comparison with coal mining and wondered if he thought we were better off without the mills and the mining. 'With the mines, initially, after they lost their jobs, they couldn't see anything in front of them. But after they'd been out of it 12 months, they wouldn't want to go back.'

And cotton? 'Yes, I suppose so, because people these days, they don't have the same outlook as they used to. Working in a manufacturing industry was like being in a sort of a family. The general manager who taught me most of what I know used to say it was like coming home here, they don't work under me, they're part of my family. That's the way the values were. People

gained from being together. There's more of a division now.
People worked as a team more, relied on one another, told each
other their personal feelings and things like that, offered a
shoulder to cry on, went out at night and had a laugh about it.
I'm not sure the high-tech atmosphere is the same.'

But Brian did not take an entirely Hovis view. He
remembered five unions in Moscow Mill, all negotiating
separately. But he put most blame for the decline of cotton on,
yet again, Margaret Thatcher, for not listening to the complaints
about cheap imports, for doing nothing about it.

You do wonder what strange folk-figure the Baroness will be in
a hundred years or so. But I don't think she should shoulder all the
blame for the death of cotton, even if she wanted to. Dr Geoffrey
Timmins, in *Four Centuries of Lancashire Cotton*, concludes:

> Essentially, Lancashire's cotton producers lost their
> comparative advantage to overseas competitors . . .
> Whether more could have been done to counteract this
> decline is doubtful. Greater investment in up-to-date
> machinery might have helped, but, as overseas
> competition intensified, there was diminishing
> confidence among cotton firms that this would be
> worthwhile. And whilst both sides of the industry
> castigated central government for failing to impose
> adequate import controls, any benefits that might have
> resulted from restrained imports were likely to have been
> outweighed by the drawbacks. Not least among these
> were the relatively high prices that domestic customers
> would have had to pay for cotton goods . . .

Other authorities have pointed out that it was European and
American imports which gave Lancashire a battering, sanctioned
by the same international multifibre agreements that placed
tariffs on cotton goods from the developing world. All very

inconvenient. But what a good economic forecaster Mr Gandhi was! And now we shall leave Brian weaving the current Moscow Mills output on his century-old looms: some tea towels for the Soroptimists, for free.

In the weaving shed, Boyd Hargreaves was bustling. Boyd is Peter's youngest son, in his late twenties, one of four Hargreaves in the business, marketing manager for the shopping village, full of the figures: 500,000 paying visitors through the till in a year, 80,000 square feet of space, more than 200 jobs created, 50 start-ups, catchment area of 1½ million people within 45 minutes' drive. I don't know whether it was his face, or his name, or his dark suit, but there was something definitely Victorian about Boyd. The group is still manufacturing textiles, specialising in bed and table linen, based at the Britannia Mill in Blackburn, but for Boyd, retailing was the thing: 'It's more exciting, throws up more problems to solve, there's always something new . . . with 10,000 customers a week, there's always something different.' I thanked him for his time and left, wondering what Mr Gandhi would have made of the mill's reinvention as an oriental bazaar.

The first time I went to Oldham was to report on the birth of Louise Brown, the very first of what we then called, rather quaintly, 'test-tube babies'. I started my report, 'Oldham is not romantic. But then, if you think about it, neither is a test-tube baby.' Ah, the slick sureness of Youth! But I wrote more truly than I knew, as some years later, my wife and I attempted to produce a test-tube baby of our own, and, no, it really wasn't romantic. We tried both publicly and privately funded routes; the main difference for me was that, when I was asked to produce my sperm, the private operation provided me with pornography and the public one didn't. Call me old-fashioned, but I decided not to have the possible conception of my first child closely aided by someone to whom I had not been introduced. In any case, we ended up adopting, which was impossibly romantic, but you haven't got time for that.

I think, probably, that I spoke true of Oldham as well. It was certainly romantic once, nestling on the moorsides of the Pennines, wild, windswept and solitary, but that would be about 300 years ago, before the mills came. And came. At its peak, Oldham was the Spinning Capital of the World, with nearly 350 mills and 17 million spindles, an eighth of the number in the entire world, 10 million more than Bolton, which was quite busy itself.

But this concentration on mills suggests a lack of concentration on other things. They've never had that much time for anything too fancy in Oldham. As Brian Law writes in *Oldham, Brave Oldham*, no one was prepared to stump up the money even for a public park in the mid-nineteenth century, at the time of the founding of the new corporation. They didn't want a big public library, either, a bit later on. Manchester, Bolton and Rochdale might build grand town halls, but Oldham wasn't interested. It called itself Brave Oldham because it had earned itself a living from nothing and that was what it was interested in: earning. 'If other places could "excel in splendour",' Law quotes a leading Oldhamer as saying mid-century, 'that was not for Oldham; rather the town would prove itself by "the usefulness of its achievements".' Hmmm. Rather too close to Yorkshire, if you ask me. (I'm working on this theory that Lancashire becomes less and less dreamy, whimsical and impractical the closer it gets to Yorkshire. Liverpool, Manchester; Blackpool, Oldham – that sort of thing.)

Engels, in pursuit of *The Condition*, went. He thought Oldham like the other towns round Manchester:

> Almost wholly working people's districts, interspersed
> only with factories, a few thoroughfares lined with shops
> and a few lanes along which the gardens and houses of

the manufacturers are scattered like villas. The towns themselves are badly and irregularly built with foul courts, lanes and back alleys, reeking of coal smoke, and especially dingy from the original bright red brick, turned black with time.

Dickens was in Lancashire, too, and Oldham would have done just as well as Preston as the model for Coketown in *Hard Times*:

It was a town of red brick, or of red brick that would have been red if the smoke and ashes had allowed it; but as matters stood it was a town of unnatural red and black like the painted face of a savage. It was a town of machinery and tall chimneys, out of which interminable serpents of smoke trailed themselves for ever and ever, and never got uncoiled. It had a black canal in it, and a river that ran purple with evil-smelling dye, where there was a rattling and a trembling all day long, and where the piston of the steam engine worked monotonously, like the head of an elephant in melancholy madness.

A century later, Walter Greenwood was equally clear, but more sympathetic:

Like any other Lancashire industrial town, Oldham's share of ugliness is complete. Offer this criticism of his town to any Oldham lad and immediately and irrelevantly he will leap to its defence by asking: 'Hast ever looked in a mirror thysen?' He might go on to ask logically when Oldham had entered a beauty competition; further it would perhaps be as well if the next time you are sitting down to a meal of imported foodstuff which has been exchanged for the products of Oldham, derived from the sweat and toil of Oldham lads

197

and lasses, you would be gracious enough to think gratefully on the smoke, grime and industry of the north.

Well said, Walter. Another 50 years on, though, and things don't look quite as set, or simple. Now most of the dirty work has gone, what are the Oldham lads and lasses getting in return? If beauty is coming, it's certainly taking its time, delayed, detained and helping New Millennial Manchester with its enquiries. Walter used to know an old man from Oldham who spent his holidays at home during the Wakes Week so that he could smell the fresh air sweeping down from the Pennines, untainted by the factory smoke. That's there most of the time now, bracingly, as the town still remains 'an overcoat colder than Manchester'; other improvements seem even less tangible.

The Late-Twentieth-Century All-Purpose Town Planning Starter Kit has provided the usual motorway barrier between centre and districts, complete with all the consequent concrete bridge and walkway paraphernalia. There's the usual disproportionate tower block, this one housing the offices of the Metropolitan Borough Council, isolated by one of the usual giant car parks. The old town hall, not grand, but with a good classical portico, stands in the middle of town, boarded and empty, a forlorn monument to (among other things) the political career of Winston Churchill, launched from these steps when he became the town's MP in 1900. (Did you know, by the way, that in 1955 he contemplated 'Keep Britain White' as a vote-winning slogan?) Still, the usual shopping centre has now been demolished. There is the usual post-modern one now, Spindles, full, as the name implies, of the usual PM references back to the gone days, a modern view of the mill.

But the new art gallery is open; there are plans for a new library, theatre and museum, an Arts Quarter for Oldham. It's hoped that the town hall will provide a home for the theatre.

The Metrolink extension to the Manchester tram system should be on its way, providing it doesn't take another U-turn. The town hall and bus station are up for mixed redevelopment. In the words of Brian Law, whose history of the town is published by the council, 'Existing parking will be augmented; the heritage core of old Oldham preserved, refurbished and enhanced by design initiatives and new focal points, and more pedestrianised public squares created to uplift the visitor experience.'

I hope so, even if they were saying much the same, minus the buzz-wordery, about the unfulfilled plans of the '50s. This visitor's experience, meanwhile, in the waiting time, was melancholy. Much of it, I think, was to do with the mills. There are still some 138 left. Some of them are in a more decrepit state than others (all those windows are particularly tempting) but most are being used for something else.

We are surrounded by the vast but obsolete works of the Victorians and cannot compete. London can get away with clever conversions of, for example, Bankside Power Station; but in Oldham, it is like living with 138 Banksides.

Down at the other end of the town centre from Spindles, at the other end of Yorkshire Street, stands the old NatWest bank, a stolid riot of cupola, pediments, columns, embossed shields, urns, cherubs and polished granite, faced by another once-grand Victorian office building, also empty apart from something going on in the basement. This turned out to be the very early days of the Epona Club, name taken from the Internet, some reference to an alternative world, run by Bryn with help from James, with hopes of expanding up to the ground floor if it went well, although they didn't seem that confident, stood alone at the bar in the early evening. Not too confident about Oldham, either, given the trouble. 'If we're not all going to get on, there's no future,' said Bryn, telling me that people had started cancelling their orders since some Asians had taken over the local newsagents.

Ah, yes, the trouble; the riots. That's why I had come. In particular, I wanted to gaze upon the Peace Barrier, the only barrier built to protect and divide warring communities in mainland Britain, a large obstacle to my vision of Lancs. So I hailed a cab. Dr Virinder Kalra has written a book about Asian immigration into Lancashire, based on research in Oldham, detailing the arrival of Kashmiris in the town in the 1960s. They worked the night shifts that had been brought in to maximise the benefits from the new improved machinery that Lancashire had introduced at last, but too late; the night shifts that the existing workforce, male and female, didn't want to work. Dr Kalra also details the subsequent efforts of the newcomers to get another job when the mills began to close in the '80s. The lucky, younger ones managed to find work driving taxis, or opening and working in takeaways. (The older ones, in a remarkable example of the law of unexpected consequence, relieved their unemployment by working in and setting up mosques, those very visible signs of a different sort of settlement that seem to provoke and disturb so.)

Dr Kalra has entitled his book, *From Textile Mills to Taxi Ranks*. My cab driver was almost complete proof of the doctor's findings, so I decided he could prevail over the professional veto I was talking about in Wigan. Mohammed was 48. He had travelled to Britain with his parents from Kashmir, had come to Oldham to work in a mill and had been made redundant. I asked him to take me on a tour of Oldham. While he drove, he talked. 'I've lived in Oldham for 20 years. There was no problem in Oldham, never, ever, when I used to work in textiles and then when I started driving a cab, I didn't have a problem with anyone, not at all . . . I have two neighbours who are English, I have no problem with them, not at all.'

We drove up into Glodwick, one of the main Asian areas, and scene of much of the rioting. Pressed, Mohammed conceded that not all was unproblematic in Oldham. 'It's the youngsters

who cause the problem, from both sides. They are a bit senseless
. . . the National Front, they came into Oldham . . . after that,
we have a lot of problems.'

Indeed. Six months of trouble began in Oldham in January
2001 with the stabbing of a young white man by a group of
Asian teenagers. The local police chief described a pattern of
attacks by 'predatory' Asian gangs on lone white males. The
National Front began to take an interest, leafleting the area, and
threatening a march. There was a continuing debate over
whether, as the graffiti suggested, Glodwick was a 'no-go area'
for whites. A white pensioner was attacked and beaten by Asian
youths. An Asian man was attacked and beaten by white youths.

Reading this and the timetable of violence in the independent
report commissioned into the rioting, you can see everything
ratcheting and tightening towards the weekend of riots in May:
the trouble at a local school, the increased presence of
extremists, the skirmishing and abuse, the scuffle, the fight, the
attacks on Asian houses, the attacks by Asians on pubs, the petrol
bombs, the fire-bombing of the local newspaper offices. And you
can see all the causes and resentments, the culture clashes, the
attacks on symbols of those cultures, even down to the pubs, one
of them called, I promise, the Live And Let Live.

The independent report was part of a wider series into the
similar disturbances in Burnley and Bradford, including an
overall government review which came up with those national
recommendations you might remember about introducing an
oath of allegiance and 'working out a shared definition of
nationhood, encouraging cohesion while celebrating
multiculturalism, and undertaking a very frank and honest
analysis of the separation' that had grown up in communities like
Oldham.

And it is quite some separation. Apart from names like 'Paki'
being the normal, routine and accepted way for white people to
refer to Asians, the two communities live apart and are schooled

apart. One Asian told the government review team that after talking to them she probably wouldn't see another white face until she came back to the inquiry the next week. 'At present,' the review reported,

> some pupils entering the education system at the age of five have rarely, if ever, had the opportunity to play, socialise with or learn alongside children from a different culture. In the current structure this may not happen until the child enters secondary education at the age of eleven. It may not happen then. This occurs because parents choose their local school in their community, and Asian schools and white communites are quite separate.

The government review also acknowledged the potency of the vote-winning complaint of Robin Evans in Blackburn; it found that 'one cause of friction between white and ethnic minority communities . . . was the perceived imbalance of financial help from the state. There was a view among white residents that money was channelled into ethnic minority areas only because they were minorities, not because their need was any greater.'

In Oldham, the most common form of this is the widespread belief among the white community that mosque-building is publicly funded. Interestingly, the government review took a pretty straight BNP line: 'There is an assumption that black and ethnic minority groups are in need and in general that their needs will be the greatest. This may in fact not be the case.'

The solutions? The independent report wanted an Oldham Community Plan, a new Local Strategic Partnership, and a new Urban Regeneration Company. It also wanted central government departments, coordinated by the Home Office and the Department of Transport, Local Government and the Regions, operating through the Government Office for the North West, to consider urgently entering into a new Compact with Oldham Metropolitan Borough Council, which should also work with the Citizenship Foundation and the Local Learning Partnership, and set up a Race and Diversity Strategy Committee. The citizens of Oldham, meanwhile, should consider a referendum on the question of an elected mayor. It also found that there had been 'a scattergun approach to regeneration'.

Right. Someone from one of the four consultancies brought in to help the above lot regenerate Oldham couldn't get over the irony that one of the principal causes of the riots was not deprivation, but different parts of the communities worrying about other parts getting more than their fair share of all the money available from any number of sources, local, national and European.

My thoughts, less economically and socially literate, were simpler, and went like this: in an economy in which everyone is being paid to provide services to each other, where does the money come from? Who makes things? Other people, somewhere else, who haven't yet had the benefit of all this service, leisure and pleasure? What happens when they do? What happens when the music stops? Will it be what happened last time? Will it be Cotton, again? Another one for Mr Gandhi.

Mohammed, meanwhile, was driving me towards a footbridge over one of the encircling dual carriageways. 'Look at that footbridge, look at all that glasswork. It cost £1 million and you see one person a month using it if you're lucky.' He drove me to the boarded-up town hall. 'Look at that. A very nice building. They closed it down. They don't care. We pay a lot of council tax in Oldham and they spend it on useless things. There must be something for the youngsters to make them busy. When they are busy in work, they don't cause problems. There is no problem in Manchester, but in Oldham, we are far, far behind, you know.'

Now, said Mohammed, white people were insulting him, telling him, 'black bastard, get back to your own country . . . If

I had a chance to move, I would definitely move, but my children are still at school . . . I've been to Slough, I've been to Watford, they don't stare at you there because they've got no time . . . I respect everyone, and I expect the same from everyone.'

I asked Mohammed to take me to the Peace Barrier, but he had never heard of it, he said. He dropped me off back in the town centre. A few weeks later, Israr Hussain, a 42-year-old Oldham taxi driver, was stabbed to death by a white passenger. I began to wonder whether Slough might be more fit for Asians now.

I continued alone my quest for the Peace Barrier, and went to Royle Close, alleged site of this new iron curtain between the divided communities. I couldn't find it. Royle Close is a new development, the kind where the road bends rather than goes straight. There were several entrances into it, including a winding and narrow alley leading in from the Ashton Road end which was conspicuously unblocked. It was a little hard to see how this 'ringing of a neighbourhood' condemned by David Blunkett and highlighted by the *Daily Mail* worked. Joe Royle, the big Everton centre-forward and Oldham Athletic manager after whom the close is named, was never so complicated.

I asked an Asian man working on his car where the Peace Barrier was and he looked at me as if I was mad and went inside his house. A blonde middle-aged woman came down the road. I asked her. 'It's there, over there,' she said. I looked at the rusty bit of iron fencing, about eight feet high and ten feet wide, across an alley leading into Honeywell Lane. What did she make of it? 'I don't like it,' she said. 'I used to take a short cut to work through there.'

She was a care coordinator and didn't want to give her name, so we'll call her Thelma. I asked her about the trouble. 'It's the whites,' she said. She told me that the alley had been used by white youths as a rat-run during the riots. 'The young whites, they cause the trouble. They hang around street corners. They're bored, they're drinking and they're doing drugs.' Nothing else for the young to do: the eternal mitigation, first offered up, if I remember correctly, in Sodom and Gomorrah. (By the way, I know about the other lot, but what exactly were they up to in Gomorrah, do you think?)

Thelma wanted to leave, too. But she couldn't sell her house. It had been on the market for three years. She'd bought it in 1984 for £10,000. Eighteen months ago, the house next door had sold, but for £6,000. And now the white youths were setting empty houses in her street on fire in case they were given to asylum seekers. Oldham, Brave Oldham.

Thelma arrived at the house she had to visit. It was close by Maple Mill, where Thelma had worked for a bit, where they made kitchen fittings now. Just one side of the four-storeyed mill had 144 windows, necessary to combat the heat from the old ring-spinning frames. In the winter sun, just outside the mill's shadow, an Asian man and woman, traditionally dressed, deep in conversation, were sitting on the kerb of the pavement as if to present some kind of poignant allegorical tableau of the type beloved by the Victorians, entitled 'At the End of the Thread' or some such. Something else about them nudged me, too, but I didn't realise what it was until some months later, in Bolton, as I watched some Asian women pass by: the Lancashire shawl has returned, only it's now called the hijab.

Did I tell you, by the way, that much of Oldham's ascendancy in spinning came from its move away from American raw cotton to Indian raw cotton, which allowed it to survive the Cotton Famine better than most other Lancashire towns? And just to complicate my earlier picture of implacable and selfless moral solidarity, I suppose I ought to say that prior to this it had been a hotbed of support for the Confederacy. Sometimes, you know, it can be a little difficult to follow the command of that great journalist, Ephraim Hardcastle: 'Shepherd the facts, laddie, shepherd the facts!'

Parked nearby was a new and shiny open-topped Mercedes sports car. Two men in their twenties, with short haircuts and wrap-around sunglasses, were sitting in it, their racial mix indeterminate and irrelevant. The car moved off. As it did, the passenger slowly and deliberately extended his left arm out of the window, opened his hand and let a carton of Ribena Lite fall into the road. There was something in the casual contempt of this display that I found depressing beyond all sensible measure.

Chadderton was a bit depressing, too, on a winter afternoon, in the Asda car park. Apart from the Asda, a triumph of the neo-conservatory style, single-storey, with the odd twiddle of a gable, there didn't seem to be much to the centre of Chadderton, one of the outlying townships which had resisted administrative incorporation into Oldham long after the physical fact, right up until the local government reorganisation of 1974.

The swimming baths, second home of the great Henry Taylor – 1885–1951, three swimming world records, four Olympic Games, eight medals, four golds – had been given a leisure centre addition not so much unsympathetic as indifferent; the cupola-capped town hall now received callers round the side, not through its grand frontage. A plaque at one corner of the Asda car park celebrating Chadderton's twinning with the German town of Geestacht was accompanied by a note that it had been relocated to its present site after the Commemorative Gardens at the corner of Broadway and Middleton Road had been 'lost to roadworks'. Indeed.

In the other corner, there was a struggle going on against the wind to inflate and erect a large white tent with spikes on. Or 'bizarre spikes', to give the *Daily Express*'s full description. For this was none other than the infamous 'Thought Bubble', which had been touring Oldham as part of the 'visioning process' for the future of the town. Rarely had apostrophes been so angry, particularly when it was revealed that '£3,000 of public money' had been spent on the Bubble. Ah, well. I thought it sounded an interesting way of sounding out public opinion, and significantly more stimulating than yet more people on the street with clipboards or one of those dreary mobile office things. I was also interested to see that the brains behind the scheme belonged to Charlie Baker.

Charlie Baker. A man with a gift for alternative thought, especially about towns and cities and houses. Not exactly an unreconstructed punk, but rather a punk in a constant state of construction. In the '80s, when everybody had wanted to knock tower blocks down, when deck access had been anathema, Charlie had fought to save the Hulme Crescents, a fine Mancunian example, for an alternative community of young artists and the like, which was when I first met him. He failed, but didn't stop, pressing on with his housing co-op, Homes for Change, a splendidly organic and irregular complex of four- and six-storey maisonettes and flats with deck access, of course, built around a courtyard and known in Hulme as Fort Hippy, despite Charlie considering 'hippy' to be the worst form of insult.

And now Charlie was a consultant for Urbed, the urban design company (not-for-profit, of course) which had saved Covent Garden and had been hired by the new Local Strategic Partnership to save Oldham, which was why Charlie was now fighting to blow up his Bubble in the Asda car park, aided by a team of young volunteers from the Prince's Trust and the government-funded Groundwork agency, and watched by Dave and Paul, Asda trolley-gatherers.

Dave and Paul didn't feel entitled to speak for Chadderton, being from Oldham, but they did think the Bubble was a good idea. One of the basic problems Charlie and Urbed had identified in Oldham was 'liveability', making the place somewhere where people wanted to live, so I was interested to hear Dave and Paul both say that living in Oldham wasn't too bad. I asked them where they would live if they could. Paul said

Torquay; Dave, who was older, plumped for Lytham St Annes.

The Bubble was up. Charlie had to dash off for a meeting and left his team to begin the visioning process. 'What's this in aid of, then?' inquired an Asian woman on her way in to Asda. 'It's a thinking bubble,' said John, one of the volunteers. I couldn't quite see how it was going to work, but it did, and soon the Bubble was pretty full. Parents and children were prompted to stick yellow Post-it notes on boards with their thoughts about what was good, what was bad, and what could be better about Oldham. Suggestions were varied. You will gather the range of the suggested improvements from 'More manufacturing jobs' and 'A bigger Asda'. One of the things wrong was 'No ice-skating'. People were also asked to say where they were from. Most gave a particular district, hardly any said Oldham. While I wasn't looking, somebody put up on the Good Things board: 'Life is easy.' Life is easy! Could this be a person unique to the country, let alone Lancs? But of course I couldn't find him, or her. On the other side of the Bubble, two nine-year-old red-headed twins were laboriously writing down how they would like to see Oldham in 20 years' time. 'Nice and quiet,' wrote one. 'Nice and noisy,' wrote the other. No one said it would be easy.

I popped into Asda for a chat with Father Christmas. What did he think Oldham and Chadderton needed? Santa pondered before coming up with a splendidly trademark mix of goodwill and commercialism: an improved shopping centre and more people coming together. Charlie returned and had a cup of coffee. I wondered what he thought about the mills, and put to him my intimidating-ghosts-better-got-shot-of theory. I should have known that Charlie would be a Mills Man. Sure, he said, most people living near the old mills wanted them dropped, but that was because they had no faith in alternative uses. Mills in the middle of Oldham shouldn't be used for storage and distribution, that belonged to a business park somewhere outside Warrington between the M6 and the M62. Hardly any jobs created, no social function. He didn't want yuppie lofts, either; no, Charlie, of course, had a vision of neighbourhoods where the mill was the social hub, with housing, studios, workshops, hi-tech communications. Charlie had looked at Oldham and he had seen its future as the media, arts and cultural workshop for Manchester, small businesses in affordable premises fuelling the glossy output of the City, people happy to live in a great spot close to the centre but next to the moors, new mills for the new millennium, producing creativity not cotton.

I wondered about this fantastic proliferation of agencies and acronyms involved in regeneration. Wouldn't it be better to have a Mr or Ms Big, a local Heseltine, a benevolent Gradgrind, to force things through? But this was far too fascist a solution for Charlie. I asked him how hopeful he was for his new millennial mills. Charlie had been in Manchester long enough to acquire some of its tempering realism. Well, he said, he would be quite happy with ten, disappointed with fewer than five and gutted with zero.

Outside, John, the volunteer, said that he had done his dissertation on community relations in Oldham. One of his central tenets had been that young Asians were showing how well they had integrated by behaving just as loutishly as the young whites. His tutor, he said, hadn't been impressed. I talked to a nice old lady about the bad old days and how she had always saved for her retirement and spent a lot of time listening to Radio Four and learning Italian and how standards in Chadderton had gone down since 'all the . . . all the . . . foreigners' had come in.

Ah, yes, foreigners. I went to see Shamim Miah, who is something of an unofficial spokesman for the young Asians of Oldham. Shamim's father came to England from Bangladesh (or East Pakistan as it was then; Bangladeshis form the other main Asian community in Oldham) and worked in Bedford before spending 35 years at another Greenfield Mill, this one in Oldham. Shamim left school without any GCSEs, worked in a takeaway, 'dossed around' for five years, and then somehow got himself together and into Manchester University. He has a degree in social sciences and a Masters in orientalism. His wife is a schoolteacher. When he went back to his old school, a teacher asked him to spell 'university' to see whether he was lying about his academic success. Now he's teaching sociology at one, the new Oldham University Centre, when he's not doing his other job as a policy officer with Oldham Council.

Shamim was clear about the main causes of the 2001 riots, putting the blame on the casual, insensitive and accepted kind of racism displayed by the local media, police, council and white community, the attitudes and behaviour that, before the riots, meant he couldn't even go shopping on a Saturday afternoon in the town centre with his wife and young child without risking abuse and insult. But he was also clear that all of this has improved since the riots, that there are some signs of the communities working together, of better policing. He had been encouraged, he said, by the way community leaders had met in Oldham in the immediate aftermath of 7 July 2005 – something that would never have happened before the riots – and was convinced this had helped prevent any local backlash.

Optimistic, but not foolishly so. Racism, institutional, personal and casual, remained. The best test for this was the way taxi drivers like Mohammed were treated. 'Someone who's sober might very well tell you how great he thinks Muslims are. Get a couple of pints down his throat and he will often start to articulate a different kind of response altogether.' And there was, said Shamim, in his opinion, quite some way to go before his Two Pint Test would start to show really positive results.

Against this, because of this, he said, there is a deep-seated disaffection among Asian youth, who feel demonised and despised. Another Asian social scientist, said Shamim, compares this with the famous cry of Millwall soccer supporters: 'We are Millwall, no one likes us, we don't care.'

That's why he hadn't been exactly surprised by the London bombings: they were the most extreme effect of that disaffection. There were plenty of things that could be done; he, for example, had plans to take young members of his community to Auschwitz, to Bosnia, to show them 'the logical consequences of extreme ideas'. But nothing would be achieved without economic progress. 'You can talk about multiculturalism, dead, alive, good thing, bad thing, too much, too little, Britishness, lack of it, for as long as you like, but it won't mean anything at all until we've achieved equality, socially and economically. It won't mean anything to the young lad up in Glodwick who just wants a job.'

That wasn't all, either, of course. One of the most important factors in the disaffection was the generational thing. Shamim's father and his generation had accepted racist behaviour to the extent that they had stopped noticing it. His generation, born here, hadn't really expected it and didn't see why they had to put up with it. His father and his generation had seen themselves as Asians, Shamim's generation wasn't quite sure how to see themselves. 'My father still has an idea that he wants to go back to Bangladesh. But I'm second generation, I don't feel any connections with Bangladesh or that.'

Shamim said he hadn't really finished working out what he was, but if you asked him now what his identity was, he would describe himself as a British Muslim. But, he said, he did feel proud of being British. And he felt, proud, too, of Oldham, despite everything. And those, I felt, were the type of prides we don't hear nearly enough about.

We finished talking. It had been lunchtime during Ramadan. Shamim had pressed refreshment on me, but had taken nothing himself. At the door, we looked across and down at two old mills. Shamim gave me one of his big grins. This was where the

211

posh people, the millowners, used to live, he said. The thought occurred, as we were looking, that a mill would make the most marvellous mosque, its chimney a fine minaret. Shamim gave me another of his big grins. He liked that.

I had another appointment, to see Father Phil Sumner, a Roman Catholic priest who had done doughty work in Manchester's famously troubled Moss Side before arriving in the newly famously troubled Oldham on 11 September 2001, a day to focus anybody's thoughts.

Father Phil talked with enthusiasm, and, as he said, he was an optimist because that was part of his job. Father Phil was a New Catholic priest, not like the Old Catholic priests I grew up with; the Old Catholic priests were men of culture and wit, supporters, essentially, of the established order, who enjoyed their relaxation time, usually involving strong drink and lively conversation, with the Catholic middle classes. 'Could you put another shepherd in the pie?' was the way one of my childhood favourites used to broach a pastoral visit. New Catholic priests like Father Phil are men who see injustice and work for change and are at ease with the talk of accessing and identity and alienation and cohesion, and usually have rather more pressing things to do than exercise their culture and wit on the middle classes. Which is a great gain for everybody else, but a sadness for us.

Father Phil wanted to start the change where it should be started, in education, with a recognition of difference, not a pretence that it wasn't there; instilling pride, explaining worth, encouraging belonging. But there was a long way to go, and the size of the problem shouldn't be underestimated: in the 2001 election, 16.4 per cent of the Oldham West electorate had voted for the BNP candidate, the highest ever for a fascist party in a general election.

Increased prosperity, said Father Phil, would cure some of the disaffection with the Labour Party which that vote represented;

but it wouldn't work by itself. Nor would just a will to change things: 'Oldham is at the stage at the moment of having the will and the commitment, and that's the first stage that's necessary. But it will take time to get the training to understand the issues in the proper way. Sometimes the best will in the world can achieve the wrong things.'

Which brought us to faith-based schools. I fumbled my way through a bit of reporting in Northern Ireland in the early '80s; even to me it seemed there was one clear message – the problem, the death, the hate and the distrust wouldn't disappear until these two religions were educated together. So here, 20 years later, we had a government that wanted to increase segregated education, and a government inquiry into the rioting in Oldham, Burnley and Bradford which concluded that 'the development of more faith-based schools may, in some cases, lead to an increase in monocultural schools'. And a recommendation that all schools should offer at least 25 per cent of places to reflect 'other cultures or ethnicities in their area'.

Father Phil was, he said, concerned that faith-based schools in an area like Oldham could become part of the problem. His parish primary school had succeeded in introducing 20 per cent of non-Catholics, even if it wasn't the policy of the governing Salford diocese so to do. But shouldn't Catholics abandon their segregated schools altogether? 'We're not ready to go that far,' said Father Phil. 'We haven't got the structures to go that far. It's too radical a suggestion at this stage for the Catholic Church in this country. They fought for Catholic schools for many years. They see it as an important battle that they won. They feel it would be to sell out those who have gone before us in that struggle.'

So, an Old Catholic message: time. Let me quote Brian Law again, about how it was in the 1860s and 1870s:

> Street fights, fights in public houses, fights with the police, were common in the poorest areas . . . as

elsewhere the Irish immigrants were living in the most crowded and squalid circumstances in the worst streets in the town. In the aftermath of the Great Famine they were usually destitute when they arrived and until they got some kind of work they had little choice but to double up with friends or relatives . . . They were viewed with deep hostility because of their Roman Catholicism and because, in their poverty, they were a threat to the livelihood of the other working poor . . .

Popular resentment towards the Irish at the time, less in Oldham than elsewhere, surfaced on the occasion of the Whit Walks in 1861. A procession of children from St Patrick's Catholic church clashed with a similar Anglican procession in the marketplace. The incident led to violent anti-Catholic riots the same evening and the following day when gangs of youths stoned and smashed the two Catholic churches.

Heavy rain on Whit Sunday seems to have quietened the mob, but incidents, more or less serious, continued over the next week involving as many as 15,000 people. The *Chronicle* [the local newspaper] condemned 'lawless and outrageous' behaviour, but spoke of 'ignorant and turbulent Irish', 'a dangerous element in our society', 'alien in blood, language and religion, opposed in their feelings and interests to the people of England'.

Time, then. That which, as the great Mr Tom Paine said, 'makes more converts than reason'. And, also, the one thing we don't get now. Humanity's three great curse-blessings, curiosity, ingenuity and impatience, drive the whirligig ever faster. We spent most of last century attempting to wipe out whole races; now we want peace and harmony at the same pace as our faster food and swifter gratification. Why should we be patient when we are omnipotent? Patience predicates events beyond our control, and we have stopped believing in that, despite all manner and scale of warnings to the contrary. Thanks, Herr Nietzsche. He died mad, you know. Do you remember the graffito: 'God is Dead – Nietzche. Nietzsche is Dead – God'? Not that I can decide between them, being caught in a perpetual and broadly well-intentioned Lancastrian type of dither. So this would probably be a good time to tell you that my wife and I recently decided to have our children educated by the Benedictines.

Did I also tell you that I have written a large number of leading articles, the ones that opine anonymously down a side column in the middle of the newspaper? Exactly. Do as I say. Lots of ideas, though. And I had another one, about Oldham. It was too close to Manchester. True, the connection had a lot of promise, but it didn't mean that Oldham shouldn't regain and retain its identity by a shrewd piece of differentiation. It should declare itself Lancashire again. Walter Greenwood had called it 'this most Lancashire of Lancashire towns'. The town could move forward through the past, recapture the pride.

Before long Rochdale and Bolton would follow, then St Helens, then Wigan, then Warrington, then Widnes, Ulverston, Barrow, Southport, all demanding a radical Red Rose revival. What a vision! Can you see it, hear the shouts and laughter, the delighted exclamations of 'Well, I'll go to the foot of our stairs!', as Wiganer embraces Warringtonian, Sandgrounder hugs Sintelliner, friends reunited at last? But, by now, you will have realised that I am above all a realist; it is perhaps fanciful to dream of reclaiming the two great lost cities, which are now big enough and old enough to stand on their own feats, as long as they acknowledge their proud parentage. Sorry? Sandgrounder: Southport; Sintelliner: St Helens. Bonus – Sand Grown Un: Blackpool.

I tried my dream for Oldham on Shamim. He was polite, but a bit doubtful; everyone, in fact, had seemed a bit doubtful, even

Charlie Baker, who was normally up for a good alternative concept. Too late, too old-fashioned, its time past.

So I was pensive as I made my way into the Spindles centre to buy my mum a mobile phone. Well, she is in her 80s. One thing you'll never be short of in a post-modern shopping centre is a mobile-phone shop. I started with the Carphone Warehouse. Aminul Hoque served me. Amin was in his early twenties, doing a degree at Manchester Metropolitan University, but he was taking a year off, 'because I need to make some money'. Amin was going to be a teacher. Nice long holidays, I said. Yeah, that was right, said Amin, fourteen weeks when you could be buying and selling. One of his old teachers ran a chain of launderettes. He and about ten of his friends were going to make a lot of money, teaching and doing the same. Amin was going to have a helicopter. You could land them up on Saddleworth Moor, at the posh end of town, he'd heard you could get one, second-hand, for £50,000.

Oldham? He liked Oldham, it was a good place, all the trouble had been exaggerated by the media. He'd been to London, couldn't stand all those dead-eyed people, looking straight ahead. Amin seethed and buzzed with the future, in Oldham. When I told Father Phil about Amin, he said he was an exception, but I couldn't help but be buoyed. I'll tell you what it was: it was like meeting my grandfather, the first-generation Lancastrian, just before the Great War, behind the bacon counter at Stringfellows in St Helens, seething and buzzing with all the shops he was going to open and run. Or, indeed, my other grandfather, the first-generation Cockney, father up from Devon, who, as it happens, was already selling phones around then. Thank you, Amin. You cheered me up almost as much as the BNP collapse in Oldham at the last general election. Charlie Baker did get his plan for the mills through, too, although there's nothing about making them into mosques, yet. I also liked something else that's supposed to be coming: in an obvious nod over to Southport's proud tradition, Oldham's big main roads are to be 'boulevarded'. Boulevarding – cutting out all the alienating elevations and underpasses – is so named because of the superior amount of traffic the Champs Élysées can manage without the need for such things. And where was it tried first? Bury.

What else? Well, Bryn and James and the Epona Club have gone; the new tenants are running a children's activity centre. And the last time I was in Royle Close, it was Hallowe'en, and a group of lively Asian children were demanding tricks or treats, which is, I suppose, a measure of some sort of progress.

Back in Salford, there didn't seem much more left of Engels. Ermen and Engels had another mill, in Eccles, but I couldn't find any trace of it. So I went back into Manchester by way of Salford Quays. I'd last been there in the early '90s, before the Lowry Centre and the Imperial War Museum of the North, when the idea of luxury, state-of-the-art accommodation in Salford at the side of the Manchester Ship Canal had seemed most novel. Down there, I came across Karen Cobbin, a hotel sales manager, and David Loft, a financial services consultant, on the patio of their canalside apartment. They were from Brighton, and they liked Manchester; the people were more friendly, not so worried about what other people had got. Mind you, Karen had never seen mushy peas before they came here. Did she eat them now? 'God, no, definitely not.' Ah, yes, mushy peas, as much a Lancashire cliché as Mr Lowry and his matchstick men.

I liked the Lowry Centre, and, even though its architect, Michael Wilford, was outraged by it, I appreciated the Mancunian way in which the Lowry Designer Outlet shopping experience extravaganza had been plonked down in front of one of his key vistas, conforming to the tradition which has also seen the hallowed Free Trade Hall become a five-star hotel. And yet a great deal of money is to be made here, sir! When they built Manchester Town Hall, they had a triangular plot available, so if they wanted a grand classical effort, they would have had to buy more land to square it off into the correct classical proportions. Manchester Town Hall is triangular, and Gothic. Like I said, just a little too close to Yorkshire.

Don't worry, I'm not going to go on about Lowry, except to remark on the way he conveys that strange affection for ugliness which you must have if you come from an ugly place. The romance of Lancs is there. I like, too, his love for the Pre-Raphaelites, and the way he painted to the sounds of Bellini and Donizetti. And the quotes: 'Painting is damned hard work,' and 'P.S. This art is a terrible business.'

And this story, told by Keith Waterhouse:

> Many years ago the late L.S. Lowry had an exhibition, which, unusually for this master of crowded street scenes, was dominated by single figures, including the famous one of a man lying on a wall with a bowler hat on his chest. The art critics made much of this development and wrote reams about the artist finally homing in on the essential loneliness of his characters. At the opening night party, Mr Lowry provided me with his own interpretation: 'Y'see, Keith, I had a ten by eight to do for Merthyr Tydfil Corporation, but at the same time I'd this exhibition coming up and I'd promised to give them at least half-a-dozen new pictures. But with this big job on the best I could do was to dash off some of what I call me ones.

Splendid.

The Granada TV studios are just over the border from Salford, on the way up to the city centre. I worked there once, on a year's contract as a production office assistant, with a view to a powerful career in current affairs. I never quite got the hang of it, though; most of the year was spent as a 'call boy', knocking on dressing-room doors, ensuring that the stars of things like *Coronation Street* were in the right scene at the right time. I always managed to forget someone, somehow. I suppose I should have made a tidy income, too, selling the secrets of the stars to the tabloids, but I never really managed to discover any, except that Doris Speed, who played the snobbish landlady of the Rover's Return, Annie Walker, was in reality really nice, while Margot Bryant, who played the sweetest of old ladies, Minnie Caldwell, was in reality really horrible, a foul-mouthed old cantanker.

My, how I enjoyed it the day that Margot tripped over a camera cable and Violet Carson, who played Ena Sharples, tripped over Margot and fell on top of her. You must have heard of Ena Sharples. Ah, well. You're unlikely, then, to remember Albert Tatlock, played by Jack Howarth, who used to transform himself into Albert by the simple, and only, device of putting a bit of burnt cork on his top lip.

But surely you remember Doris, if only for Annie's exquisite stare into the middle distance above pursed lips which greeted yet another piece of coarse badinage from the appallingly ignorant clientele foisted upon her by a cruel fate when she should rightly have been running a tearoom in Lytham. What a lady Doris was, a good ten years older than we thought she was, but the one who remembered my name, the one who never uttered a single reproof, no matter how many times I called her for the wrong scene, late, or forgot to call her at all.

I used to love *Coronation Street* in the days when it was a sitcom masquerading as a soap. Try some of these voices, sounding faintly, quaintly across the years: 'Hilda, will you stop that singing! It's like a lump of coke stuck under the back gate'; 'If she lived in India, she'd be sacred'; 'He'd skin a flea and then sell it a vest'; 'The day I have to look like that to attract the fellers is the day I give up the struggle as a female fatal'; 'Give him a chance? I wouldn't give him the steam off my tea'; 'When you've made gravy under gunfire, you can do anything' . . . the true sound of Lancs, captured, preserved, and already out of date by then, overdubbed by the samey blandness of national broadcasting and newspapers.

I liked Neville Buswell, too. He played Ray Langton, a bit of a tearaway, married to Deirdre (the one with the big specs), partner of Len Fairclough. Blimey. Is there anything more far away and forgotten than a dead or departed soap character? Neville, though, came and had a drink when I left and used to put one on for me at the bookies. I read later that he'd ended up as a bank clerk in Las Vegas after a spell as a croupier, which seems a remarkably whimsical, Lancastrian thing to do, even if he is from Derbyshire. I had this idea that I should go to talk to him about it, on the same trip on which I checked whether there is still a family of Lancashire fish-friers frying the finest fish and chips in all America at Fall River, Massachusetts. No, really. But then, remarkably even for a soap series, he turned up again, to acclaim, after 27 years, so that Ray could look back on his life and die at Ken and Deirdre's (second) wedding reception in, naturally, The Rover's. Death follows Ken, you know. His first wife electrocuted herself with her hairdryer, and there's been worse since. Neville's boss in Las Vegas gave him six weeks off to do it. He's a mortgage adviser now. I also now discover that he made an earlier one-off reappearance in a video-only *Coronation Street* spin-off, *Viva Las Vegas*, playing Ray as a gay barman. Unimprovable, really. Which just leaves the fish-friers.

Now where were we? Ah, yes, Engels: Jonathan Schofield, one of Manchester's Blue Badge guides took me to Chetham's Library, the oldest free public library in England, part of a fifteenth-century school and hospital whose wardens once included Dr John Dee, the noted Elizabethan magician and alchemist, a man who clearly learnt much from his exposure to Lancs, if not quite the trick of turning muck into brass, which came later.

We sat at the table in the library where Engels and Marx sat and touched some of the books they had read. The librarian said East Germans, once the most plentiful of visitors, were seldom seen these days; but the Chinese kept on coming. And, he said, should anyone be contemplating making them a gift, they still had more than enough busts of Marx to keep them going. Outside, in the new Exchange Square, there was more bomb-recovered space, dominated by the monolithic glass-clad Urbis building, designed by Manchester's Ian Simpson, housing the museum of the modern city and not doing half as well as it might have done if it had concentrated exclusively on Manchester and Lancashire (a somewhat biased observer writes). Jonathan, in the usual guide's way, reflected that the swanky water feature was just about where the old open sewers and ditches of the Irishtown and Little Gibraltar slums used to be. Jonathan was an excellent guide. I forgot to tell him that, according to a survey, there are more open-topped cars sold in Manchester than in the whole of Spain, but I expect he knew it anyway. A key fact on the whimsical front, though, I think you'll agree. Oh, and while we're on architecture, did I mention that Norman Foster is a Mancunian? Thank you.

I think you'll know, too, about the 2002 Commonwealth Games, the success, the feeling that this really is a great European city again, its naming as Britain's most creative city, its finest mix of innovation, cultural diversity and sexual tolerance. For more of this special Manchesterness, go to Canal Street, centre of Manchester's pioneering gay village, the largest in Europe. There you should talk to Iain Scott, owner of the Taurus cocktail bar, restaurant and occasional fringe theatre, and as far removed from Basil Newby in Blackpool as it is possible to get while sharing the same vowel orientation.

There is nothing pink about Taurus. And Iain is very good on why Manchester is the North's gay capital, rather than, say, Leeds, Birmingham or even Liverpool. 'I think it's because historically there has been a tolerance here in Manchester to all sorts of things for a couple of hundred years or so,' he said, pointing to the large number of different and long-established communities in the city, Chinese, Jewish, Polish, and to the size of Manchester compared with other Northern cities, which allowed people to be different.

I, of course, was most anxious to get Iain to confirm that there was a Lancashire gene, a tendency towards the fey and whimsical that made Lancashire men more likely to be gay. You are aware, of course, that George Formby is a gay icon? He is. But Iain, apart from allowing that the Northern warmth and friendliness made for tolerance, gave that as much shrift as my proposition that Manchester's gayness might have a connection with its busy rag trade. Iain's gay vision was solid progress towards a moneyed sophistication rather than the screaming frivolities of Basil in Blackpool. Another of his points was that gay culture and lifestyle had inspired and to some extent led the regeneration of the city, the loft living, the bars, the restaurants, the smart consumerism.

Very Manchester, even if he was keen on horoscopes and, I'm pretty certain, Doris Day was singing in the background. I wondered what Engels would have made of it. I do have a clue, though. He wrote to Marx: 'The pederasts are beginning to count themselves and find they make a power in the state . . . It is only luck that we are personally too old to have to fear that on the victory of this party we shall have to pay the victors bodily tribute.' The last bit sounds like the early version of a Bernard Manning gag.

I went back to Weaste, to Engels' pool. The Chandos Sports and Social Club is next to it. You have to be a member to fish. The Chandos used to be the works sports and social club for Winterbottom's, the bookbinding company that took over the mill. It was a sunny Saturday morning at the pool, but no one was fishing. I went into the club. Most people were in the room on the other side of the bar, watching Manchester United. Let's not start on them, either, as we all know far too much already; but it is interesting that they were a far more romantic team while Manchester was sleeping.

A small, round, bald man was sat in the front room on his own, with a pint of Guinness. 'Now then, young man,' he said. He was, he said, the secretary, although he didn't really have to, as I have been into enough Northern clubs, and watched enough programmes about Northern clubs, to recognise a secretary when I see one. I explained about Engels. He hadn't heard that one, he said, but he'd be happy to show me round. I asked him why he wasn't watching United. Wasn't he a fan? 'I can't support myself, never mind them,' he said. We looked at the pool. What was it called? 'Everyone calls it the Rezzie,' he said. Rezzie, reservoir. Oh, yes, there were a lot of fish in there. They'd caught a 30-pound carp in there, massive. Did he fish? 'Only at the chippie.'

Have you ever seen *Phoenix Nights*, the TV comedy about the Phoenix Club in Bolton, written by and starring Peter Kay, Lancashire's latest comic gift to the world? Kay plays the bouncer, and the secretary, Brian Potter, who is in a wheelchair. Brian is, of course, a romancer, a man dedicated to making the Phoenix the equal of anything in Las Vegas, firm in the belief that he's almost there. I used the phrase 'whimsy with attitude' earlier on, and it works well here, too. The wheelchair is there for edge, not sympathy.

I could try to analyse Lancashire humour, starting off by confiding that it's based on life being the bit of a bugger that it is and that rather than cry, they've decided they might as well get their own back by teasing it and everybody else. I could say that the humour, like everything else, gets harder as it moves east, from Dodd to Manning. But I think it would be more helpful to tell you about Kay the bouncer and his partner taking a contract to kill a husband, and preparing to follow the husband's car. The husband pulls away, Kay and the partner begin to follow. 'Stop!' shouts Kay, making sure the in-car tape player is playing the right music to shadow somebody by. Or his shout as, for some reason which I have forgotten, a group of dwarfs advance on the club: 'How far away are they?' Personally, though, I prefer the more whimsical Kay, the stand-up Kay, the Kay of Comic Relief's 'Is This The Way To Amarillo?', which shows the true Lancashire comic genius, the mark of Dodd, Dawson and Morecambe, the mockery which is funny but friendly, and, equally crucially, includes laughing at yourself as well.

'This,' said the secretary, 'is an oasis in Salford.' He showed me the concert room upstairs, with its new sound system. They had some very good acts, he said. 'I get them to do it cheaper because they try their new gear out on us, and then I give them a fiver for petrol.' Did he watch? 'I'm a vaults lad,' he said. 'I don't go upstairs. I'm not into it. I'm in the engine room down here. This club was dying. I got a nudge off my mate. Somebody's got to be the secretary, he said, got to apply for a licence. The old secretary was packing it in, he'd had enough. I'd never run a bar, I'd never waited on, I'd done nothing. What a shock! The hours you have to put in. I live here. Me and my wife don't have a row any more because we don't see each other.'

He'd been through five bar stewards in five years. 'It's only a job for them. The less people come in, the better for them. I need to build the place up . . . I'm a bit busy, if you know what I mean. When there's a do on upstairs, I put ten pee on across the board, on everything. Well, they had a right go about that. They was going to lynch me. "This is a non-profit-making organisation," they said. "Fuck you," I said. "Who's going to replace the chairs and the carpets?" They haven't got a clue and they're going on about non-profit-making! I said, "Shut up!" I swear a bit, but that's me.'

224

I asked him if he'd ever seen *Phoenix Nights*. He said it was filmed at a couple of the clubs he went to in Bolton. The secretaries there meet once a week, he said, free buffet and bar, hints on health and safety and that sort of thing, very useful. I said he should do a turn. 'Who, me? Mind you, I'm told I'm a character.'

He was, he said, 58. He had six children, five lads and a girl. 'The wife is into plants, animals and kids.' He'd worked at Manchester dry docks, before becoming a painter and decorator, before this. He showed me, at the back, the bowling green. It was in splendid condition. 'We get all sorts here. Herons, ducks. They were playing bowls one night and a duck and her ducklings walked right across the green. Like I said, an oasis in Salford.'

What did he think of the Manchester regeneration? 'It's not coming to us. And what is it? All the industry's being taken away by people you don't see in secret meetings in different parts of the world. This country's turning into a holiday island and we'll just be waiters. Tony Blair? He's just Margaret Thatcher in pants. There are two Tory parties, and one's called New Labour.'

He'd got no problem with Engels, he said. He was a Tory Communist: 'You've got to be a bit busy, but you've got to be right with people at the same time.' As a matter of fact, his dad had been a Communist. That's why he'd called him Leon. Sorry? That was his name, Leon Thorpe, after Trotsky. Leon! Well, well, well.

I thought I might as well tell Leon about Balzac, and women dying of love. Leon laughed out loud at this. 'Very good,' he beamed through his spectacles, 'Very good. Ee ba gum, stretch my braces!' Of course he was a Lancastrian! 'When I do the pools, I still put Lancs on the address. It's my little protest. I've been doing the same numbers for 30 years. They're birthday numbers. Do you know, if my father had been born on the second instead of the third, I would have won £230 once, instead of £7 15 s.'

It was time to ask Leon about Walter Greenwood's dream in 1950 of the future, when 'all the dirt, smoke, filth and intolerable overcrowding and ugliness will remain only on films for later and luckier generations to marvel at and wonder what sort of people their forefathers were to put up with, aye, and even defend, such intolerable conditions'; and when boys would be able to fish in the Irwell again. 'It's swarming with fish since it's been cleaned up,' said Leon.

Quite an improvement, then. 'Not for me,' said Leon. 'I'm against the Quays. It upsets me when I see the Lowry and all that. I remember when it was a docks with lots of people going to work. People had a reason to get up. Now they stay in bed all day, because what's the use of getting up? Now you have to pay £240,000 for a flat over there. And do you know what really annoyed me? They took the cobblestones out of our street and put them down in the Quays. Now we've just got tarmac.'

Thanks, Leon. Sorry, Walter. Sorry, Fred. But at least there is fishing, here, and on the Irwell. Do you remember, Fred, how you and your old friend imagined the perfect day under the new world order: work in the morning, fishing in the afternoon, philosophical conversation in the evening? Almost there, then. Always almost there.

Chapter Eight

The Lancashire Toreador

Blood and Sand quite near Benidorm

I first came across Frank Evans at Bury's football ground, Gigg Lane, which was being shared then by the Swinton rugby league club. Swinton had, in the way clubs do, come down in the world. I don't mean this as any reflection on Gigg Lane, which is quite a smart, compact little ground; but it is in Bury, not Swinton; and it is not Station Road, Swinton, one of the great rugby league grounds until they pulled it down and built houses on it, which makes a change from a supermarket.

Station Road was not smart, but it was big: in the '60s, it could hold over 40,000, and did sometimes, for Test matches, finals, semi-finals and such. Station Road may have had old stands, shale banks not terraces, but it also had the sense of the big occasion and the authentic rugby league smell of old beer and strong tobacco, lost for ever beneath the hamburgers, hot dogs and onions.

They had a good team, too: Gowers, Buckley, Speed, Fleet and Stopford, names that don't mean much now, but ones I enjoy typing for the memory of all their fizz and dash, and for the marvel of a three-quarter line containing Speed, Fleet and Stopford.

But now they were in Bury, and playing St Helens in the Cup, and given so little chance of causing an upset that the rugby league correspondent of *The Independent* had chosen to go elsewhere, despite the attendance and optimism of his editor in chief, a very big fan in an admittedly specialised field which was getting more specialised by the season. I like to see such devotion as evidence of the same Lancashire whimsicality which had led him to accept the job at *The Independent*, but then I would. I was attending as his guest, a difficult role for a St Helens supporter and his employee. How are you at sympathy without condescension? Exactly. The difficulty would be to avoid punching the air too noticeably as the St Helens players sliced contemptuously through his team and his dreams. I had the same trouble, once, cuckooing on the press benches at Central Park, Wigan, as the Saints pulled off a wildly improbable victory and my right arm developed a Strangelovian mind of its own, which, mindful of the impartiality of the fourth estate, I managed to convert into several sharp raps on the bench, thus doing rather better than the scrupulously fair radio commentary on the very close Celtic–Rangers match which ended with a last-minute breakaway goal and the loud cry, 'Fuck me, we've scored!'

As it turned out, and as I might have known, St Helens helped by making a right pig's ear of it. Swinton played rather well, and although we won, a couple of injuries at crucial moments to key Swinton players allowed plenty of scope for the saving grace of what might have been. So the editor in chief was still talking to me as we filed out; and he pointed to a man ahead of us, and said: 'That's the bullfighter from Salford.'

The bullfighter from Salford! Could such things be? I was, as it happens, familiar with one of George Formby's lesser works,

'The Lancashire Toreador', but I had no idea there really was one. But there was: Frank Evans, famed as the kitchen-fitter who practised in the park with a supermarket shopping trolley fitted with horns, the butcher's son who had fallen in love with the *corrida* one hot afternoon in Granada, the matador who had been knocked to the ground by half a ton of black fighting bull in the Plaza de Toros at Benalmadena and had said afterwards, 'The wife's hit me harder.'

Frank was there because one of his sons was playing centre for Swinton. That was another thing about Frank: he wasn't young. He was already in his fifties then, and though the great matadors, El Cordobés, Curro Romero, fought on into their sixties, they were living off their legend, while Frank was still trying to make one outside Salford, Swinton and Spain's smaller rings.

I found all this out later, of course. I lost sight of him that afternoon somewhere between the bar and the directors' lounge, where Tony Barrow, a former St Helens player and Swinton's chief executive, was putting his arm round the referee's shoulder and saying, in a confiding sort of way, 'As your friend, may I say you were a complete load of shite today?' As your friend! Marvellous.

Anyway, when I decided to write this book, Frank was a pretty obvious, stand-out selection. True, there were other Lancastrians engaged in some fairly unlikely and equally whimsical and risky activities; Steve Bennett, from Manchester, the man aiming to fly his own rocket into space, is just one that springs readily to mind. But what better illustration could there be than Frank for Lancashire's peculiar affinity and romantic weakness for the Latin way of things? Shakespeare felt it and Napoleon III felt it, as did the good burghers of Blackpool. And Frank felt it, although as I discovered when I finally got to meet him, he couldn't really explain it.

Finally. What I hadn't appreciated when I first made contact with Frank was that it's only the very top bullfighters who fight frequently, and that the promoters and management of bullfights and bullfighters would have their counterparts in boxing, previously regarded by me as the nonpareil in the department of the serpentine and the chicane, shaking their heads in awe and admiration.

What I also hadn't appreciated was that it's only the very top bullfighters who make any money out if it. The current big young name, El Juli, can earn £50,000 in an afternoon. Frank gets around £4,000, with more than £2,000 going on tax, expenses and to pay for his team, and he has to support his fighting with all manner of commercial activity at home and abroad, including the kitchen-fitting, nursing homes and importing Cuban cigars. So when he said on the phone that he was fighting on Sunday, I should have dropped everything and gone. As it was, quite a few months went by before he got another one, and I was going to be there even if it was the first weekend in January.

And there had been time to do some research. I had discovered that Frank had fought his first bull in 1966, in Montpelier, in France, and that he had achieved full matador status in the ceremony known as the *alternativa* in Cuidad Real in 1991. I studied the matadors' league table, the *escafalon*, and noted that Frank, who fights under the name of El Inglés, usually finished about halfway down the table of 200, which registers fights fought and the award of, in ascending order, according to the acclaim of the crowd and the judgement of the Presidente of the Corrida, ear, ears and tail.

Much more impressive, though, was that, since the retirement of the legendary El Cordobés and the almost equally legendary Curro Romero, Frank seemed to be the oldest matador still fighting; and that, since the forced retirement of the Japanese matador, El Niño del Sol Nasciento (The Rising Sun Kid), he was the only non-Latin *torero*, too.

I had also attempted to temper any Anglo-sensitivity about

blood and ears and tails by reading Hemingway and his leading text, *Death in the Afternoon*. How are you with Hemingway? I have tended to find him a bit too rich and mannered, and slightly ruined by Alan Coren's retelling of *For Whom the Bell Tolls* starring Winnie the Pooh and Piglet: 'The wounds, Pooh, the wounds.'

I wasn't that encouraged, either, by 'All stories, if continued long enough, end in death.' Right. But then I began to see how well Ernest and his subject were suited, in the way it turned flirting with death into a high operatic art, with the suits and the poses. Here he is, for example, on the *faena*, the last act of the fight, where the skill and grace of coordinated, choreographed passes with the cape, the *muleta*, leads to the death of the bull, which, done really well,

> takes a man out of himself and makes him feel immortal while it is proceeding . . . gives him an ecstasy that is, while momentary, as profound as any religious ecstasy; moving all the people in the ring together and increasing in emotional intensity as it proceeds, carrying the bullfighter with it, he playing on the crowd through the bull and being moved as it responds in a growing ecstasy of ordered, formal, passionate, increasing disregard for death that leaves you, when it is over, and the death administered to the animal that has made it possible, as empty, as changed, and as sad as any major emotion will leave you.

Yes, I know, I thought he was into short sentences, too. And there's more:

> The essence of the greatest emotional appeal of bullfighting is the feeling of immortality that the bullfighter feels in the middle of a great *faena* and that

he gives to the spectators. He is performing a work of art, and he is playing with death, bringing it closer, closer to himself, a death that you know is in the horns because you have the canvas-covered bodies of the horses on the sand to prove it. He gives the feeling of his immortality, and, as you watch it, it becomes yours. Then when it belongs to both of you, he proves it with the sword.

And this, on the death of the great Gitanillo:

The bull turned very quickly and Gitanillo turned with the *muleta* to let him come by on the left, raised the *muleta* and then rose himself into the air, his legs wide spread, his hands still holding the *muleta*, his head down, the bull's left horn in his thigh. The bull turned him on the horn and threw him against the *barrera*. The bull's horn found him, picked him up once more and threw him against the wood again. Then as he lay there the bull drove the horn through his back . . . all of this did not take three seconds . . . There was a horn wound in each thigh and in each wound the quadriceps and abductor muscles had been torn loose. But in the wound in the back the horn had driven clean through the pelvis and had torn the sciatic nerve and pulled it out by the root as a worm may be pulled out of the damp lawn by a robin.

I also read of the death of the two legends: Joselito, the one they said no bull could ever catch until one did, just after the First World War, in Talavera de la Reina; and poor Manolete, the one the country wouldn't let retire, booed into proving his courage again and again until he bled to death from a thigh wound in Linares just after the Second. And I read that one in ten matadors was killed, and one in four crippled. I tried to tie this in with the cheerful Lancashire tones at the end of the mobile phone and, mostly, I got a picture in my head of George Formby, when he panics and goes, 'Ooooh!'

Frank certainly seemed calm enough, though, in the garage under his hotel in Fuengirola, just down the coast from Benalmadena, where he would be fighting the next day. He cut a slight but athletic figure, as befitted a former winger at rugby union for Sale and rugby league for Salford, neat and confident in movement. He was wearing his hair in what I discovered to be the typical torero half-mullet, curly at the back; all in all, he rather reminded me of the sort of Mancunian who wore white clogs and a black shirt and went to the disco in the '70s and bumped into George Best, which he did.

He had spread his bullfighter's big scarlet cape, the famous red rag, over the bonnet of his car and was using a wire brush to clean off the mud that had got on it while he had been practising on a *finca*, a country farm, in Andalucia, inland from the Costa del Sol. He talked as he brushed; Frank is a great talker. He has that Lancashire combination of low tones and hard vowels, and he swears more than most people I have met. He adds his preferred Anglo-Saxonisms to his fluent Spanish, which makes for an interesting effect, particularly when it is copied by his entourage, his sword-handler, and his *banderilleros*, the ones who wield the long barbed darts. To save space and repetition, you should add your own to Frank's conversation.

'I'll tell you what I'm not doing this time,' Frank was saying, 'and that's kneeling down, waiting for the bull to come out. Normally that works very well, the bull just swerves past you, but the last time I was here it didn't, and I got knocked all over the place. The next time I did it again, though, just to show, and nobody seemed to bother much. The early stuff always gets forgotten, anyway, it's the end they're interested in. And there's nothing worse than doing something that's not appreciated. Sometimes my wife bakes a cake for someone, and I often think of the amount of effort she puts in that should be appreciated more than if she'd given them a fur coat.'

Not appreciated. It is fair to say that, at home and abroad, there has been a refusal to take Frank entirely seriously as a matador. His search for acclaim has been hindered by British sensitivities towards the great Spanish spectacle and Spanish scepticism towards a foreign torero. He has not been given the fights in the places he thinks he deserves, in Seville and Madrid. There is a quote, from an anonymous Spanish aficionado, which invariably surfaces in any story about Frank: 'He has not an iota of talent.'

In Britain, when they are not condemning him as a barbarian, they are cheerfully bracketing him with Eddie the Eagle. These things rankle. Frank rather resents, too, the greater respect that he feels was accorded to his English predecessors, Vincent Hitchcock in the '40s and '50s, and Henry Higgins in the '60s, even though neither progressed as far as he has: 'But they were public schoolboys, weren't they, and I'm just a ragamuffin from Salford.'

And there's the nub, and the rub, what we might call the George Formby Factor, the complications and implications of being the son of a butcher from Salford and practising in the park with a horned supermarket trolley. These are the things that, I think, produced my initial reaction that day at Bury, rather than awed respect. To be fair, Frank might not look anything like George Formby, but then he doesn't look anything like El Cordobés, either, or any other image you might have of a dark and brooding bullfighter. Frank, I have to tell you, has a resolutely Lancastrian face; so much so that when you see him in his *montera*, the distinctive hat of the matador and the banderilleros, he might as well be wearing a flat cap.

All this, to me, makes Frank's bullfighting all the more splendid. Because, although Frank can't help being a bit of a Lancashire cheeky chappy, and giving out quotes like the one about his wife having hit him harder, and wrapping his *banderillas* in a beer towel bearing the name of the pub in *Emmerdale Farm*, he does still have his dreams, dreams of strutting glory, gasps and ovations in the blood and the sand.

Frank wants to fight in every country where they kill bulls. He has fought in Spain, France and Venezuela. After this fight, he was off to Mexico. And then there is the Big One, the Last Great Dream, Frank fighting at the torero's Old Trafford, the Plaza Monumental de las Ventas in Madrid. Frank wants to march in there accompanied by a Salford pipe band playing 'The Lancashire Toreador'. That's what I mean about him. That's why all of us love to see George, no matter how gormless he is, no matter how unlikely it is, win the race and get the girl. Sorry? Well, perhaps not all of us. Actually, if you press me, I'll admit that I don't think I know anybody else who does like George Formby films, even if no less an authority than Thora Hird once declared him to be 'a legend sent by God', a sentiment I compare with the look on my wife's face if I try to play my CD featuring 'Leaning on a Lamp Post'.

Still, when I asked David Bret, George's biographer, about 'The Lancashire Toreador', he told me that it was probably written to be part of the bullfighter film George had always wanted to make but never did, something along the lines of Valentino's *Blood and Sand*. No, really. George was, as I've said, something of a gay icon. David Bret says that *Bell-Bottom George*, his wartime Navy film, 'is also unique in that the majority of the cast and almost every one of the male extras were unashamedly gay . . . and the scene in which George sings, "It Serves you Right", surrounded by a bevy of well-proportioned, posing matelots, was a potent exercise in camp homoeroticism revered by George's surprisingly large, closeted gay following in wartime Britain – as indeed is the whole film.' Oooh!

We really should get back to Frank, but I must tell you a few other interesting things about George. You might know that he died only three months after his formidable wife of 36 years, Beryl. You might also know that he almost got married again on his deathbed. But did you know that his fiancée left a large part of the royalties from his songs – such masterpieces of double entendre as 'With My Little Ukulele in My Hand', 'You Can't Keep a Growing Lad Down' and 'With My Little Stick of Blackpool Rock' – to a convent near Wigan? Or that Yana, the statuesque '60s songstress, had an affair with him on the rebound from her gay lover? Or that one of Beryl's favourite forms of address was 'Who's pissed on your chips?' Or that George very nearly made a movie of Strindberg's *Miss Julie*, in Swedish? Ooh! Perhaps my favourite, though, is that one of George's big hits, 'Auntie Maggie's Remedy', had been written by his undertaker.

But we are back now, in the garage under the hotel in Fuengirola, where Frank was saying, 'I carry on because I love the applause, because I would be bored if I didn't, because I want to keep in touch with my youth, because I want to master this thing and because I'm a fucking egomaniac.' And, he was also saying, there was a promoter from Madrid coming to watch him tomorrow. The dream was still there.

Today, though, there was rest and lunch. And that continuing tension between Salford and Spain. Frank drove us through Fuengirola, past the Three Lions pub, the Old Bailey pub, the Chequers Golf Bar, the Shakespeare ('under new management'; do you ever wonder what horrors lie behind that message?) and the Rose and Crown, advertising the best Tetley in town (note that: how many Tetley outlets can there be?).

Gaspar Jimenez, the promoter at Benalmadena, which is the next resort up the road, was a big supporter of Frank, seeing him as a potent draw for the Brit holidaymakers and the retirees crowding the area. A rather splendid mural of El Inglés had just appeared on the outside of the ring. Frank, meanwhile, was being bothered about business on his mobile phone. 'Don't talk to me about hotels,' he said, employing a line that cannot be employed by too many British entrepreneurs, 'I've got two bulls to kill tomorrow.'

We lunched at an excellent seafood restaurant on the front at Fuengirola. Frank explained that tomorrow it would be just scrambled eggs, in case he needed to be operated on. We touched on courage. 'My first corrida was in Montpelier. It was all a blur. They weren't that keen on an Englishman fighting, but I'd trained, I'd been taught, I'd got my licence from Madrid. But nothing quite prepares you for the real thing. I found, though, that I could stand still, confront the bull. I had it. A lot don't. It's accepted that you must have it, have that kind of courage. What the Spaniards say is that if you haven't got it, what are you doing down there, because you're going to get paid and we're paying to watch you do it.

'If there's no element of danger, then there's no emotion. And it's emotion that makes the corrida. Of course there's a risk, but I train every day, I work on my fitness, I practise my passes. I know a lot about bullfighting. I know what I'm up to. I have a good reputation with the sword and I take it very, very seriously. But you're taking on an unpredictable animal that could kill you. Every now and then you can make a mistake, and you do make a mistake. You need to be lucky.' So far, Frank has been gored only once, training, on a finca, up his backside, miraculously little damage, mostly due to it being a clean bull's-eye, if you follow. (If you don't: 'It went straight up my arse.')

We talked, too, about the cruelty to the animal. 'The bull definitely feels frightened,' said Frank. 'It's because he feels frightened that he attacks. If anything troubles me, it's that. But at the end of the day, the species is bred to sit on somebody's plate, and to get it onto the plate, it has to go through something a bit nasty, whether it's the bullring or the slaughterhouse.' It was the same, he said, with fox-hunting: there were people who objected to the killing of something being accompanied by enjoyment. What would he say to them? 'Bollocks,' said Frank.

Frank has had hate mail, and an intercepted letter bomb. Animal-rights protesters have demonstrated outside his home. 'I don't know why they did that. I know where I live, my neighbours know where I live. They'd have been better off doing it in the centre of Manchester.' Actually, he'd had this idea about putting a bullfight on at the old Belle Vue stadium in Manchester, but there had been a certain amount of opposition.

The main course arrived. It was a rather tasty piece of fish. Frank mentioned that he had once thrown a live lobster he had ordered back into the sea because he had suddenly felt sorry for it. 'I was even more sorry,' he said, 'when I found out it was 1,100 pesetas per gram, not for the whole thing.' Did I mention that Frank started out butchering with his father?

He moved on rapidly to a story involving a promoter in some small-town ring not wanting to pay him his money, and the Mayor getting involved, and Frank getting out of town rather quickly. Then he talked about how the previous year had been a very bad one for gorings, with much graphic description of horns going in here and coming out there, and bullfighters touched with premonition and forebodings.

And every so often Frank would return to talking about the two bulls he was going to face the next day, worrying about them in the way a cricketer worries about the pitch, or the weather. He was desperate to impress the Man from Madrid, and a lot depended on the bulls. A hesitant bull means that the matador cannot build up any rhythm, provide any form to the series of passes that leads up to the killing of the bull, display the art that is as important as his courage and his skill with the kill. A strong bull, unwilling to take direction in the choreography of its death, can have the same effect.

But I couldn't see any nervousness in Frank. 'Some people play golf at weekends,' he said. 'I get chased by bulls.' We went up to the bullring to see the new mural of Frank, which he posed beside for photographs. The bullfight was due to start the next day at 5 p.m. Someone, it might have been me, made a weak joke about it being 'Death at teatime, then'. Everybody laughed. 'Don't forget that refers to the bull,' said Frank. I started wondering how whimsical it would be if Frank were to end up on the same bill as Joselito and Manolete at teatime tomorrow.

The next morning, we went up to the bullring for the *sorteo*, the allocation of the bulls. Benalmadena, it is fair to say, is not in the front rank of bullrings. The bill was a mixed one: Frank was the only full professional; the other two toreros were young novices. But the Man from Madrid had telephoned; he was coming down despite a cough and cold. We watched from above as the bulls were coaxed and goaded from the pen at the back of the bullring into their large, numbered, trap-like stables.

There was a hubbub and huddle from which Frank stayed slightly detached: members of the *cuadrillas*, or teams, the *banderilleros*, the *picadors*, still in mufti, various interested parties meeting with Gaspar Jimenez, the promoter, in his office, forms to be signed, cash handed over, and various aficionados, several of whom turned out to be British, some visiting and some resident. I've talked before about how it is when hobbyists gather together; I preferred the Sons of the Desert to the Anglo Aficionados. A little too ready with the animal-rights lines – 'The bull has had four or five years of absolute bliss on the best pastures in Spain. The average head of cattle is lucky to see 12 to 18 months penned up . . . I don't think this is as cruel as the meat you pick up in Sainsbury's . . . If it wasn't for this business, there wouldn't be an animal like the fighting bull. It wouldn't exist.' – and a bit too serious for me. Still, it's not every day an estate agent hands you a list of the matadors who have made him weep with emotion.

Frank wasn't on it, though they were proud of their boy, if a little dismissive of the venue. Gaspar, meanwhile, having done his morning business, was celebrating his birthday with a paella, cooked by his charming wife, whose talents also included killing bulls (she had been one of the very few female matadors). Gaspar said that Frank was an '*ebulliente*' matador, with '*fuerte*' (loose transation: Frank has *cojones*). Manuel Fernandez Maldonaldo, from the local TV station, also enjoying the paella, said Frank had a '*corazon grande*' (loose translation: Frank has *cojones*).

And Frank, Frank had gone back to the hotel for the scrambled eggs. Frank today was much more Spanish Frank than Salford Frank. I was reminded of the great Lorca's description of the bullfight as 'the last serious thing'. And of this, from Hemingway: that American sports lovers 'are not fascinated by death, its nearness or avoidance. We are fascinated by victory, and we replace the avoidance of death by the avoidance of defeat. It is a very nice symbolism, but it takes more *cojones* to be a sportsman when death is a closer party to the game.'

So I didn't laugh, giggle or even smirk as I watched Frank being dressed for the fight by Matthias, his sword-handler, straining to get into his scarlet suit of lights and pink stockings. I didn't look knowingly at Frank's glass case with his rosary and holy cards inside it. And I didn't laugh, either, when we went back down to the underground garage and Frank practised his passes on his chief banderillero, Moreno, who charged him with two horns attached to a black binliner to act as the bull's head, making all the right grunts.

And I certainly didn't laugh as Francisco, Frank's trainer, drove me to the bullfight using only the hand that hadn't been bitten by a dog, leaving the steering wheel to its own devices while he changed gear. Frank was being driven in a slightly more seemly fashion by his son Matthew, one of the rugby league players, who had flown in with a friend that lunchtime. At the Plaza de Toros, the crowd was building up nicely, considering it was January. The aficionados were there, and so was this young English boy, David, in his early teens, parents living on the Costa, who wanted to be a matador, which seemed odd, as he wasn't even from Lancashire.

The Man from Madrid had arrived, too, satisfyingly *ebulliente* in the promoter's universal standard kit of camel-hair coat and cigar. I may be imagining it at this remove, of course, but I'm pretty sure he had the coat draped round his shoulders.

There was another hubbub of huddles in the *patio de caballos*, the yard where the matadors and their cuadrillas wait to be summoned into the ring, the banderilleros splendidly subverting their ornate outfits with last snatched cigarettes. And then they were on, following the *Alguacil*, the mounted master of ceremonies, into the ring, accompanied by the small band up in the stand blaring out a brassy *paso doble* of just the right raggedness. It was cold, but the sun was still out. The stands were only about a quarter full, though.

I don't remember much about the first bull, taken by Frank as the senior man. This was only my second bullfight, the first years ago, in Nîmes, and it takes a bit of time to get your eye in. I remember the bull suddenly arriving in the ring, black, solid, threatening, and bringing with it, for me, the sudden realisation that the fight was going to happen and it hadn't all been an elaborate charade which would make a nice chapter for my book. I remember watching Moreno and the other banderilleros feinting at the bull with their capes and then sprinting away to give Frank, watching now from behind the *barrera*, the chin-high wooden barrier that runs round the ring, clues about how it would fight. And I remember Moreno jumping in front of the bull and reaching over the horns to place the first banderillas in the bull's withers, and, slightly, the mounted picador screwing his lance into the bull like some sort of giant bradawl.

But Frank's passes, this way and that, and the kill, aren't really there in my memory, which throws up mostly the bull at one point pawing the ground in accepted cartoon fashion, but then going into reverse, and the flurry of white handkerchiefs as the aficionados showed the approval which would grant Frank an ear. And I remember Moreno sawing it off with a small sharp knife, then wiping the knife on the carcass, and the carcass being dragged off, one leg still twitching, by a man on horseback.

I remember the next torero, a perfect contrast to Frank, tall and dark and slender in his impossibly turquoise, impossibly tight suit of lights, the very model of a matador, enough to satisfy Goya, Picasso, even perhaps Hemingway, drawing himself up on his toes, narrowing his eyes above his impossibly sharp and angled cheekbones, showing his teeth in a sneer of impossibly donnish disdain, and barking, '*Toro*!' And I remember Frank watching, and giving his verdict on his first effort, 'Shit bull, wasn't it?'

The British aficionados were not impressed with the young, beautiful bullfighter, and, as if to prove them right, he took one risk too many and found himself slapped to the ground by a horn. The banderilleros were out from behind the barrera in an instant, drawing the bull away from the downed matador with their large capes. He got up gingerly and continued. Before arriving in Spain, I had spoken to Bill Lyon, doyen of American aficionados, domiciled in Madrid. 'Whatever you do,' Bill had said to me, 'just promise me you won't call it a sport. Call it a spectacle, but don't call it a sport. It's not a sport, because the bull dies.'

The bull dies. The young bullfighter was not making a very good fist of it. He was trying to plunge his *estoque*, the killing sword, into the small area between the bull's withers which allows a way into the heart. He couldn't find it, though, and had to use another, heavier sword, the *descabello*, to sever the spine, which, finally, after several jabs, he managed. The bull bellowed and fell. The bellow was a shock, because it was the bull's first, a loud cry of woe. The small knife was used again to finish him off.

The sun was still out, but it was getting chillier. Matthew, Frank's son, was sitting with his friend, Gary, reading text messages about soccer scores back at home. Earlier, Frank had said a lot of the smaller bullrings reminded him of Doncaster rugby league ground on a foggy Saturday afternoon. It seemed clear to me that the spectacle and style and operatic quality that reduces men to tears would be easier to appreciate on a simmering afternoon in Seville than in a small ring on the Costa del Sol a quarter full with 300 people on a late afternoon turning chilly with bewildered bulls and botched killings.

Frank's second bull was not like his first. The first liked to reverse; the second didn't seem to know how to. Frank went through his passes, but the bull wouldn't play. It crowded Frank, keeping tight in on him, turning back too quickly after going through the cape, not allowing Frank any grace or poise. At one point, Frank, frustrated, stopped, and the bull stopped too, leaving them facing each other, both blowing hard.

The Man from Madrid was shouting advice. Francisco, Frank's trainer, was shouting advice. Frank decided that he would get no further with this bull. He went for the kill. To kill, to hit that spot, he must reach over the bull's horns to sink the blade, exposing his body fully to the horns. This is the famous Moment of Truth. Frank trailed his cape on the ground to make the bull lower his head, and went for it. But he went too high, and the estoque hit bone and bounced out. It hit the ground along with Frank's cape. The bull charged and Frank sprinted for it; you could see he used to be a winger, dodgy left knee or not. Oooh!

I think I began to understand the bullfight better then; and without wishing to get too metaphorical, too life and death, or even too Spanish on you, I could see, all the same, that the slightly raggedy band, the slightly tacky suiting, the proud poses and the sudden indignities captured much of humanity's mix and mess of seriousness and farce, grace and brutality, courage and fear, nobility and pointlessness, its need to challenge, to dominate. Oooh, indeed.

Frank tried again. This time the sword went in deep. But the bull wouldn't die. Frank finished it off with the *descabello*. There were no white handkerchiefs this time. And he had been given an *aviso*, a warning for taking too long.

It was getting dark. The beautiful young matador fought as bravely and flashily as before, went down again, botched the kill again. The third matador, whose bottom did look too big in a suit of lights, was, nevertheless, a local lad, and got carried off in triumph. Over in the tourist stands, there were, despite Gaspar's hopes, few British onlookers. Quite a lot of Americans had turned up, but they hadn't realised that El Inglés was English. I asked Matthew if he or his brother had ever fancied a go. 'No,' he said. Frank's wife, Margaret, isn't keen, either. She stays in Salford. 'You don't want your wife coming to the office, do you?' But he did call her on the mobile after the second bull, as emotional as a commuter. 'I'm at the bullfight.'

Afterwards, Frank was a bit detached, 'mildly pissed off' about the corrida. 'The first bull didn't want to fight, and the second one didn't want to stop.' Still, the Man from Madrid hadn't been entirely dismissive; there was still some sort of chance. We drove back to the hotel. 'For God's sake, Matthew,' said the man who had just fought two bulls, 'Slow down! Why do you have to go so fast? Don't drive so close to that car in front! Matthew, slow down!'

Chapter Nine

523 Seconds

A brief encounter with *Brief Encounter*

Don't tell me you haven't heard of *Brief Encounter*. Even if you haven't seen it, mid-afternoon, rain outside, or late at night, minority channel, or videoed it at either time, you will surely know enough about it to attempt a brief *rencontre*. Middle-aged, middle-class woman from Middle England, Home Counties Division, wonderful vowels, married to marvellous husband, solid, steady, reliable, with two sweet children, one of each, falls for nice doctor at railway station, goes out with him a couple of times, but doesn't do the indecent thing. Sacrifice, restraint, duty. Written by Noel Coward, directed by David Lean. Lots of loud piano music. Light relief from comedy couple in the station buffet, lots of trains.

No, I'm not a big fan. I do like old films, though, generally. Particularly, I like old films if Joseph Cotton, Cary Grant, James Stewart, William Holden, Burt Lancaster, Alec Guinness, Audrey Hepburn, Marilyn Monroe, Ava Gardner, Frank Sinatra, Sophia Loren, Fred Astaire, Jack Lemmon, Bob

245

Hope, Groucho Marx, Carole Lombard, Gene Kelly, Peter Sellers, Kenneth More, Peter Lorre, Humphrey Bogart, Orson Welles or George Formby are in them, or if John Ford, Howard Hawks or Preston Sturges made them. I like David Lean's other films, too, up to *Lawrence*. I like Noel Coward, when he's not serious.

Coward, of course, as you might expect, owes much to Lancashire: his early mentor was a typically eccentric Lancastrian of wide and musical tastes, Ned, the third and last Earl of Lathom, who died young, tubercular and penniless after spending his money on the theatre and ancillary activities like entertaining Coward, Ivor Novello, Beverley Nichols and many others at his Lancashire home, Blythe Hall, obvious inspiration for *Blithe Spirit*. The details I like best are that footmen used to be dispatched to London by sleeper for chocolate almonds; and that the earl had had his own special perfume, 'Suivez-moi, Jeune Homme'. Very French, very Lancs. (And it also rather reminds me of the French Navy's famous anthem, 'A l'Eau, C'est l'Heure!' Unfamiliar to you? Try saying it out loud.)

After Ned died, Blythe Hall eventually ended up in the hands of a Catholic order, the Passionists; make of that what you will, although I should add that my mother and father helped put on fund-raising dances there which were most decorous and lacking in any sort of chocolate almond, thank you very much, although a road haulier did once fall into the earl's neo-classical swimming-pool.

I like *Blithe Spirit*, though. I like the Coward and Lean *Blithe Spirit*, too, even if they didn't. 'You have just fucked up the best thing I ever wrote,' Coward said to Lean after he'd seen it for the first time. 'I'm sorry,' said Lean. But I like Rex Harrison in it, and Margaret Rutherford. Did you know that Rex was from Lancashire, Huyton, near Liverpool? He was; his family, depending on whether you asked Rex or somebody else, were lawyers, insurers or butchers. He was also the local champion ballroom dancer. When I asked him about it many years later, in his fine suite at the Ritz, and even finer suit, a shimmer of dark green, he wasn't very forthcoming, but then he wasn't very forthcoming about anything, including why he had been married so many times. 'I married my mistakes,' he said, eyeing me coldly through the magnificent wreckage of the face he deserved. 'I didn't have to live with them.' Robert Morley fared better; to him, Rex lamented 'my wretched marriages', continuing, 'How different from you, only one wife . . . and, if I may say so, only one performance.' One of his ex-wives, Elizabeth, said Rex was the only man she had known who sent back the wine in his own house. When he was knighted, he complained that, 'The Queen wasn't properly briefed, she didn't seem to know who I was.' He had a house in Italy, where he insisted on driving mostly on the left. His final words, on his deathbed, to his son Noel, the one who had that hit with 'Windmills of Your Mind', were: 'You never could play the guitar.' Marvellous, and proof that you can take the Lancashire out of the man.

But, *Brief Encounter*. I can't engage with Celia Johnson and her Laura Jesson. I know I'm supposed to sympathise with her dithering between duty and desire, convention and Cupid, but I don't, even though I can see it was a brave film to make, and a brave story to write, especially because Coward and Lean subvert her sacrifice by having her ready to fling herself under a passing express à la Karenina, but making her fail through cowardice, not duty. Perhaps that's the subversion too far, making it too complicated, too much like life. Certainly, that seems to be the bit that's overlooked in all the talk of restraint and responsibility.

So I'm left thinking about how much better the original thought, Roger Livesey, would have been than the improbably and wildly wet Trevor Howard; about the splendour of the Rachmaninov score; about what an unexpectedly fine pair of legs

Celia had; and about what it would have been like without the trains, the station and the buffet.

Carnforth nearly found out. Carnforth, minutes from Lancaster, not far from Morecambe and the Bay, provided the station used by Lean as his model for Milford, the town of the film. You might be a little surprised by this, not because Lancashire doesn't strike you as the ideal romantic setting, but because Milford seems so very suburban and home county. *Brief Encounter*, though, was made in 1945, and there were worries about lights and bombs if filming took place in the south. Celia wasn't looking forward to it: 'We have to go up north for four weeks' location on some horrible railway station.' But, much warmed by the stationmaster and his fire, she found she quite liked it. 'You'd think there could be nothing more dreary than spending ten hours on a railway station platform every night,' she wrote, 'but we do the whole thing in the acme of luxury and sit drinking occasional brandies and rushing out now and again to see the expresses roaring through . . . all the guards and porters and people are most awfully nice.' Everybody liked Celia, apparently, even if she wasn't that keen on the food, but Trevor Howard was thought a little stand-offish. (Trevor did have a position to maintain; it emerged recently that he'd invented most of his service record, and had to be quietly warned to stop boasting about a non-existent MC. Nor were his colleagues too impressed by the intellectual rigour he brought to the part: 'Why doesn't he just go on and fuck her?')

When Lean gave *Brief Encounter* its first showing, in Rochester, the audience laughed. But they didn't laugh in the North, thank you, or anywhere else. It remains one of the most praised and successful British films; even the French like it, if only because it confirms their prejudices about British inhibitions. That, though, is as nothing to the acclaim it has received in Japan, where, you will be endlessly assured,

248

particularly in Carnforth, it is considered a vital illustration of correct social behaviour, and, according to persistent legend, is still on show daily in a Tokyo cinema.

Carnforth station did not fare so well. Dr Beeching and the Death of Steam pretty well did for it. The great marshalling yard of what had been one of Britain's major junctions stilled and rusted. That was diesel: when electrification came, the north–south west-coast mainline trains stopped stopping, and the platforms were taken away. Soon the station buildings, including the famous refreshment rooms, were closed and boarded, and Carnforth was just 'an unmanned operational station on the Furness to Leeds line'. All was waving weeds, peeling decay and broken glass. The clock, so urgently watched by Celia and Trevor, had not only stopped, it had been sold off. Carnforth's time had gone. They were going to knock everything down. That totem of progress, a supermarket, was planned.

I restrained myself there from adding 'and dreams' or possibly 'and memories' after 'broken glass'; nevertheless, you will get the picture. The scene was set. Enter Peter Yates, local garage owner, then chairman of the local chamber of trade, looking for a project to help the town. The previous chairman had built a new toilet block; Peter was about to become director and producer of the Carnforth revival. The Carnforth Station and Railway Trust was formed. A 99-year lease was taken out on the buildings. Money rolled in, slowly, then more quickly. Grants came in from the regional economic and tourism agencies. More than a million of the £1.5 million restoration costs have now been raised. The entrance buildings and ticket office have been restored, and the great thing, the resonant, redolent thing, the Brief Encounter Tearoom; next will be the David Lean Tribute exhibition and the Brief Encounter Trail. In short, it is the very model of those countless tourist/heritage projects you must have read about and, if you have children, visited by the score.

Except that there seems to be something more about Carnforth, something that happens, perhaps, when the fanaticism and romance of film meets the fanaticism and romance of steam. Take, for example, the clock, which is back now, repaired. But it wasn't just any repair: its replacement electrical bits have been thrown out in favour of the original workings, discovered – after the most dogged, tireless detective work going from dealer to dealer, from false lead to good one – in a shed on the banks of the Thames at Twickenham.

I think it's a lot to do with Peter Yates. It was Peter, of course, who helped track down the clock parts. But there's more to Peter than the essential restoration enthusiast's qualities of doggedness and attention to detail. Peter is not so much romantic as mystical about Carnforth Station. The station is in his soul. It worried him. In 1992, he was watching the Cup final between Liverpool and Sunderland on the television when he was suddenly moved to get up and go down to the station, and not just because it was a dull game. 'When I came down there were five Japanese tourists stood under the clock having their picture taken. And I thought that if somebody was prepared to come halfway round the world to have their picture taken under a derelict clock in a derelict station, something had to be done.'

Do you remember that baseball movie with Kevin Costner where he is moved by ghosts and voices to build a baseball stadium in the middle of nowhere? 'If you build it, they will come,' the voices said. Maybe I was a little bit carried away, but Peter, at the station, slight, smeared of face, in his overalls, earnest behind his glasses, in between yet another recovery trip with his breakdown truck on the nearby M6, rather reminded me of that. If you rebuild it, they will come, though, in his case.

Obviously, the Japanese were important in all this, practically and mystically. I hadn't seen any while I'd been at the station, but it was still quite early. Peter showed me round, even though he was a bit pressed. The station was taking up too much of his time. 'The wife's not happy, not happy at all . . . You get trapped, don't you? You start something and you've just got to finish it . . . I'm just trying to save a little bit of what there was. When you think of all the history and all the lives that have gone through this station, it was a tragedy to see it in ruins. We've got to save the best of what was there . . . From the past you see the future. The future comes out of the past.' Peter was warming to his dream; the M6 and its cold hard shoulder were far away, the message of *Brief Encounter* was close at hand. 'Let's try and get those old-fashioned values back,' he said. 'We definitely need them, things like restraint and decency and respectability, all the things that you and I were taught as kids and kids have forgotten today or have never been taught, people caring for others, niceness, humour. We should all be sociable and say hello to each other, not like down south, if you say hello to them down there they look at you as if you've crawled out from under a stone . . . hello?'

Peter's mobile had gone off. The M6 was calling. 'I've spent a lot of my life on the M6,' he said, leaving. 'Between junctions 34 and 36. My wife's going to scatter my ashes on the M6. Then they're going to get stuck in someone's exhaust, and a green young mechanic is going to be called out on his first job. It's the cycle, isn't it? Everything goes in cycles.' I told you he was a mystic.

I wandered round the station. There were still no Japanese. It was in colour, not black and white, and there were no steam trains; I was having difficulty summoning Celia and Trevor. I concentrated hard on the spot Peter had shown me, where they had said one of their aching, tremulous goodbyes, but in vain. I should tell you, though, that you are in the company of a man who once spent the night alone in the Chamber of Horrors at

Madame Tussaud's and didn't experience very much then, either.

Mr Waring, retired school bursar from Grange-over-Sands, was waiting for a train with his bicycle, in hard hat and shorts. I asked him where he was going. 'John O'Groats,' he said. 'I'm on the way from Land's End, but I stopped off at home for two years.' It was going to take him about nine days, he said. He liked bicycle touring, he said, because it was the right speed to see the countryside. He'd be staying in B&Bs, or a hostel if he got short of company. Oh, yes, he knew they'd filmed *Brief Encounter* at the station, but he'd never really thought of Carnforth as romantic, more as a transit sort of place. Did he know that Lancashire was the county where women died of love? Mr Waring liked that. 'Die for love, don't you mean? You'd better ask the wife.' Where was she? 'Playing golf,' said Mr Waring. Mrs Young, at the other end of the bench, said she was proud to be from Lancashire. 'It's got a sense of humour,' she said. 'And they're the type of people who'd share their last crust with you.' Mrs Young was from Crosby, but she was widowed now, and living with her daughter in Arnside, nearby. It was lovely, she said, but she did miss her old friends a bit.

Their train came and went, leaving a quiet station behind. I took a turn up the High Street, an upward-curving, small-shopped kind of a street, its air of best Northern no-nonsense relieved by the boasting (entirely justified) of the local sausage-maker and the splendidly entitled Naughty But Nice Bakery and Coffee Shop, which I entered immediately.

There are those who find the badinage in *Brief Encounter* between Stanley Holloway's cheeky-cheery cockney railwayman and Joyce Carey's effortfully preserved and mock-posh refreshments-room manageress a bit grating. Coward saw it as essential to counterpoint and ease the tension, as with Shakespeare's mechanicals. I rather like it, particularly when Holloway grabs Carey for a kiss across the counter and knocks over a pile of cakes and Carey says, 'Now look at me Banburys, all over the floor.'

But then I do enjoy an eavesdrop, although I haven't ever done as well as my wife, who was behind two women in their fifties on the No. 159 from Brixton to Oxford Street discussing their respective husbands: 'He bothered me again last night.' Or, for that matter, my mother, in a pub near Frinton, at the next table to a little girl with a teddy bear and her parents, who were talking about a recent trip to London. The girl looked at her teddy and announced, to no one in particular, in a resigned kind of way, 'Poor little bugger's never even been to Colchester.' I've always liked that. I should clear up, though, while we're on Stanley Holloway, that there was nothing Lancastrian about him, even if he did do 'Albert and the Lion' and 'Sam, Sam, Pick Up Tha' Musket'. But I can tell you that he wanted to be an opera singer, if that's any use. And that, unsurprisingly, Rex Harrison couldn't stand him. There was rather too much of the music hall in him for Rex; and rather too much of Holloway in *My Fair Lady*.

'Salad cream or mayonnaise with the ham salad sandwich?' said the girl behind the counter in the Naughty But Nice Bakery and Coffee Shop. 'Aren't they the same?' asked the customer in the overalls. 'No,' said the girl. 'I'll just have to guess, then.' 'Salad cream,' said the customer in the overalls. Not Stanley and Joyce, I grant you, but it does give the flavour. The girl was called Vanessa. She didn't think there was a great deal of interest in Carnforth in *Brief Encounter*, not among her generation, anyway. Sharon was also serving. She agreed. But, she said, she had bought the film last year: 'It was on special offer at Asda.' What had she made of it? 'I haven't watched it yet,' she said. And Carnforth, I asked, was it a romantic place? 'There are,' said Sharon, or it might have been Vanessa, 'no interesting men round here.' I left.

In the bookshop, I asked the man at the counter if he had a

book by the local celebrity, Roddy Wright. He was from the second-hand department upstairs, helping out, and he didn't know what I was talking about. You know, I said, the Catholic bishop from Scotland who ran off with the divorcee. He'd settled in Carnforth and written his autobiography. 'That's a bit of local gossip that's escaped me,' said the second-hand bookseller.

Honestly. What sort of priorities did he have? Here was the sort of conjunction that any journalist with the slightest pretension towards significant social comment would put both his arms, legs and nose in the door for; here was as fine an example imaginable of journalism's greatest grail, that which we call 'Irony'. Give us irony and we are content. Balzac agreed. He said irony was the essence of the character of Providence. And here was a man, a bishop, no less, who had abandoned duty for love and then settled in the setting for the country's most famous film of the exact reverse. Why, it's almost as good as David Lean's father leaving his mother when Lean was a teenager and almost as good as Lean leaving his first wife and two-year-old son for a girl he had met on his honeymoon. Lean left five wives in all, two more even than Rex. 'I've never seen a man . . . who was in more of a subconscious dilemma between his sensuality and his strict sense of morality,' said Anthony Havelock-Allan, the producer of *Brief Encounter*.

None of this, however, is as good as my all-time favourite head-shaking, wry-smiling irony: did you know that the man who wrote 'Pack Up Your Troubles in Your Old Kit Bag and Smile, Smile, Smile' killed himself? I could tell you about it, but it's a long story and, as you might imagine, rather sad.

But, the Bishop: why would he come to Carnforth? In defiance, or to punish himself further? Surely he couldn't have been ignorant of the irony? Unfortunately, the bookshop hadn't got a copy of his autobiography, *Feet of Clay*, but I did order one, before having a wander around the estate, Cragbank, where he had bought a house. One of the roads was called Jesson Way, after Celia's character. At the post office, there was a little note advertising the Jesson Clinic: 'Modern Acupuncture. Remedial Massage'.

As you can see, it can be difficult to turn the irony detector down once it gets going. On the way back to the station, I pondered on the new Brief Encounter Tearoom. The exterior of the refreshments room in the film was, in fact, 'flats' specially erected on the station. The interior was a set at Denham Studios. So the reconstructed tearoom is based on the set which was based on the tearoom. I should also tell you that the Station Trust's archivist, Peter Davies, has calculated, painstakingly, how much of *Brief Encounter* was filmed at Carnforth: only 523 out of the 4,920 seconds.

If you rebuild it, they will come. Peter Yates met me at the station, with the visitors' books. There were a lot of entries, including two from Japanese visitors, which a local lady had translated. The first had written, 'I have seen the film in Japan.' The second had written, 'I've found Europe thrilling and will see the film in Japan.' And he'd added a Japanese proverb: 'In travelling, a companion. In life, sympathy.' I was reminded of the account written by Mizuhiko Yamaguchi, a journalist with the *Yomiuri Shimbun* newspaper, of Tokyo, in which he described his visit to Carnforth in 1988. '"How is it that such a typically English film attracts such interest from the Japanese?" I was asked during an interview by the local broadcasting company on the platform. As I turned to the microphone to answer, an express train passed triumphantly through the station.' And that's how he ended his piece. Splendid. They're also very keen on Beatrix Potter, you know: up in the Lakes, there is even Japanese signage to her old home at Near Sawrey. (Sawrey was just inside the old Lost Lancashire border, too, but to be honest, speaking after too many bad bedtimes with impenetrable

Nutkins and twee Tittlemice, Cumbria and Tokyo are welcome to her.)

Peter was in a hurry. He was, though, plainly used to a bit of scepticism about the Japanese. 'They were all accusing me of making it up. And then, one Civic Sunday, everyone was gathered in front of the council offices, waiting for the parade. And suddenly this coach appears, and the driver asks, "Where is the station?", and then everybody can see there are Japanese hanging out of its every orifice.' Not for the first time, the thought occured that this would all make the most terrific film.

Peter was now describing his further vision. Of course they would come. And not just the romantic romantics, but the steam romantics, too. What he wanted now was to get the mainline trains stopping again, to put back the platforms. And then there were the plans for the old marshalling yards, in private hands at the moment, used for steam train repair and servicing. Why, over there, in a shed, was nothing less than Harry Potter's school train, the Hogwarts Express. Contractual, copyright and lots of other problems at the moment, but Peter was confident it would all be sorted, eventually. The Hogwarts Express! I was seized by a vision of the ultimate all-family themed film experience: *Harry Potter* and *Brief Encounter*; surely room could be made, too, for *The Railway Children*, *The Great Escape*, *The Lady Vanishes*, *The 39 Steps*, *Oh, Mr Porter!*, and, of course, *Thomas the Tank Engine* and *Trainspotting*. I was about to share it with Peter, but he had to get back to the M6.

They're another breed, railway people, aren't they? This is a friend of the station, Richard Crane, describing the last steam train to pass through it:

> The clank of the motion, the squeal of the wheels, the
> smile from the soot-stained face of the driver, another

hoot on the whistle, a bark from the chimney as the train gathered pace after crossing over and passing through Carnforth's long, curving platforms . . . More than 30 years have passed but the image of that last freight train has never paled from my mind and the very thought of it still sets my heart racing.

Remember, then, next time you see those people at the end of the platform with notebooks, what beats beneath the anorak. Remember, too, that Paul Simon wrote *Homeward Bound* in Lancashire, sitting at Widnes North railway station, and I know what he meant, as that was the one I used to wait on to go away to school, although I don't remember seeing him there.

I went off to see Elaine Maudsley. Mrs Maudsley, now in her seventies, deserves a full footnote in the History of Modern Celebrity. At the beginning of *Brief Encounter*, Stanley Holloway watches the express pass through Milford Junction, checks the time on his fob watch with an approving smile, then jumps down from the platform, crosses the line and clambers up on to the opposite platform. Behind him, further up the platform, is Elaine Maudsley. No doubt Peter the Archivist would be more precise, but I calculate that she appears for 12 seconds. That is the part Elaine played in her brief encounter with *Brief Encounter*.

I asked her, in her pin-neat, freshly plumped home in Carnforth, how many times had she been interviewed about it? 'Oh, my goodness me!' sighed Mrs Maudsley. 'I wouldn't know. I've been in magazines, on television, and in practically every newspaper, except *The Times* and the *Daily Telegraph*. And you are?'

Elaine had been working on Carnforth Station, in the book stall, since she was 14. When the war broke out, she wanted to join up, but her mother was ill and her four brothers were away fighting, so she was asked to work in the refreshments room at the station, which she did throughout the war. 'I loved working on the station. I thought it was a lovely, lovely place. It was always bustling, always plenty going on. There were boys going home, and tears when people were seeing them back off to the War again. Yes, it was a romantic place, very romantic.'

It was her friend who worked with her in the refreshments room who suggested that she ought to do something in the film. The crew used the room, and so it was arranged. She should have been nearer to the camera, but Stanley Holloway kept grabbing her ankle as he clambered up during rehearsals. 'I was quite young and attractive in those days,' said Elaine, elegant in powder-blue cardigan, matching slacks and gold sandals, hair just done. 'Stanley Holloway was a bit of a joker, and he kept doing it, so they said, "Elaine, I think we'd better have you out of his way, go a bit further down." And that was it. To be perfectly honest, I wasn't in any way star-struck. These things meant nothing to me. I used to laugh and say, "You do know you're talking to a film star," just stupid nonsense, really, and I never thought much about it after that. It's been more exciting since, although I'm getting bored with the interviews now. I did Victoria Wood, you know, for *Great Railway Journeys*, she interviewed me down at the station, and *Woman's Weekly* did a lovely article one Christmas.

'Yes, I think it's a lovely film, but I wouldn't say it was my favourite. I like *Casablanca*, I like most films of that era, *Mrs Miniver* and that sort. I'd have loved to have been an actress, I was in the local drama group, but you don't get chances like that.'

So Elaine kept working at the station. And met her husband, John, there. 'He was working nearby. He used to come in for his coffee in the morning and his tea in the afternoon. The girl who had got me that part noticed him. She said, "That chap over there's got his eye on you. He won't let anybody else serve him." Anyway, eventually he asked me out. I said "No", I wasn't bothered, I had lots of boyfriends, but he kept persisting, and one day I said "Yes", and we were married for 47 years. It was much against my mother's advice, because he was 16 years older than me, and I was quite flighty, or as flighty as you were in those days, not like today, but it lasted all those years. He was a lovely guy, and I miss him very much.

'John had been one of nine, and I was one of six. He went out to New Zealand when he was 16, under the Church of England scheme that used to place them with families. His father had gone out to New Zealand and promised to come back, but he never did. John saw him out there, but it didn't work. He never talked about it. His brother Ray followed him out, and they both went into the New Zealand Army during the War. Ray was shot dead next to him, in Crete. I kept up writing to the family Ray used to live with. The son still visits, he's a professor at Christchurch University.'

After they were married, John worked for John Menzies at the station for many years. They had two daughters. They got a council house in Carnforth, the one Elaine still rents, and John worked away at the garden. Elaine stays there because it reminds her of him. 'I love the garden, that's why I don't want to leave. I'm doing it now. Sometimes I can't quite work out what to do and I'll say out loud, "Oh, John, why didn't you tell me about that?" People must think I'm crackers if they're listening.'

John died from cancer. She nursed him, and she nursed her friend, too, the one who had got her the part, through her last days. When her friend's husband died, Elaine found they had left her enough money to take a trip to New Zealand, to visit John's old haunts, and Ray's adopted family.

Elaine was waiting for a heart operation. She had, she said, still got some living to do. She had a 'gentleman friend', but no one could replace John. She rose carefully to show me her wedding photograph. They were a handsome couple. 'They used it in *Woman's Weekly*,' she said, proudly. 'He was a lovely, lovely man. I wouldn't say that we didn't have our ups and downs, because we did. I'd just love one day for him to pop his head round the door and say something silly, because that's what he used to do.'

I told Elaine about Lancashire and women dying of love. 'Aah,' she said. 'How sweet! Oh, that's lovely!'

Earlier, at the station, I'd noticed a nun. I do tend to notice nuns, as I was educated by them from the age of four until eight, and I've always rather liked them. I think I've mentioned elsewhere that it was a hesitation to push one out of the way as I raced down some aeroplane steps onto a hot story which convinced me that I would never be a journalist of the very highest calibre. They used to say something similar about Frank Bruno: lacks the killer instinct, too nice. I put this to his manager and trainer, Terry Lawless. 'He's not nice in the ring,' said Lawless. 'Not nice at all.' Sadly, the same could not be said of me.

Anyway, I asked Peter about the nun, and he said she was from a convent at Hyning Hall, just outside Carnforth, and that the nuns there had given some money to the project. Well. This was interesting. Was this their way of supporting the moral values of *Brief Encounter*?

I went to see them. Hyning Hall is a splendidly gracious house which once belonged to the Peel family and is now the Monastery of Our Lady of Hyning, home to a community of 13 Bernardine Cistercian nuns. The Abbess, Sister Mary Lucy, came into the parlour to see me. I thanked her. 'Well, I'm in,' she said, with a smile and a twinkle in her brown eyes, within the wimple. The Bernardine Cistercians are not an enclosed order in the same way as the Carmelites, but they do not 'go tripping out for amusement', as Sister Mary Lucy put it, with another twinkle.

I asked her about the contribution to the station. It was very small, she said, and, no, it was not to do with *Brief Encounter*, which was now rather 'an archive film' that she doubted half the community had ever seen; no, it was because the station was useful to the monastery, for the people who visited it on retreat. 'First and foremost we are a monastery,' she said. 'Our first work is prayer and our community life. What we also try to do is provide a place for those who wish to share in some way in our peace and prayerfulness.'

I complimented Sister Mary Lucy on the beauty of the house. She said, with another smile, that they lived in the old maids' quarters. A group had come to visit from the church built near the ancient Cistercian abbey at Whalley, near Blackburn. 'Now you've seen some living ruins,' Sister Mary Lucy had told them. I told her that I had just been at Hoghton Tower doing some research into Shakespeare, Lancashire and Catholicism. Sister Mary Lucy said that there were some excellent sentiments in Shakespeare, for example the lines, 'What a tangled web we weave, when first we practise to deceive.'

Although I didn't really notice it until later, this last splendidly pointed up the quandary I was in as I sat there: my instincts as a journalist and obsessive ironist were urging me to ask the Abbess about the shamed bishop, while my instincts as a convent-trained irregular Catholic and devout coward were urging me just as hard not to. So I deeply embarrassed myself with some dreadful faltering and waffling about not wishing to embarrass Sister Mary Lucy but wasn't there perhaps an irony about the bishop, Carnforth and *Brief Encounter*, but, please, she mustn't answer if she thought this was all in bad taste, and similar other hawing and haverings, by the end of which I was both sweating and blushing and the Abbess was, of course, completely unfazed. 'Oh,' she said, 'they're long gone. They're up somewhere near Kendal now.' I stumbled through something about it being a sad story. The

261

Abbess agreed that the newspapers were full of sad stories. I persisted with *Brief Encounter*'s message of duty and sacrifice. The Abbess said that duty and sacrifice were not exactly fashionable. I said these things went round in cycles, and no doubt they would be back. The Abbess didn't seem so sure. These old films, she said, were like fairy stories. *Brief Encounter* was very big in Japan, I said.

The Abbess told me she had visited Japan, and Africa. She had been head of the order at one time, but she told me this in a way which was entirely unboastful while also entirely unapologetic, a rare gift. I can't even find the right tone to concede that I was at Oxford. I think it's something to do with the look on Sister Loretta's face when I was six and she asked John Brown who had been the best speller and he answered, 'Myself.' The only person I know who could match Sister Mary Lucy's ease was the late Duke of Norfolk, but he had a rather more robust approach: 'I am – pompous arse, you might say – Earl Marshal of England,' was the way he put it to me.

I asked Sister Mary Lucy why she had become a nun. 'It's always a very difficult thing to say. How does anybody decide, whether they are a doctor, or a solicitor, or a pilot, or whatever? It was something I felt I should do with my life. We've all got a vocation, and we'll only be fulfilled and happy if we respond to that call, whatever it may be.'

She was about to leave Hyning, she said, though she didn't know where she was going or what she'd be doing: 'You don't retire in the order, you get recycled.' I bade her farewell and returned to the station. There was a man outside taking photographs, but he turned out to be a surveyor on the project. If I was interested in visitors, he said, he'd heard that there had been a big coachload of Japanese round the other day.

The man in the bookshop sent me the ex-bishop's confessions. He had come to Carnforth, it turned out, because another priest who had left for love was living there. He noted that *The Times* had drawn the *Brief Encounter* comparison, and called it 'clever', but not in an admiring way: I wouldn't say the ex-Bishop was big on irony. But then that strand of Catholicism is no longer fashionable, although I do remember a fine sermon in Westminster Cathedral recalling the pleas of the Israelites for God to do something after yet another attack by the Chaldeans: 'And God replied, "But I have done something," and the Israelites asked, "What have you done?" And God replied, "I sent the Chaldeans."'

But the Bishop does have a piece of dialogue that makes an interesting comparison with Coward's:

> We sat in my kitchen one day and reached our decision.
> It was a dark, comfortless room at the back of the house,
> not much of a place for making life-changing plans.
>
> As we sat at the old table with our cups of coffee,
> Kathleen spoke: 'Roddy, what are we to do?' I put down
> my cup. 'Kathleen, we can't continue like this. We
> mustn't. Neither of us is living in the real sense!'
>
> 'We have each other,' she said, 'we're certain of that.
> And we have no illusions about what might happen.'
>
> 'I know too well what all of this will cost your family.
> We've spoken of it over and over. Whatever, we must be
> sure of these things. And I know what pain I'll cause my
> own family, and so many others. God knows we've
> prayed and thought about it. We want to be together,
> and that means we must leave. I want us to spend the
> rest of our days together. But what about you, Kathleen?
> Will it cost too much in your life?'
>
> 'Roddy, you know the answer to that very well.'

Kitchen Coward, then, but not a bad alternative ending for Trevor and Celia, all the same. Later, I looked up Sister Mary Lucy's reference to tangled webs and deception, only to find that

I had misunderstood her: it's not Shakespeare, it's Walter Scott. But that's probably enough ironies, even for me.

Besides, we should end without irony, toasting the success of Peter Yates and all his friends and helpers, in the magnificently restored refreshments room, which has just obtained its drinks licence, where Betty and Sheila, volunteers, are doing their bit behind the counter until a professional couple take over on a permanent basis, shortly. When not efficiently dispensing, they are chatting to John, the volunteer guide, who makes sure that *Brief Encounter* plays continuously in one of the display rooms all the time they're open. Take that, Tokyo.

It's not been open for business long, but they've had three Japanese already, they said, so there'll be a lot more soon, when the word spreads. John is from Yorkshire, but he's been in Carnforth for 20 years, so he's a good man to ask about Lancashire and Yorkshire senses of humour. He says that when a Yorkshire person is being funny, you can't always tell, which explains a lot. And then he mentions that the Orient Express passed through the other day, on its way to Barrow, which is having a bit of a renaissance, cruise ships, Gateway to the Lakes, and I feel ashamed for having ever, for a moment, doubted the romance of Lancs.

So I ask Betty and Sheila what they think about Lancs being the county where women die of love, and they're not sure, but they think Lancashire women might be a bit more down to earth than that, like our Gracie. Betty had seen Gracie once, in Rochdale, she said, proudly. I told them my favourite story about Kathleen Ferrier, how, towards the end, recording in Vienna, she had sung Mahler so beautifully for Bruno Walter that there had just been this silence at the end, broken by Ferrier going over to Walter and asking him, 'Was I all right, love?' Everybody likes that. Sheila says they're interesting, these things, aren't they, because in Staffs, where she comes from, they would say, duck, not love. And Betty says, 'It's love in Lancashire.'

Chapter Ten

Bard Beginnings

Or Shakespeare in Lancashire, Love?

I arrived at Hoghton Tower a little late. On the hill, just below the house, next to the long, arrow-straight drive, the battle was all over bar the shouting, one or two loud bangs, and some puffs of smoke. 'Right,' said one of the Roundheads, a touch too loudly, 'everybody die now!' And they did, rather convincingly. The small crowd clapped politely. Another Sunday, another stately home, another Sealed Knot spectacular.

A small, stocky, portly Knotter came over to show everybody the size of his carbine. There are quite a few small, stocky, portly Knotters; at any rate, there seems always to be one when they feature as extras in all these history programmes Dr Starkey and Professor Schama make. This one was a painter and decorator from Preston, and rueing that he was not quite as fit as he once was: 'I used to be able to run around like that all afternoon,' he said. Like all Knotters, he was bang on top of his subject, and very knowledgeable about the tower.

Which, confusingly, isn't there any more, and hasn't been

265

these last 350 years or so. The tower in Hoghton Tower, the house's great central keep, blew up just after it was captured by the Preston painter's predecessors during the Civil War. The tower had been used to store gunpowder: the explosion, which killed some 200 people, may have been sabotage, retribution or, as some have it, caused by careless soldiery taking a puff while off-duty, which would make it one of the first examples of the dangers of passive smoking.

What remains and has been restored is a small, solid, walled and courtyarded kind of place, a reminder of that confident Tudor unpretentiousness which, along with the tower, wouldn't survive the Stuarts, even if James I, that presciently fanatical anti-tobacconist, provided Hoghton with its second-greatest claim to fame by visiting in 1617 and being so impressed by the local beef that he knighted it: Sir Loin.

I'm surprised he noticed it, coming as it did in the first course at dinner, along with the capon, mutton, chicken, duck, veal, venison, turkey, swan, goose, rabbit, tongue, heron, curlew and pig before the second course of pheasant, quail, partridge, lamb, pigeon and bacon, which came before a supper of most of it again and a breakfast the next day of most of it again, although, personally, I might have had a bit of difficulty with dried hog's cheek, first thing. I was pleased to see tripe pie on the menu, too. I also like the idea of Sir Richard Hoghton taking the guests down to the cellar after the King had gone and staying there for the next two days, 'as merry as Robin Hood and all his fellows'. No wonder he ended up later in the Fleet Prison for debt.

But, Hoghton's greatest claim. I've mentioned it already, and it's there in the guidebook, not in a strident way, but rather with the same confident unpretentiousness of the building, a statement of incontrovertible fact: 'Shakespeare Was Here'. 'We know it for certain,' is the way the charming and middle-aged lady guide, straight from wherever it is they produce all the charming and middle-aged lady guides, put it as we followed her round the house. Well. Indeed.

Imagine this calm confidence as a room, the William Shakespeare Lancashire Room. You have entered by one door. Over there is another. Open that one, and you are hit by a phenomenal frenzy of sound and fury, cries from the lectern, sources in fierce conflict, authorities in hand-to-hand combat, footnotes in foot-to-foot combat, bibliographies struggling for supremacy, an unceasing clicking of keyboards, and any number of further doors with excited voices behind them and mostly all you can hear is names, names, names: Bacon, Oxford, Marlowe, Shakeshaft, Southampton, Essex, Leicester, Worcester, Campion, Burghley, Elizabeth, Southwell, Garnett, Gillam, Cottom, Hoghton, Hesketh, Fawkes, Catesby, Parsons, Stanley, Borromeo, Weever, Arden, Debdale, Hunt, Allen, Sterrell, Chambers, Hotson, Simpson, Honigmann, Keen, Rowse, Honan, Wilson, Asquith; and that's when you're not hearing half-remembered familiar quotations followed by interpretations your keynote and nutshell cribs never dreamt of.

Shut that door, quickly. We need to be strong, take this gently and slowly. I am inviting you instead to mix metaphors and tiptoe with me across a slippery plank over an abyss of highly addictive over-information. One stumble and it's all over as you tumble into 30 years of intense study with only the promise of limited publication and the dismissal of your peers. Trust me, I'm a journalist. Too much information for us is like water for a 12-year-old boy.

Before we tackle Big Bill, though, as he is known in the publishing trade, I think we might perhaps limber up and work towards full fitness with Hoghton's third-greatest claim to fame: a visit by our second-greatest writer, Charles Dickens, during his researches in nearby Preston for *Hard Times*, his beady verdict on the spiritual consolations and life-enhancing potential of the

Industrial Revolution as represented by Mr Gradgrind and his 'Facts, sir; nothing but Facts!'

Hoghton had certainly fallen on its own hard times: the Hoghton family had moved away to more modern and convenient accommodation at Walton Hall and the rest of the house was slowly falling down, with some hand-loom weavers living amid the ruins, poor but picturesque. Dickens spotted it while out on a walk from Preston, a mere six miles to him, and decided that another half a mile up Hoghton's steep hill to the house would be just the thing. I see that Dickens' ferocious energy is now put down to his 'bipolar disorder', which is what we used to call manic depression.

No one is allowed to have any inexplicable talent, now; we can explain everything, and so El Greco and the Impressionists had eyesight that made them see like that, and Newton was autistic which made him anti-social which gave him lots of time to invent things. I must just tell you my favourite facts about Newton: he invented the cat flap; but not only that, he also made a second, smaller flap for his second, smaller cat. Remarkable. Perhaps we would be better leaving Shakespeare alone, in the way that archaeologists, with remarkable modesty for our times, have reburied the Globe until better-equipped future generations can have a go.

Dickens was so struck by Hoghton that he put it in his short story 'George Silverman's Explanation', featuring, as usual, a poor boy from humble beginnings who makes his way in the world and does and doesn't fall in love with an ideally beautiful girl. And yet there is writing and observation and comedy and sadness in the 20 pages hurriedly written for 'a cool thousand' for the American magazine market that would make a properly modest writer chuck it in now. 'A house, centuries old, deserted and falling to pieces,' he writes of Hoghton in the story,

its woods and gardens long since grass-land or ploughed
up, the Rivers Ribble and Darwen glancing below it, and
a vague haze of smoke . . . All over the house I was awed
by gaps and chinks where the sky stared sorrowfully at
me, where the birds passed, and the ivy rustled, and the
stains of winter weather blotched the rotten floors . . .

George Silverman, the hero, who, unusually, doesn't have a
happy end, is a poor orphan from Preston. Dickens had distant
relations in Preston, the Parkers. Robert Parker was a business
partner of John Dickens, Charles's father. This was never a good
idea, and they both ended up in the Marshalsea. Parker's son,
Thomas, became one of the founders of the Mormon Church in
Preston; his son, Robert, emigrated to America in 1855, seen off
from Liverpool, according to reports, by Charles Dickens, who
later wrote about it in *Monthly Magazine*.

By now, you are beginning to wonder why I am telling you
quite so much of this. Bear with me. Robert's son, Maximilian,
or Maxy, was 11 when they emigrated. Maxy, after working with
his father and other Lancashire immigrants in a textile mill in
Beaver, Utah, settled, if that is quite the right word, in high
Indian country, North Creek, where his first son was born in the
middle of a raid by Ute Indians. The son's name was Robert
Leroy Parker, who would later team up with Harry Longabaugh,
a German-descended Pennsylvanian who preferred to be known
as the Sundance Kid. Parker, for his part, preferred Butch
Cassidy.

Yes, that Butch Cassidy! And you see the implication: Butch
Cassidy, one of the West's most famous outlaws, almost certainly
spoke with a Lancashire accent! 'Ay-up, it's a stick-up,' that sort
of thing. My number-one line in this area is the nervous bank
robber in Florida who stormed in and shouted, 'All right, this is
a fuck-up, motherstickers!' Butch is a bit like that in the famous
film, too, what with the hold-up in Bolivia where he is using a

Spanish phrase book to make his intentions clear. William Goldman, the screenwriter of *Butch Cassidy and the Sundance Kid*, based his script pretty much on the Butch literature, even if he missed the Lancashire connection.

The more I think about it, though, the more I realise what a Lancashire cowboy Butch was, particularly as realised by Goldman and Paul Newman: a beguiling dreamer, not quite as clever as he thinks he is, who has never actually killed anybody and ends up in Bolivia, over-optimistic and under-prepared, then enters into legend with the Sundance Kid in that frozen frame as they run out to do battle with what they think is a few soldiers and is in fact almost the entire Bolivian Army. The bit with the bike, too, and Etta Place, Sundance's girl, is pure Laurel or Formby.

And that's only part of the legend. Butch is as much a Robin Hood as Billy the Kid and Jesse James, defenders of the little man and the old ways against the cattle barons, the railroad kings, the power brokers, and progress. And just as Billy the Kid and Jesse James refuse to die, with reports still of switched identities, cover-ups and demands for DNA tests on disputed corpses, so with Butch. Butch's sister, Lula, who was still alive in 1969, when *Butch Cassidy and the Sundance Kid* first came out, told everyone who asked that Butch wasn't killed in Bolivia, but had come back to the States, living on until 1937. Other reports have him fighting for Pancho Villa, living and dying in Paris, Ireland, Chile, Uruguay, Argentina and a New Mexico brothel. A particularly fine detail is that he was a big fan of Dickens, and that Butch, Sundance and Etta went to see *A Christmas Carol* in New York in 1899.

I like the idea of him living out his days in Paris; but not quite as much as I like the idea of him living out his days back in Preston, telling all these wild stories of trains and banks and nobody believing a word he said: 'Bloody hell, there's old Butch on about bloody Bolivia again.' More reports, please, while I linger for a moment to admire the style of Mr Paul Turner, proprietor of the Butch Cassidy Museum in Richfield, Utah: 'Myself, I like to think the old boy's still alive out there, whoopin' it up. Anybody who'd like to hear a Butch Cassidy legend or two, give me a call . . . what I don't know, I'll make up.'

But now we must get on and back to Big Bill, where research is taken rather more seriously. Facts, sir; nothing but Facts! Very well, to begin with, at least. We know that Shakespeare was baptised on 26 April 1564 and given licence to marry on 27 November 1582, that his daughter Susanna was baptised on 26 May 1583, as were his twins, Hamnet and Judith, on 2 February 1585, and that the first mention of him as a playwright was in September 1592. Apart from that, a big, round 0: the Legendary Lost Years.

The convention used to be that this 0, and its continuation as a 0 in the face of 400 years of intense interest and research, was one of the most powerful arguments for Bill being someone else. How could the son of a Stratford tradesman who left school at 14 and married at 18 with no record of attending university suddenly materialise almost fully formed as our greatest poet and playwright, formidably fluent in history, classics and philosophy, wielder of a way with words unequalled in casting spells and touching hearts? Surely the infant prodigy would have been noted and celebrated? Surely the adult phenomenon would have been acclaimed and explained far more than the surviving records and writings show? Step forward Bacon, Marlowe, Oxford, any one of whom must be more likely than this balding Black Country bloke.

I remember Enoch Powell, another Black Country bloke, if not particularly balding, at lunch at the *Daily Telegraph*, announcing in the same portentous Black Country tones that announced the imminence of rivers of a worryingly red hue, 'I will tell you one thing: the Bard was not the Man of Stratford.'

Where were the mentions of Shakespeare in diaries, at dinner or other engagements? It could not be, was not possible. We all nodded gravely, in the way hacks do when confronted by Knowledge. And then Jeremy Deedes, the *Telegraph*'s managing editor, son of Lord Deedes, with some of the same style, said, 'Well, I expect he was rather busy, writing all those plays.' I don't think Enoch even noticed our happy sniggers.

But what if the facts were known and available, but were inconvenient, and remained inconvenient even until this day? What if it were convenient that we should know as little as possible about our greatest writer, our proud national symbol, so as to make him all-inclusive and all-embracing? Consider the use to which he has been put just in the last century: portrayed by Olivier in *Henry V* as the wartime articulator of our stubborn nationalism and invincible spirit; promoted as the national muse of the new Elizabethan age, harking back to the original Elizabethan values of England as the home of sturdy independence and challenging enterprise. Consider the most pervasive literary theory of the last century, propounded by such critics as Eliot and Foucault, Blanchot, Barthes and Borges, that the greatest art is anonymous, and is produced from nothing. Consider, too, the academic and commercial interest in keeping Shakespeare a London playwright, Writer for the People. Consider the implications for all this and, particularly for previous centuries, if our greatest writer were, and now I must whisper in the manner of Joel Grey in *Cabaret* . . . Roman Catholic, a protégé of the old Catholic nobility, dedicated to the dissemination of Catholic propaganda, a follower of the old ways, the now suspiciously foreign ways, involving exotic, mysterious and dangerous creatures like the Jesuits; what if, then, our greatest writer was a traitor, dedicated to the overthrow of our greatest queen?

Quite. And you are doubtless impressed, too, by the fine sweep and my ease with the historical, sociological and literary landscape. I gained it over lunch in the restaurant below St Paul's from Professor Richard Wilson, Professor of Renaissance Studies and Director of the Shakespeare Programme at Lancaster University, a man of shaven head, great charm and an enthusiasm remarkable even by the standards of others in this book.

Professor Wilson, you will not be altogether suprised to learn, is the present principal purveyor of Shakespeare in Lancashire. The Prof has visions of Hoghton Tower. He sees a £20-million programme producing an annual Shakespeare conference, a Renaissance Library housing the returned and priceless Hoghton library, lecture rooms, accommodation, research fellows, exhibitions, seminars, workshops and, above all, or, rather, set in the side of Hoghton hill with Lancashire as a backdrop, entered from the Great Barn above, an architectural coup, a theatre seating 500, to which the great players, British and American, will come. And standing there, looking over to Pendle and the Pennines, I can see it: the Lancashire Bayreuth, the apex of the Lancashire cultural triangle, with the new vivacities of Liverpool and Manchester at the bases.

The facts, though, the facts. On what, exactly, is all this to be erected? Let me introduce Sir Bernard de Hoghton, the 14th baronet, born in 1945, unrivalled expert on all things Hoghton. *Parti pris*, clearly, as who wouldn't want a Shakespeare connection, particularly if you rely on paying guests (though only of a quick-visiting, non-staying nature)? But also a man of academic rigour; a man full of fine and sensitive feeling for the family home, distinctly unmoved by what he calls the 'hurdy-gurdy' end of stately-home promotion. A man, too, with the sense of historical proportion a family tree reaching back to Lady Godiva tends to lend. You will recall that other baronet, Sir Walter Elliot, in *Persuasion*, whose chief delight was studying his entry in the Baronetage; Sir Bernard has the same interest in his antecedents, but none of the vanity.

He is interested in them all, and can hold you in thrall, over the distance, by way of proof. But it is Alexander Hoghton, who died in 1581, who is the prime source for Shakespeare in Lancs. In his will, dated 3 August 1581, Alexander bequeathed his stock of costumes and all his musical instruments to his brother Thomas or, if he did not choose to keep players, to Sir Thomas Hesketh, of nearby Rufford Hall. Then he added: 'And I most heartily require the said Sir Thomas to be friendly unto Fulk Gillam and William Shakeshafte now dwelling with me and either to take them unto his service or else to help them to some good master, as my trust is he will.'

William Shakeshafte, player! Not exactly Shakespeare, I grant you, but near enough for a man who never seemed quite sure how to spell his name, surely? And hadn't his grandfather's name been recorded as both Shakstaff and Shakeschafte? The dates fit, as William would have been 17 at the time, having left Stratford Grammar School a couple of years before. It fits, too, with the history of the Hoghtons, who have always taken it rather nonchalantly as read and were surprised when the rest of the world began to get excited.

'It was just passed very simply down to me by my father,' said Sir Bernard, sitting in his office at Hoghton. 'He died in 1958 and was born in 1880. He just happened one day to say, "By the way, darling, you do know that it's well known in the family that William Shakespeare used to work here?" And that was it, finish, you know, end of story. I, aged 12, said "Gulp," and left it rather, you know, like that. But I did say to him later, "Who told *you*?" and he said, "Oh, my father." Now Sir James, granddaddy to me, he was born in 1852, and we then worked out that his father, Sir Henry Bold Hoghton, was born in 1799, so we can get back quite quickly.'

There is a lot else that fits and no shortage of fitters. Remember those porers and searchers and underscorers and determined keyboard tappers, the hum of fierce study and the

274

occasional shout of excitement or exasperation. Allow a humble hack to attempt a sketchy tour. John Aubrey wrote that Shakespeare 'had been in his younger years a schoolmaster in the country'. Aubrey had that from the son of Kit Beeston, a friend and fellow actor of Shakespeare. Why would Hoghton be the place in the country? Well, the Ardens, his mother's family, had Cheshire branches and Lancashire connections, including one with the Stanleys, the Earls of Derby. Shakespeare belonged to the troupe of actors known as Strange's Men, under the patronage of Ferdinando, Lord Strange, the Earl of Derby's son and heir. That troupe, which later became Derby's Men, and then the Chamberlain's Men, had been joined by the players of Sir Thomas Hesketh, into whose charge William Shakeshafte had been entrusted. Later friends and associates included Edward Alleyn, whose mother was a Townley, another Lancashire family, and Thomas Savage, fellow trustee of the Globe, who was related to Sir Thomas Hesketh and came from Rufford. John Weever, a Lancashire poet, wrote a book of epigrams addressed to various Lancashire notables, mostly related, and included one to Shakespeare.

Pretty good so far, you must concede; and the better is yet to come. Four out of five consecutive schoolmasters at Stratford Grammar School were Lancashire men. They were also Catholics. There. Out of the bag. Sniff that incense, hear those bells. The Old Religion. John Shakespeare, William's father, was a recusant, a Catholic who refused to attend Church of England services. His ostensible and well-attested excuse, that he feared debt proceedings, has been exposed as unlikely by recent research proving his excellent financial resources. Then there is the document, discovered by workmen in 1757, hidden under the roof tiles of the Shakespeare home in Henley Street, Stratford. It has now conveniently and mysteriously disappeared. It was a handwritten English version of *The Testament of the Soul*, the great, ringing counterblast of the Counter-Reformation, composed by the movement's spiritual mentor, St Charles Borromeo, the Cardinal of Milan. In it, John Shakespeare promised that he would 'patiently endure and suffer all kind of infirmity, sickness, yea and the pain of death itself' rather than abandon his faith.

How did John get it? Who gave it to him? Enter the dark villains of Elizabethan and Jacobean England, the Jesuits, Soldiers of Christ, the shock troops of the Counter-Reformation, set on their doomed, fanatical, alarmingly brave bid to persuade all of England to refuse the new Church and re-establish the old. These men were suicide bombers of the soul: some 30 of them were executed in the attempt. The Jesuit numbers included Edmund Campion, the orator of Oxford and the day, as magnetic as his phrases, as disarming as he was inspiring; Robert Southwell, the sweetest poet, as beautiful as he was gentle; but there were also Robert Persons, elusive, conspiratorial, too sharp for the scaffold; and Henry Garnet, elucidator of the dangerous doctrine of equivocation, economy with the truth in the service of God.

Despite their protestations about renderings to God and Caesar, it is difficult to see, given Elizabeth's position as Head of both Church and State, how their mission couldn't be treasonable, even without recent evidence that Persons was plotting to kill the Queen. It was Persons, it seems, who gave John Shakespeare his *Testament*, in the first great mission, with Campion, in 1580; Robert Southwell was related to the Shakespeares through the Ardens. And more: Richard Wilson believes that William went to Lancashire with Campion.

You can see why there would be resistance to a close Jesuit association with our national poet. Despite the Campions and the Southwells, the Jesuits have never quite shaken off the Persons and the Garnets. As late as 1851, for example, the Norwegian constitution banned Jesuits and Jews from entering the country. I, on the other hand, must declare an interest: they educated me. I suppose I should have gone to Stonyhurst, their great Lancashire school. But my father said that Stonyhurst boys thought 'the world owed them a living', so I went over the Pennines, to the less grand Mount St Mary's in Derbyshire, which was fine, although the Stonyhurst library, still packed with secrets, according to Richard Wilson, sounds fun.

What should I say about these fabled creatures, the Jesuits? I found them clever and pragmatic in matters of discipline, and I have never encountered anyone who could beat the headmaster's record for saying the Mass in 11 minutes, but there was no inspiration to insurrection and certainly no claims to have taught the boy Shakespeare all he knew. These were the '60s, the days of peace and love and ecumenicism and the cuddly Holy Father, John XXIII. The Church Triumphant and Militant was unfashionable, even if we did spend many hours listening to sermons describing the intestine-strewn and blood-boltered deaths of the Forty Martyrs, the victims of Elizabeth and James whose suits for sanctity were then being urgently pressed. You might see reconciliation of such apparent conflict as Jesuitical; certainly I'm hard pressed to explain how they managed it and avoided turning us into some Fawkesian fifth column, but they did. When my father died, I wanted to sing 'Faith of my Fathers' at his funeral, because it is a rousing song and one of the few I could remember; I was surprised when the parish priest rejected it, saying he didn't like 'tribal hymns'. The strength of its call for a Catholic restoration had been completely lost on me, despite the interminable times we'd sung it. Clever Jesuits, or not.

But there was sweetness, too: my old English teacher, beloved even if he did stop me from dozing off by continually addressing all his wisdom in my direction, always took the lesson off when it was time to examine the death of Lady Macbeth. He felt for her, but couldn't condone suicide, even for dramatic purposes. How I would like to discuss all this with him now. I did ask the Jesuit I know best about it recently, but he clearly regarded it as

277

no more than a loopy distraction from soldiering for Christ.

Richard Wilson, though, is most persuasive. In late 1580, Campion travelled from Lapworth Park, home of the Catesbys, one of the Stratford families, along with the Treshams, the Grants and the Winters, who would be involved in the Gunpowder Plot. Travelling with Campion was an escort of young Catholic boys, all chosen for the priesthood: the seminary waited across the Channel, in Douai. It had been founded in 1568 by William (later Cardinal) Allen of Rossall, Lancashire, friend of his neighbour, Thomas Hoghton, who went into exile with Allen 'for Blessed Conscience sake', and who helped pay for Douai with the proceeds from Hoghton's alum mines. When Thomas died in 1580, still away, Hoghton passed to his half-brother, Alexander, as Thomas's son had become a priest at Douai prior to returning on a mission to Lancashire and dying in prison in Salford in 1584. Priests, priests, priests. Simon Hunt, Shakespeare's Lancashire schoolmaster, also took the Douai route, as did the brother of another, Thomas Cottam, who accompanied Campion and, like him, was hanged, drawn and quartered.

There was a reason why Campion had spent six months, in 1580–1, at Hoghton and in the vicinity: its library. Shortly after his arrival at Dover, Campion had issued his famous challenge, for all the world like some spiritual knight errant:

> I would be loth to speak anything that might sound of any insolent brag or challenge, especially being as now a dead man to this world and willing to put my head under every man's foot, and to kiss the ground they tread upon. Yet have I such courage in avouching the Majesty of Jhesus my King, and such affiance in his gracious favour, and such assurance in my quarrel, and my evidence so impregnable, and because I know perfectly that no Protestant, nor all the Protestants living . . . can

maintain their doctrine in disputation. I am to sue most
humbly and instantly for the combat with all and every
of them, and the most principal that may be found:
protesting that in this trial the better furnished they
come, the better welcome they be.

Little wonder that, despite the rather disingenuous disavowal,
this has always been known as Campion's Brag. You should use
your own faith or philosophy to consider that when the time
came for him to live up to such temerity, he had been racked.
Four times he was put up against different panels of Anglican
divines; the best they could manage was to trip him up on his
Greek, which must nevertheless have been galling to such a
scholar. Catholics were arrested, either as a result of his
confessions, or to make it look like the result of his confessions.
He was pursued even to the scaffold by a divine wishing to argue
about justification by faith alone. His last speech was shouted
down by foppish courtiers. But at least he was probably dead
before his entrails were torn out by the butcher and thrown into
a cauldron of boiling water.

That was all ahead in 1581, although he knew it was coming.
Then, he had gone to Lancashire, according to one of his
biographers, Richard Simpson, 'because it was furthest from
London and best affected to the Catholic religion, but also
because there was more hope to find there the books to help him
answer the heretics'. Campion boasted, writes Richard Wilson,
that 'the day is too short and the sun must run a greater
circumference, before he could number all the epistles, homilies,
volumes and disputations' amassed at Hoghton. 'If Shakespeare
was Shakeshafte,' Wilson continues, 'he was a member of a
household which for six months, it seems, was nothing less than
the headquarters of the English Counter-Reformation.'

If Shakespeare was Shakeshafte? You want more? Well, Sir
Bernard could take you down to Lea Hall, another of the old

Hoghton houses, predating the Tower, although you wouldn't think it if you only saw the side which faces the road; then you'd think it was just a farmhouse. It is a farmhouse, lived in by a gentle tenant farmer of Sir Bernard, alone with the centuries; but on the side facing the Ribble estuary you can see what was, and up in the roof there are mighty beams and signs of a great open hall. Out there Sir Bernard will see barques and luggers bound for the Low Countries, linked into a network of trade and intrigue established by the exiled Thomas in Antwerp, the Venice of the North. You might see only Lancashire mud, but that fits in with the 'desert country near the sea' of *The Winter's Tale*. Lancs, naturally, as Bohemia.

This takes us to the search for references. I've had a go at this myself, not uninfluenced by the wind that whips up around the Tower, a pretty sharp breeze that had me muttering, with a certain pride in my learning, 'Blow, blow, thou winter wind', as I wandered around. It is pretty clear that the Bard had been memorably exposed to a wind from the northerly direction. The dying King John, for example, defines cold comfort as the bleak winds of the north kissing his parched lips; in *Pericles*, 'the grizzly north disgorges such a tempest forth'; Ariel recalls 'the sharp wind of the north'; in *Romeo and Juliet*, the north wind makes for a frozen bosom; both *The Winter's Tale* and *The Rape of Lucrece* mention the 'northern blast', while *Timon of Athens* has 'an angry north wind'. Beyond that, I didn't do particularly well, though. I suppose my best spot is from *Henry VI*, where Mortimer declares, 'Strong fixed is the House of Lancaster and like a mountain not to be removed.' And Sir Bernard was polite, but only that, I felt, when I wondered if there might be something in the Lea in Lea Hall being pronounced 'Lear'.

The professionals, the ones behind that door, the real glossers, would be rightly dismissive. Just to show you what we're dealing with here, one of Shakespeare's biographers, Park Honan, has noticed that even when a scene is on the east coast, the sun sets in the sea: ergo the Bard is recalling the Ribble Estuary of his youth. Much, much else besides concentrates on the Catholic Shakespeare. Richard Wilson gives a gentle introduction, pointing out the 'affinity between Catholic belief and the stage where Romeo kisses Juliet "like a holy shrine" and atones to his "ghostly confessor"', and then listing only a few of the Catholic references in the plays: Richard III is haunted by the spirits of All Souls; Hamlet's father is in Purgatory; an abbess appears from 'sanctuary' to unravel the Comedy of Errors with 'holy prayers'; Petruchio swears he loves Kate 'by God's wounds' so loudly that the priest drops the book; Olivia is catechised by servants.

'No wonder,' writes Wilson, 'Shakespeare's works were excoriated by Puritans as "prelatical trash such as clergymen spend their canonical hours on", or that they became the favourite reading of the imprisoned Charles I.' What is striking, says Wilson, 'is the stark difference from all other English drama of this Gothic theatre of dark towers, moated granges and silent convents, where statues weep in private chapels, and friars emerge from hiding places to resolve each plot'.

A mere starter. At lunch, for more than two hours, Wilson ranged around and up and down, reference following name following allusion, libraries to visit, books that simply must be read – Greenblatt, *Hamlet in Purgatory*, Arlidge, *Shakespeare and the Prince of Love*, Shell. Did I know about that formidable researcher, Professor Hildegard Hammerschmidt-Hummel of Mainz University, known to all as the Miss Marple of Mainz? She was working on this theory that Shakespeare had become a Jesuit in the Lost Years and was a secret agent for Rome.

Did I know about Steve Sohmer, the former Hollywood studio chief, now Hoghton trustee, who had some amazing theories on the chronology of the plays, their astrological significance, and the fact that Shakespeare has Caesar stabbed 33 times, the age of Christ at his death? And what about another simply remarkable fact, that in 1581 there was a family called

Shakeshafte living in Preston, and its head was called John, and that, exactly like the Stratford John Shakespeare, he was a glover? Really, where I ought to do some research was on Fulke Gillam, the other man in Alexander Hoghton's will, a lot more to be done about him: he was related to the Ollernshaws, hereditary bear-wardens to the Derbys, who used to lead the bears through Wigan, to the consternation of the townsfolk.

By now we were back at Wilson's flat, in Blackfriars, which he had bought because it was near the site of the Gatehouse, purchased by Shakespeare, leased by him to an agent of the Jesuit school at St Omer and used as a bolthole for priests on the run. There Wilson produced from the shelves of books on Shakespeare two papers which we went off to get photocopied, one on 'Venus and Adonis', the Bard's first poem, showing that it is really a coded discussion of Catholic loyalties and dilemmas, and another on *Macbeth* as a condemnation of Jesuit extremism, featuring Edmund Campion's thumb, the martyr's relic which soon afterwards was inserted into the vagina of a possessed girl to aid her exorcism. Oh, yes, and a 33-page lecture to the British Academy on Shakespeare's sense of an exit.

Too much information. Trust me, I said, I'm a journalist. We were just popping over for a quick look at Hoghton. But, as you will have noticed, I am drawn to enthusiasts and pursuers of passions. The attraction of opposites. The vital source for the hack's confident, speedy, superficial judgements. Their subjectivity contrasted with our objective, distanced, quick tiptoe over the surface. They are dotty and a bit sad, really, with none of our balance. Wilson, it is true, rather irritatingly failed to conform to this, even if he did have a shaven head. But I had seen others. And it was Shakespeare that seemed to do it to them more than anything else. I remember this bloke, young chap, who was obsessed with the shape of the Globe when Sam Wanamaker was reconstructing it on Bankside. He could argue for hours that Sam didn't have the right number of sides. I can't remember his name now, or how many sides it was, but it made a piece for me, ending with, pretty cleverly, I thought at the time, 'Who said the play was the thing?' Of course, nobody took any notice.

I remember, too, Peter Levi, a poet and Jesuit priest, greatly admired by the young Scholastics, the trainee Jesuits, at my school, almost a modern Campion to them. Then he left the priesthood to marry Cyril Connolly's widow. 'Private life with someone you love is the greatest of human pleasures,' he wrote in his numinous autobiography, *The Flutes of Autumn*. He became, after one of those silly Oxford elections, its Professor of Poetry. And he was going along very well until he got tangled up with the Bard.

During his research for a Bard biography, he had come across some verses which he thought might very well be by Shakespeare. He didn't put it any stronger than that, but such qualifications got lost in one of those marvellous brouhahas publishers and newspapers love to contrive, especially when one paper has an exclusive and the rest can knock it down. It was noisily and speedily and easily proved that the verses weren't by Shakespeare (on closer examination the 'W Sh' on the manuscript turned out to be 'W Sk', his unregarded contemporary William Skipworth) and Levi was left looking foolish.

I remember him now, after a rowdy press conference, bemused and saying to himself softly, as if to reassure himself, 'Good old Shakers, good old Shakers,' while inscribing a copy with his signature, a drawing of Shakespeare, and on the page facing the frontispiece, a parrot, whose significance now escapes me, although it will no doubt excite intense interest sometime next century.

Then there was Dr Rowse, Alfred Leslie Rowse, the son of a Cornish china clay-worker, who, by dint of his native genius for study and advertisement, had become a Fellow of All Souls of a suitably eccentric character, an acclaimed, if perhaps too prolific Elizabethan historian, and a poet in a manner too traditional, and perhaps too sentimental, to attract the attention he thought it deserved. He too got tangled up with the Bard, making a great discovery: the identity of the mysterious Dark Lady of the sonnets.

The Dark Lady, according to Rowse and corroborated 'in every circumstance and detail', was Emilia Lanier, mistress of Elizabeth's Lord Chamberlain. It made a bigger, and earlier, splash than Levi. But the corroboration was only circumstantial. There was no document spelling it out, no note saying, 'I love Emilia Lanier, signed W. Shakespeare'. And so it was not proved to everyone else's satisfaction. They couldn't disprove it, but they wouldn't approve it. The Doctor, though, knew it to be true, and those who doubted him doubted *him*, a man uniquely qualified as both poet and historian.

The doubters included Lord Dacre (maiden name, as Rowse loved to put it, Hugh Trevor-Roper) and Stanley Wells, director of the Shakespeare Institute and general editor of the *Oxford Shakespeare*; they were nevertheless dismissed as 'second-raters and third-raters' in the high-camp style and impossibly patrician tones Rowse had made his own. 'I have the advantage of ambivalence in every respect, dear,' is the way he would put it, often while caressing the nearest young male knee. (Once, a limousine left the Athenaeum for the late J.P. Getty's Sutton Place treasure house, bearing a cargo of John Julius Norwich, Sir Roy Strong, and, in the front seat, the Doctor. 'Did you see the chauffeur's knee?' said Norwich to Strong afterwards. 'Positively burnished.')

It was a highly entertaining and droll turn for the broadsheet newspapers, especially when the Doctor combined another attack on the literary establishment with his contempt for 'the idiot people'. The refusal to recognise his theory ate away at him. It is possible to see it now as his King Charles's Head, the obsession that knocked him off his academic balance and coloured all views of him subsequently. Shakespeare, again. 'Lord, what fools these mortals be,' Puck's verdict in *A Midsummer Night's Dream*, has long been a guiding maxim of journalism (always excluding ourselves, of course).

While I was comfortably pondering on this, I came across an article in the *Times Literary Supplement* offering a new analysis of Shakespeare's bogglingly dense poem 'The Phoenix and the Turtle' showing, with the aid of no fewer than eleven numbered points, that the poem was in fact all about Roger Line and his wife Anne, one of the famed Forty Martyrs, executed at Tyburn in 1601 for giving shelter to Catholic priests. I particularly liked the way the article took part of the poem's eighth stanza, 'Distance and no space was seen/Twixt this turtle and his Queen', and then asked: 'What has "distance and no space", length and no breadth . . . no area? A line – by extension, Ann and Roger Line. Complementing the password given by stanza eight's wordplay is a visual play of structure. As the poem begins its formal lament on the occasion of Ann Line's death, its quatrains become tercets: a line has been lost.'

The name of one of the two co-authors of the piece both surprised and didn't surprise me. It was John Finnis, my old Oxford law tutor. I hadn't known he was interested in Shakespeare, but the rigour of the approach was most familiar. It was Dr, now Prof., Finnis and my other main tutor, Mr Leonard, now Lord, Hoffmann, who convinced me that law was not the discipline to which I was best suited. The bright sharpness of these men's minds, honed, uncluttered, forensic, had me lost in awe, particularly as their favoured teaching method was to put to you a premise to which you would agree, and which we might call 'A'. They would then point out that if the A was the case, then B would follow, and I would say 'Yes'. They would then point out that if B was the case, C would follow, and I would say, with even more hesitation, 'Y-es'. They would then say that if C was the case, D would follow. I would say, faltering further and with, to be absolutely honest, not a clue what they were talking about, 'Y-e-s' and they would then pause and say, 'No'.

It was done with finesse, courtesy, even amiability, without blunting the point. Let me demonstrate the excellence of their all-round game: I could take a slim, elderly volume from the highest, dustiest shelf of the college's law library, attempt to pass its opinion off as my own, imagine I had got away with it, only to hear, just before the end of the tutorial, Dr Finnis enter the single deadpan parenthesis in his dry Australian accent, 'as Daintith says'.

So I had to go to see him. He invited me down to lunch; I took the train to Oxford, just as I had a few years before with Dr Rowse, whom I was escorting to Stratford in the hope of some fine Rowsean antics. On the way, as we passed through Slough, in one of the old compartments, the Doctor had started loudly declaiming Betjeman's lines about the friendly bombs and the rest of the compartment had ignored him, in that English way, which only egged on the old Celt to further outrage and the steady drop of names with disobliging comment attached. Happy days. This trip was far less eventful. When I got to the college, though, I found a small, polite demonstration going on outside against the treatment of the Kalahari Bushmen. The Professor told me it was because the President of Botswana had come to lunch. 'He was here with you, wasn't he?' said the Professor, 'Or maybe it was a bit earlier.' Earlier. Bill Clinton had been a postgraduate the year before I arrived. In the Old Members' notes in the 1993 College Record, his entry came alphabetically and immediately after six lines on someone who was making videos for accountants and solicitors. It read: 'W. J. Clinton was elected President of the United States of America on 4 November 1992.' No more. There's all I like and dislike about Oxford in that.

The Professor didn't have much time. He made it clear he

didn't have much time for the Lancashire theory, either. His main interest, he said, was in William Sterrell, secretary to the Earl of Worcester; the Earl succeeded the doomed Essex as Master of the Horse. Sterrell, a philosophy don at Magdalen, was acquainted with Southampton, Shakespeare's patron, and, of course, intertwined with more Papists than you could shake a shaft at. He was also, said the Professor, a double agent on both sides, acting for both the Catholics and Elizabeth.

A double agent on both sides! I was back in a tutorial straight away, struggling with another befuddling concept. I was further confused when the Professor said, 'Good question,' the first time this had ever happened, and such a surprise that I have now forgotten what the question was. I know I took the low hackish point about why Shakespeare would want to conceal all these hidden meanings and exactly who was supposed to understand them; the Professor thought very few people would have understood even by 1620 what he was on about, but that this was his protest of conscience. I could also see the usefulness of the argument that anything on the face of it anti-Catholic in the plays would have been ironic. Almost Jesuitical, you might say. I knew, too, that the Professor was himself a Catholic.

But, most of all, I noticed how much the Professor enjoyed the subject. I suppose it made a welcome change from teaching law to people like me, but I had never seen him staring into the distance and discoursing with such enthusiasm about, say, torts. He was full of surmise and delight over Elizabethan intrigue and detail. At one point he said, 'We just don't know!' with the pleasure of a man liberated from the certainty of statute and the constraint of precedent.

I'm sure he will say all this is completely fanciful, but it did give me a moment of revelation, in the senior common room, as, with fork poised at the halfway mark between plate and mouth, his shining eye suddenly lit up the worth and excitement of all this arcana, the intense enjoyment and noble bravery of intellectual engagement, and exposed the sad limitations of watching and occasionally mocking. And then he mentioned, unbidden, that his interest in deep Shakespeariana had first been fired by the theories of Dr Rowse and others about the sonnets. And I remembered that the best thing about our trip to Stratford had been the Doctor's enthusiasm: how he had wept at the great poet's grave; and how, when I took him to one of those World of Shakespeare audio-visual experiences, in the hope of fireworks at 'the idiot people', he was absolutely entranced, sitting there among the restless rucksacks and the lethargic leisure-wearers. I remembered, too, how he had told me that only Shakespeare could 'make your heart turn over'.

So let me now cast aside the lazy cynicism and easy condescension and bid you back to Elizabethan England, with that sudden exuberant energy infusing everything from expeditions to espionage, from the swagger of Raleigh and Drake to the spidering of Walsingham, Elizabeth's chief spy, and Burghley, her cunning chief minister and chief pursuivant, with all manner of people between, actors, writers, priests, poets, nobles, spies, magicians and chancers and forgers and double-dealers, touched by plot and counter-plot, enemies abroad and within, real and imagined, horsemen in the night, the knock at the door, gables and garb the only things that are black and white, fate never more arbitrary, consciences pricked, bodies racked and hacked, accommodations made, beauty and butchery accomplished, twins the starker for the contrast, the birth of the modern.

And the world of the boy genius turned upside down by the arrival in Stratford of the uncompromising Campion compromising his recusant father. And the consequent despatch of the boy to Lancashire, adopting, as they all did, aliases, and ending up at Hoghton, home of the patrons of his schoolmasters and of the books which would inform his writings, a boy amazed by the bravado and brilliance of Campion but also aghast, shocked into worrying at the themes which would inspire and invade his writings, best summed up by whether it is nobler to suffer the slings and arrows of outrageous fortune or to take up arms against them.

I could, with my new enthusiasm for deep learning, take you on to the rest of the texts, but that is far better left to Professors Wilson and Finnis and colleagues. My gift is for easy, over-confident précis: Shakespeare was thoroughly steeped, as is entirely clear from much of what he wrote, in Catholicism. But, as is entirely clear from everything he wrote, he was too inquiring for the ultimate certainties of faith. He might well, as was recorded in the seventeenth century, have 'died a papist', but he lived, thank God, as a feeble, fallible one who preached between the lines rather than from the scaffold. And anyone who can write comedy as broad as that must have learnt his trade in Lancs.

At Hoghton, meanwhile, they were having a ghost tour, one of Sir Bernard's wheezes to bring in a bit of income. This being Hoghton, our guide was the estate foreman, Ian Barrett, who had come from Blackburn to mend the boiler 25 years ago and stayed to take a great interest in Hoghton's history. This being Lancs, Mr Barrett was a stand-up kind of a guide, lugubrious and droll, and not beyond a little affectionate light teasing of the Hoghtons. He solemnly informed his audience in the candlelight that Hoghton had seven ghosts and retold Sir Bernard's literally hair-raising experience with some ghostly footsteps, which he had implored Mr Barrett not to tell the cleaning ladies about the next morning. 'So,' said Mr Barrett, with native timing and an accent extravagant in elongated vowels even for Blackburn, 'when I told the cleaning ladies the next morning . . .' Or, 'We had somebody die a couple of years ago. Quite ruined the evening . . .'

Down in the passages underneath the tower, the laughter became a little more nervous. Mr Barrett showed us the dungeon, now containing, in the approved 'heritage' manner, a waxwork tableau. This one was a representative of the other local Stuart celebrities, the Pendle Witches, a collection of blind old biddies with sharp tongues and retarded children, who didn't live to regret their boasting of curses and mutual incriminations involving dead men, dead cows, black dogs, familiars called Tibb, Fancy and Dandy, soured milk and a stroke-struck pedlar. Eight of them were hanged in 1612 after an enthusiastic prosecution by the Lancashire gentry, anxious to prove their loyalty and their distaste for the sinister and the exotic and the dangerous, which might explain the inclusion of Alice Nutter, convicted on even flimsier evidence than the rest, a Catholic woman of noble birth whose family included two martyred Jesuits.

When James I, as firm a believer in witchcraft as he was in the evils of tobacco, made that visit to Hoghton in 1617, he summoned the ones that had been acquitted and looked at them from behind a screen, to avoid the evil eye. Mr Barrett, with an eye for a good story, deftly wove the young Shakespeare into this, pointing up the *Macbeth* connection, which seems compelling.

But here's a funny thing. *Macbeth* was written in 1606: Prof. Wilson argues that it is a fierce critique of the extremism of the previous year's Gunpowder Plot. Certainly the Porter makes mocking (and, thinks Prof. Finnis, secretly ironical) reference to Henry Garnet, the equivocating Jesuit hanged for his part in the plot. Macbeth, in the full-on Catholic reading, is Catesby, leader of the plot, a noble man corrupted who, like Macbeth, died fighting with sword in hand. Fine. But what of the witches, foreshadowed six years before they emerged into notoriety? Spooky, as you might say on a ghost tour.

We were outside by now, where Mr Barrett was explaining why the free sample of dishwasher powder in the new dishwasher in the converted flat in the east wing had never been used:

nobody could live in the east wing because nobody could sleep there, because it was the site of the house's gallows. Is this the first time dishwasher powder has taken top billing in a ghost story? I like to think so. Mr Barrett went on to point out some stone orbs which were the symbol of Hoghton power. 'The de Hoghtons,' said Mr Barrett, 'had a lot of balls.' The ghost hunters liked that. It reminded me of the favourite local newspaper story, featuring the young girl reporter who wrote a piece about Hoghton during the time of Sir Henry, the 13th baronet, in which she reported that the banqueting hall was the place where 'Sir Henry holds his balls and dances'. Ah, well. Sorry, Sir Bernard.

The ghost hunters were mostly women. Mr Barrett told me they usually were. 'The men are the non-believers,' he said. 'It's generally the women who go to fortune-tellers, isn't it?' he said. I was reminded of something I had happened on in John Bossy's *The English Catholic Community, 1570–1850*. Bossy, like everybody else, cannot explain why Lancashire was quite so doggedly Catholic; later on, though, he notes that a fellow historian has put forward the theory that Catholicism survived in England because the wives of the gentry decided that it should, and kept to the old religion in defiance of their conforming husbands. This portrait, writes Bossy, 'of a class victorious on the Narrow Seas but defeated in the kitchen and the nursery is a comic invention of some power; it is surely also to a large degree true'.

He might have added that it was a comic invention pursued nowhere more vigorously than in Lancashire. I was watching *Sing As You Go* again recently, and was struck by the strength of Gracie Fields. That no-nonsense attitude and sheer force reminded me of so many Lancashire women in my childhood. I was struck, too, by the splendidly henpecked husbands, one of whom, the consort of Gracie's Blackpool landlady employer, seems to live in a cupboard in the kitchen. And to think it was written by J.B. Priestley of Bradford, even if he was, as usual, over-compensating for his Yorkshireness by being over-sentimental. Gracie, of course, didn't get the man. Did you know she was great friends with Noel Coward on Capri? She married a handyman out there, nice chap.

Sorry? Ah, yes, Facts, sir; nothing but Facts! Shakespeare in Lancs. There is another thing. A copy of Halle's *Chronicles*, a prime source for Shakespeare, along with Holinshed, was bought by Alan Keen, an antiquarian bookseller, at a sale in Yorkshire in 1940. When he unwrapped it, he found some 400 notes written in the margins by an Elizabethan hand. By dint of some remarkable detective work, Keen traced the book along a path that led to Hoghton at the right time for the young Will to have done his research in the margins. The Hand of Will! The only example apart from the famous varied signatures! In Lancs! Keen compiled exhaustive similarities between the notes and the plays, but once again, as with Dr Rowse, it was not enough for non-believers; the annotated volume was sold to an anonymous buyer, and forgotten.

The Hoghtons have not been lucky with the fabulous library they assembled in the sixteenth century, the one that sent Campion north, the once whence Halle came. Part of it was given as a marriage dowry for a younger daughter, and ended up with Lancaster University by way of Cartmel Priory. The remainder of the books got as far as Walton Hall, where, in the words of Sir Bernard, they 'survived up to 1860, when a young Hoghton boy taking too much liking to his father's cigars hears the old boy stepping down the corridor, thinks, "Bloody hell, what am I going to do with this Romeo y Julieta or Monte Cristo?" or whatever he was smoking in those days, shoves it behind some old books, flees out of the French window into the shrubbery, is found out by his father, thrashed and put to bed, and then later that night, "Fire! Fire! Fire!". It's absolutely tragic, but if what survives is anything at all to go by, I now understand why our dear friend Edmund Campion wanted to spend time with us in this house.'

Tantalising, to put it politely, as is the other fire which destroyed the Pantechnicon depository in London at around the same time, taking with it accumulated Hoghton pictures and *objets* that were being stored there during the restoration of the tower; as is the probability that the musical instruments left to Sir Thomas Hesketh were sold off by mistake as junk in the 1950s or early '60s. Imagine: instruments plucked by Will lying in a toy cupboard in Todmorden or on the top of a wardrobe in Rochdale. Some of George Formby's ukuleles are missing too, you know.

While I was writing this, Sir Bernard was very excited because Michael Wood was supposed to be having the famous Halle's *Chronicle* expertly examined for his BBC series, *In Search of Shakespeare*. There were some splendid shots of Sir Bernard poring over old books at Hoghton, but, of the mysterious *Chronicle*, nothing. So? Another anti-Lancs cover-up? I spoke to Wood and his producer, Rebecca Dodds: the book and the annotations had been expertly examined, but did not allow for a firm conclusion. Should you need convincing, let me remind you that Wood is from Manchester.

And, as you will know if you've seen him, he is also an expert enthusiast, a Lancashire kind of historian, full of the romance and mystery and wonder of the past. And so it was that I was again exposed to another sally of sources and barrage of books. The Stanley Connection, that was the one to pursue, especially the mysterious death of Ferdinando, the Fifth Earl of Derby, the Lord Strange who was Shakespeare's early patron, a potential claimant to the throne through descent from Henry VII, dead at the age of 35 after 11 days of agony, ascribed, depending on your source, view or faction, to acute peritonitis, witchcraft, or poison ordered, depending etc., by the Jesuits because he wouldn't join a plot against Elizabeth, by Burghley because he had joined a plot, or by Burghley to make it look as if he had joined a plot. And all further compounded by links to Marlowe's death in Deptford. And to Prague, at that time inhabited by the most marvellous mix of exiled English Catholics, spies, soldiers and hunters of fortune, alchemists and charlatans of the order of John Dee and his medium, John Kelley, the Preston-connected conman whose ears had been clipped for counterfeiting. And into which, somehow, somewhere, fits 'The School of Night', mentioned by Will in *Love's Labour's Lost*, allegedly an occult circle of scholars, poets and nobles, possibly led by Ferdinando's brother, the next earl.

But hey, nonny, no. I feel the draught of those doors of contention opening and hear the hubbub of the varied convinced rising once more, enough to test the sadly frail resolve of this recent convert to exhausting, exhaustive and uncompromising study. Quick! A dream, perchance: that Shakespeareans of all colours will sit together in rows on a steep Lancashire hillside, silent and rapt as the magic hour unfolds upon the stage with Pendle and the Pennines beyond. The play is the thing. But he was there, you know.

Chapter Eleven

Lancs Farewell

Going to Fleetwood

Fleetwood, said my friend Matthew, was where Lancastrians went to die, so I took the tram from Blackpool. The tram clunked and whirred and jarred its way north, up the coast, through Bispham and Norbreck and Little Bispham, and past Cleveleys. The Illuminations end at Bispham, which gives the places beyond that a certain Christ-stopped-at-Eboli feel, even if Norbreck is home to that marvel of castellated contrivance, the Norbreck Hydro as was, an hotel whose mere mention turns strong party-conference-covering political journalists pale and to the nearest available drink. Have I mentioned this plan to power the Illuminations with donkey dung from Blackpool Beach? Marvellous; Lancs at the technological sharp end, as ever. Well, perhaps not the sharp end. Cleveleys? I have never been to Cleveleys, but it's good to keep a few things in reserve.

The tram wasn't a fancy Blackpool prom one, rather a solid green and cream affair, not much changed over the years from the beginnings of the high-speed tramway in the 1880s. It was the sort of lazy sunny Sunday that the Kinks and the Small Faces used to put to music. A couple sat in front of me. She was in her mid-fifties, dressed in one of those coral pink raincoats you never see for sale, with an uncomplicated haircut; he was in an anorak, glasses and a parting which was too far over to the side. They said nothing to each other, like the couples you sometimes see having a pub lunch. Then, finally, she did say something to him, and he turned and gave her one of the sweetest, most loving smiles I have ever seen. I was glad when they got off before Fleetwood.

Which is a remarkable place. If you know nothing about it – and I didn't know a lot – the first indication of this is the lighthouse by the tramstop, 90 feet of finely proportioned brown sandstone, so elegant that I thought it must be some kind of folly until I saw that it was aligned with another one, over on the seafront, beyond the long curve and classical portico, again in sandstone, of the North Euston Hotel. The North Euston Hotel! There had been dreams here, at the end of the line. And it was some kind of folly.

But let's not rush. For one thing, if you come into Fleetwood by tram, you miss the roundabout. I've mentioned before my interest in roundabouts, which began as a joke for the newspaper column I was writing, following on from an interest in bus shelters which started when my attention was drawn to an article claiming that a bus shelter between Newhaven and Lewes might be the least used in Britain. Ah, yes, you say, the drollness of the banal, common currency of the post-modern columnist.

But there's more to roundabouts. The roundabout is one of the finest achievements of the twentieth century. The splendid simplicity of its solution to the problem of the traffic junction makes it fit to rank alongside far fancier technological advances. And, before dismissing late Western civilisation as, in the words of Mr Gandhi, a good idea, consider the basic courtesy and discipline that the roundabout assumes and achieves. Consider, too, my plan for alleviating road congestion by making everyone go round twice.

We have already noted, with fitting incredulity, that the first roundabout was, in fact, the Arc de Triomphe. And, if Blackpool can bow to Paris with its tower, Fleetwood can nod with its roundabout. No arch as you approach on the A585, but a statue, mounted on a mighty monumental plinth, echoing the greatest works of the Mayans and Egyptians.

And no ordinary statue, but one of startling similarity to the image of Eros, the God of Love, which adorns Piccadilly Circus. How romantic is that? Pedants will, of course, tell you that Gilbert's splendid piece of aluminium, a memorial to the great works of Lord Shaftesbury, is actually supposed to be the Angel of Christian Charity, but pedants have no soul; they are the enemies of generosity and romance and fancy, and see beauty only in earthbound exactitudes. The people preferred it to be Eros, and so Eros it is. (Mind you, I don't want to be difficult, but the statue is actually facing the wrong way. It's a visual pun: he should be firing his arrow at, 'burying' his 'shaft' in, Shaftesbury Avenue, not Regent Street.)

But why is Eros here in Fleetwood? Well, that was another reason why I'd come. You must have heard of Fisherman's Friend, the soothing lozenge and universal joke opportunity. A barrister friend of mine, for example, was prosecuting a man who had committed some perversely deviant act which we need know no more about. The man developed a bad cold and cough and was having trouble giving evidence. The judge, similarly troubled, proffered his bag of the lozenges and asked the defendant's barrister, 'Would it help if he sucked a Fisherman's Friend?'

'No, thank you, your honour,' replied his counsel, 'he's in quite enough trouble already.' I've always liked that one.

Fleetwood is the home of Fisherman's Friend. Travel by tram or car and you cannot miss the factory, a huge affair which seems to run most of the length of the town. The Fisherman's Friend formula of liquorice, capsicum, eucalyptus and menthol was first mixed by James Lofthouse in his Fleetwood chemist shop in 1865 after the local trawlermen had asked him for something to keep them going, out on the northern fishing grounds. Lofthouse made a liquid first, then the lozenge (rather easier in a swell).

The Fleetwood fishermen proved enthusiastic suckers for the next 100 years, until Iceland's extension of its fishing limits, the Cod War, EU regulations and overfishing fished out the Fleetwood deep-sea fleet. Things might not have looked good for a Friend with only a few fishermen if it hadn't been for Doreen Lofthouse, married to Lofthouse's grandson, a Fleetwood girl herself, and an entrepreneur waiting to happen.

She had started selling Fisherman's Friend as far away as East Lancashire and then all over Lancashire and, after Lancashire, the world: Norway, Germany, Singapore, the United States, more than 100 countries including Papua New Guinea. New flavours were introduced, along with a sugar-free variety. They won three Queen's Awards for Export: the annual production of lozenges would go round the world five times – my favourite kind of statistic. Lady Thatcher sucks them; so does, it is said, Pavarotti, before going on. In fact, it is also said, the Italian operatic tenor industry would fall apart without Fisherman's Friend. Madonna swears by them too, apparently.

Lancashire fishermen, Italian opera singers. I told you this was a romantic place. And what I had been told in Blackpool was that Doreen Lofthouse had bought that statue of Eros and put it on the roundabout and built a vault beneath the plinth to be her final resting place. Can you think of anything more magnificent?

So I visited the roundabout, and had a look. There, inscribed, on the plinth, was the legend, 'Fisherman's Friend Welcomes You To Fleetwood'. Nothing about a final resting place, though.

I telephoned Fisherman's Friend to see if I could talk to Mrs Lofthouse. Eventually, I was told that it would not be possible, but I could see her son, Duncan, the joint managing director. Mrs Lofthouse began to take on the magic and mystery of other confectionery manufacturers, like Willie Wonka, or Uncle Joe, of Uncle Joe's Mintballs, Wigan's gift to the world. If only George Orwell had tried one of Uncle Joe's Mintballs. Another funny thing is that no one at Uncle Joe's now has any idea who Uncle Joe was.

Mr Lofthouse was charming. He told me that his mother didn't talk to journalists any more because they tended to get things wrong. This seemed a good cue to mention the Eros mausoleum. It was wrong. The statue was nothing like that, said Mr Lofthouse. It was one of several copies that had been made of the original when it was taken down for restoration in the 1980s. His mother had seen it at a garden show and decided it was just the thing for Fleetwood, and made a gift of it to the town, to go with all her other gifts, like repaving the prom and refurbishing the hospital. Even so, the council took a lot of persuading that Eros wouldn't be a bit of a distraction for drivers. I'm surprised the Arc de Triomphe has survived, frankly.

Mr Lofthouse took me round the factory. I'm not very good at factory visits. My most disappointing was at the Royal Worcester factory during the 1997 general election campaign, when John and Norma resolutely failed to drop so much as a saucer. But Mr Lofthouse was an infectious enthusiast who couldn't forget when they got their first-ever packaging machine, back in the late '60s, and now look at it: 275 employees, nearly 30,000 square metres of factory and all sorts of machines whizzing and mixtures globbiter-globbitting and coloured tubes and glass and lozenges being directed here and there.

We were dressed in the white overalls and white hats, the ones that look like opaque hairnets. I've never seen anyone carry them off, although Nigel Lawson maintained the most dignity. But Mr Lofthouse managed well, reminding me of a more genial version of Captain Mainwaring. I couldn't get over how friendly and smiling all the staff were, until I caught sight of myself in a mirror.

A bit of a false start, then, even if I did get some free samples. So: to the lighthouse, designed by no less a figure than Decimus Burton, student of Nash, principal practitioner of the Greek style that flowered briefly between Georgian and Gothic revival, architect of the Athenaeum in Pall Mall, much of Hyde Park and much of Kew, including the magnificent Palm House: in short, the architect of the day. And, even more to our point, creator of the Wellington Arch at Hyde Park Corner, our country's greatest roundabout, Britain's Arc de Triomphe on Britain's Place de l'Étoile.

Burton was, as you might have guessed, the tenth son of James Burton, designer and builder of much of St Leonard's, which was where he first met Peter Hesketh, the founder of Fleetwood. Now I'm quite used to the idea, and by now I hope you are, too, of the Lancashire man as a bit of a dallier and a dabbler and dreamer, and Peter Hesketh was up there with the best. A second son of a family combining the Bolds and the Fleetwoods and large tracts of Lancs including most of the coast from Southport to Morecambe Bay, Hesketh had some marvellously woolly and Oxford-inspired dreams about improving the lot of the common man. He was elected Member of Parliament for Preston on a manifesto which included taxes on industry, not people, and the abolition of the death penalty. He had translated and published Victor Hugo's *The Last Days of the Condemned*. And he had met Robert Owen, the socialist reformer and tireless founder of failed utopias in Scotland, England, Ireland and America. Out of all this came the big dream: a Lancashire holiday resort to succour and salve the tired and huddled of the mills and mines. Decimus Burton called it 'Peter's Golden Dream'.

Second sons could do little but dream; the death of his brother made Hesketh a first son. A first son with a dream, vision, a grasp of opportunity, and a feel for practicality, figures and balance sheets which would make Ken Dodd a hot prospect for the presidency of the Institute of Cost Accountants. Still, he had a lot of money to start off with, even if he didn't like asking for rent. When I tell you he used his younger brother as his enforcer and that his younger brother was a vicar, you will appreciate the problem.

As we've seen, the Heskeths owned a lot of Southport, and were much involved, along with the Scarisbricks, in the early days of the resort – Hesketh proposed and devised the promenade there. But the big one was Fleetwood, a completely new town which would be a resort, fishing port and more. Hesketh was with Wellington and Huskisson and Stephenson in 1830, and was seized by the railway. He wanted to bring it, with the industrial workers of Lancashire on board, to his coast. And more: everyone knew, because George Stephenson kept telling them, that trains would never be able to get over Shap Fell from England into Scotland. If they could ever manage the incline, no brakes could hold them on the descent.

Hesketh's land included a spot at the top of the Fylde Peninsula, looking over Morecambe Bay, with the safe waters of the Wyre just inland. It was obvious: build a railway to here from the main line at Preston, and then passengers could embark on a steamer up to Ardrossan, just below Glasgow. And so the call for Burton, and, at the end of the line from London, the mighty North Euston Hotel. The Preston and Wyre Railway Company was formed, prospectuses were issued, shares offered. Hesketh underwrote it all.

And, of course, it all went wrong. The cost of the railway line alone was £300,000 (nearly £15 million today), more than double the original airy estimate by a dodgy colonel of a surveyor. In 1847, Queen Victoria came down from Ardrossan to take the train to London and pay the first visit by a Duke of Lancaster to Lancashire for 200 years. And they used to complain about the Lionheart being out of England. All the town's lights were switched on as the royal yacht was sighted, and they all failed, including the lighthouses. In that same year, almost inevitably, trains began to whizz up Shap Fell.

Hesketh had handed over control of his business affairs to a man called Kemp, who was from Essex. Lancashire dreamer versus Essex doer: no contest. Kemp showed Hesketh as little as possible about the costs of building the new town, which was an unnecessary precaution, as Hesketh wouldn't have understood anyway.

There was no income flow; no one would take up the shares. Hesketh was forced to sell all his land in Blackpool and Southport, Churchtown and North Meols, Tulketh, Bispham and Norbreck, then his personal possessions, then his home to what was to become Rossall School. (Did I mention that Major Walter Clopton Wingfield, the inventor of lawn tennis, was at Rossall? Thank you. Another gift to the world.)

Hesketh died in 1866 in his flat in Piccadilly, which was about all he had left, apart from his debt-ridden Fleetwood holdings, a baronetcy, and a second barrel: Sir Peter Hesketh-Fleetwood. His first wife had died shortly after giving birth to the fourth of their children, all of whom died young. His only son by his second marriage became a priest; his Spanish wife lived on the charity of his relations until her death in 1900. And Kemp? But, of course: Kemp, who had established an impressive portfolio on his own account, including a steamer service to Ireland, sold out in 1874, retired to the former home of Hesketh-Fleetwood's brother, the vicar, and lived happily ever after.

A melancholy tale to contemplate, on a Lancashire Indian summer Sunday, outside the North Euston Hotel, stranded since they closed the line and knocked the railway station down in 1966. Not that the North Euston is all there, either. When

Xenon Vantini was manager, it had another wing, curving away round the corner, where the Magistrates' Court is now. And there was a splendid swimming baths behind, another of Hesketh's wheezes. But hardly anyone ever used them. Vantini was a Corsican with several claims to fame: he had, he said, once been a courier to the great Napoleon – that link again! – and he had opened the world's first railway refreshment room at Wolverton Station in 1838. The North Euston, where he arrived in 1841, was to break this winning, if eclectic, streak, despite his deployment of an Italian Operatic Orchestra. It was, simply, too big and too fancy. And one night, after three years, Vantini and his wife just disappeared, but not before he had, for some reason, suggested the idea of Rossall. After less than 20 years, the North Euston was sold to the government at a loss and ended up as a barracks.

I went into the North Euston, which has been restored. The bar was doing a good trade. Burton's amazing curved ballroom was empty, but cared for, and Vantini had a room named after him. It seemed a long way from Corsica. I must go and see if he's remembered at Wolverton.

Outside, on the promenade, I saw exactly what my friend Matthew meant. There were cars parked all along it and, inside them, elderly couples, with flasks and sandwiches, some with binoculars, all looking out at Morecambe Bay. Matthew had got his idea on a close, hazy day. He'd fancied that out there, just at the edge of the haze, was a rowing boat, where sat Death in a flat cap, shouting out names: 'Stanley Ollershaw . . . Eunice Eccles . . . Frank Farnworth . . . Elsie Platt . . . Sidney Lugsmore . . . Ida Stringfellow . . .' Perhaps that's the way Vantini went. It would certainly be better than the way Sir Peter did, in his flat in Piccadilly. Have you been where Keats died, just by the Spanish Steps, with life going on loudly, blithely, unconcerned outside? It must have been like that for Hesketh.

I walked further along the prom. A man was standing,

waiting, with his pair of crown green bowls in a red bag. It will be crown green in heaven, I suppose, rather than that dull, flat Southern stuff. My father was president of the St Helens Bowling Club without ever bowling a bowl in anger, although his father had left him a fine initialled pair. He preferred to chat, and tease, in the bar. After he died, there was a tribute to him in the local paper from a member: 'When Jack held court there, probably two evenings a week, the greens remained unjacked and the snooker table lights emitted not a flicker . . . he will not only be missed – he'll never be matched.'

A radio or a tape was carrying loudly on the still afternoon air from one of the shops on the prom. 'So this man goes to the doctor, and the doctor says, "I've got some bad news, and some very bad news. The bad news is that you've got 24 hours to live, and the very bad news is that I tried to get hold of you yesterday."'

Nobody laughed, but I don't think they could hear, in their cars. They were still staring out at the bay. It was a bit clear for Matthew's rowing boat, I thought. And I thought, too, about my father dying. Which affected me a lot more than I thought it would. The usual shallow selfish reasons, I suppose, loss of anchor, intimations of own mortality. But, of course, it was not as simple as that, because I missed him, too, because I loved him, even when he was exasperating me or irritating me, his fault but mine too, the pompous part of all the education he had given me but hadn't wanted himself, except that he had, a bit, perhaps. It was the difference between us.

So, not that simple. But then the idea that everything can be reduced to one thing or the other, has to be one thing or the other, is among the great gifts my trade has given to the age, to go with the impatience and self-importance. All of which I demonstrated splendidly as I tried to find a fitting epitaph to go on his headstone, something better than the usual 'Of your mercy, pray for the repose of the soul of . . .' or, 'Not dead, but sleeping . . .'. I couldn't find anything, of course. So I decided to write something myself, which was absolutely dreadful, no matter how hard and how long I tried, and ended up being edited down by somebody, probably the stonemason. No escape, even on a gravestone.

Quite right, too. It was a pity I couldn't have used one of his catchphrases, of which he had many. But they were mostly of a secular nature, although solemnly intoned at any time for no particular reason. Early visits to the theatre had clearly left a strong mark: 'Today is my daughter's wedding day, a thousand pounds I give away! On second thoughts, I think it best . . . to keep it in the old oak chest!'; 'Once aboard the lugger and the girl is mine! What if she screams? Then gag the bugger!'; 'Six o'clock and she's not here. She must be false . . . or on the beer!'; 'The boy stood on the burning deck, selling kippers at a penny a peck. Did 'e sell 'em? Did 'e 'eck!'

Another one was the tale of Paul, who went to a fancy-dress ball, thought he would risk it and go as a biscuit, but the dog ate him up in the hall. I loved the nonsense of all this, the idea that life is mostly barmy, even while I groaned, in the same way that I loved it, even though slightly shocked, as you should be as a properly pious eight year old, when he used to grin and mug at me in church. He was a regular churchgoer, although I could never quite work out why, particularly as for many years he stood at the back of a church where he couldn't even see the altar, reading one of the Catholic papers. 'Many are called, but few are frozen,' he used to say, very regularly, in a nod to his position in the grocery trade. I wish I could have smuggled that on to the gravestone.

My two brothers went into the business and kept on after his death. But it was getting harder and harder to compete with the big supermarkets and, eventually, the business was sold. To the Co-op. Now those 28 Rochdale Pioneers, also inspired by the ideas of Robert Owen, founders of the Co-operative Movement in a little shop in Toad Lane in 1844, might well have won the admiration of the world for the nobility, simplicity and cleverness of their idea, but that world did not embrace other grocers. My dad did not like the Co-op. I think he thought they weren't playing fair, bringing all that moral crusading into it. He would have been astonished that the business had been sold at all; but to the Co-op! He would have laughed in the end, though. 'Oooh, bloody'ell!' he would have said, eventually, I think. When he died, he left me one of his shops. When the business was sold, I held on to it, and the Co-op rent it from me. Which makes me the last of us to own a grocer's shop. Another funny thing.

I was thinking about all this as I stared across Morecambe Bay with everybody else. And I thought, too, how proud we should be, and Britain should be, of this great county, of what it had achieved and had given the world; how proud we should be to have inspired Shakespeare and Paris and Dickens and Laurel and Chaplin and Astaire and Coward and George and Gracie and dear Celia and dreadful Rex and all the rest of them; how proud we should be of the great good instincts of Manchester and the peculiar genius of Liverpool and the fierce energy of the mill and mining towns; but, most of all, how proud we should be of all those deceptively gentle Stans and Sids and Franks and Tommys and Georges and Arthurs and all those deceptively fierce Eunices and Elsies and Idas and Bettys and Ritas and Ednas and Winnies who had already gone to the rowing boat after hard, forgotten lives that had made our softer ones possible.

I even spared a thought for the many more who hadn't conformed to my silly, sentimental, naive and condescending stereotype. Fool that I am, I hoped they'd all had, at least, a bit of fun of the Blackpool kind, a great gust of broad pleasure once or twice or so along the way, enough to shake the head at and laugh at the memory and hug themselves and go, 'Oooh, bloody'ell!'

306

I hoped that Frank would fight his bull in Madrid and Tom would build his statue in the Mersey and Peter would get his platforms back and Leon would end up running the biggest casino in Blackpool and the Sons of the Desert would march through Wigan once more and Ince would ring to the tales of Lancelot and Hoghton to the plays of Will. And I hoped, too, that Amin and Shamim would stay and prosper until it was their turn for Fleetwood. I thanked dry Alan and warm Walter for starting me off on all this, even if I didn't seem to have found anyone who had died of love, although I had found plenty of sense and sweetness. And I thought, too, about the Lancashire heaven, where ukuleles and meat and potato pies would be as plentiful as trumpets and foie gras, and Hornby and Barlow would be stealing runs eternally to the sounds of Fields and Ferrier, and, with any luck, Voll's try would be showing as often as *Brief Encounter* in Carnforth.

As I stared, to my amazement, although nobody else seemed very bothered, a great white number two suddenly appeared in the sky, followed shortly afterwards by a great white zero. Stone me, I thought, he's calling them in by numbers! It turned out to be the Red Arrows writing the year during a display over at Morecambe. It would be Morecambe, wouldn't it? Look, Ern! Oooh, bloody'ell! Ah, Lancashire!

307

Afterword

Blackpool still stands ready to be the new Las Vegas. The necessary legislation has been much debated, disputed, derided, delayed, revised and re-revised, but is still supposed to be coming. Frankly, I wouldn't bet on it.

Basil Newby continues to shake and move: he has revamped the mighty old 3,000-seater Blackpool Odeon, turning it into the new home of both Funny Girls and the Flamingo, and employing Joan Collins to do one of the opening honours. The Flying Handbag has also moved to grand new purpose-built premises. *Bitches In Stitches*, Basil's autobiography, remains forthcoming; he promises it will reveal all about the celebrities who have queued up to, yes, 'kiss my ring'.

Mr and Mrs Harris, formerly of the San Remo, Blackpool, are thoroughly settled and happily retired in Calgary, living with their daughter and son-in-law; they could not be persuaded, no matter how much I tried, to wax nostalgic for fresh air and fun.

Stella Siddall is still running her fantasy flats in Blackpool. Sadly, her husband, Geoff, died of cancer not long after my visit. Trade remains difficult, and now a big London entertainment company is talking about buying up her side of the street, ready for the casinos; Camelot, Pompeii and the rest appear earmarked to be the car park. Stella is now talking about retiring, so you had better hurry up if you want to visit.

The Friends of Real Lancashire continue their doughty campaign that insists upon the existence of the ancient and traditional county, whatever here-today-gone-tomorrow, compulsively fiddling legislators and administrators might get up to. In November 2005, meanwhile, a national group, County Watch, mounted a border raid, taking down the 34 'Welcome to Lancashire' road signs which were giving the misleading impression that Lancashire County Council's truncated administrative fiefdom is the true county. Lancashire County Council have now put them back up, but the struggle continues.

My **Auntie Vera** didn't hear **Mr Chesworth** shout over the fence, but then, as she says, she is a bit deaf.

Gabriel Muies has finished his book, *The Moles of Edge Hill*, which, he says, will tell all about the Williamson Tunnels, their history, purpose and rediscovery. He is now looking for a publisher. Meanwhile, he has finally located Williamson's grave under that car park and has persuaded the Duke of Westminster to turn the area into a commemorative garden. Gabriel is still talking non-stop, and has, among many other things, confirmed that, yes, he was the model for Yosser 'Gis a job' Hughes in Alan Bleasdale's *Boys from the Black Stuff*. It happened in the '80s, after the Toxteth riots, when a high-powered deputation of politicians and construction chiefs arrived near Gabriel's house. Gabriel put on his suit and joined them, and when they finally asked him who he was, he gave the reply made immortal after Bleasdale read about it in the *Echo*. And no, he's still not got one.

Adolf Hitler would still just about recognise Upper Stanhope Street, but **Ahmad** has left for Middlesbrough and a better job. I'm afraid **Phairverts** has closed on Bold Street, too, and the

Golden Hot is shut as well, following, courtesy of the the Great Ironist In The Sky, a fire. But Liverpool continues to seethe with hard hats and the buzz of change, and to offer as much optimism as is allowed before someone makes a joke about it.

Peter Halligan is working on his memoirs and Jung's Chinese connections. He is also contemplating an event provisionally entitled The Culture of Capital 2007.

Tom Murphy's statue still awaits money and feasibility studies and the like. Tom is getting a bit fed up with the delay. His wife keeps telling him to forget about it; but he can't, because people will keep telling him what a great idea it is, including me. Meanwhile, I notice, someone else has got a plan for a giant glass Stonehenge on the Wirral bank of the Mersey. And someone else wants to build a full-sized £300-million replica of the *Titanic* and anchor it at the Pier Head, although I'm a bit worried about mixed messages there. Oh, and the Yellow Submarine has now been taken to John Lennon Airport, which, in Liverpool, is far too obvious a place for it.

Quentin Hughes has died. His obituaries recorded the debt that Liverpool owed him, making clear that it was his teachings, writings and actions as chairman of the Merseyside Civic Society and founder of the Liverpool Heritage Bureau which saved Liverpool's magnificent Victorian and Edwardian architecture from the unsympathetic '60s, so enabling the city to achieve its World Heritage and Capital of Culture status. He, of course, barely mentioned any of this to me. I spoke to him a couple of months before his death; he was still chuckling about Southport, which is how I shall remember him. *Vale*.

The latest annual **Laurel and HarDay** took place as usual at the Beer Engine, Poolstock, and featured a very special guest star, Jean Darling, who was Curly Locks in The Boys' classic *March of the Wooden Soldiers*. Jean, who now lives in Ireland, got to know Stan and Ollie quite well 'because Stan fancied her mum', as one of the Sons put it. Her part in the film was silent but originally she had sung a number, which ended up on the cutting-room floor; 71 years later, she sang it again, in Wigan, which was rather splendid.

Happy Harry Ingle has celebrated his 90th birthday; his next big date is a Sons' convention in Augusta, Georgia, near to Oliver's birthplace.

Predictably, after that *dies mirabilis*, 25 June 2005, when **St Helens** beat Wigan by seventy-five points to nil (75–0), the season went on to finish in a fashion familiar to the Knowsley Road unfainthearts. Saints topped the Super League but failed to make the Grand Final, and were also beaten in the semi-final of the Challenge Cup. They did, however, report a profit for once, and there was again talk of a new stadium. By the time you read this, though, everything, I can confidently predict, will have changed. Should you want a commemorative coffee mug emblazoned with the electronic scoreboard bearing the St Helens 75, Wigan 0 result, or indeed one showing Tom Van Vollenhoven in his pomp, feel free to contact the club's store, where both are available at a very reasonable price. This will also give you the bonus, if you ring on 0870 756 5252, of listening to a uniquely Lancastrian version of a recorded options message, courtesy of, naturally, Mr Johnny Vegas, who, I notice elsewhere, has somehow persuaded John Malkovich to become a Saints fan, which seems in splendidly apt accord with club philosophy and ambience.

In December 2005, **Robin Evans** pleaded guilty to forging signatures on a nomination paper for a council by-election and was ordered to serve 60 hours' community service. The conviction prevents him from standing for election for five years.

Aminul Hoque has graduated, but has decided, for the moment, against a career in teaching. Besides selling telephones, he is also building up a property portfolio and planning a trip to China to talk imports. He remains heavily involved in youth work in Oldham, aimed at making sure, he says, that they all get to own a Ferrari.

Kathleen Jebb hasn't entirely lost her faith in New Labour, but it has been further and sorely tried. Now in her 80s, she's given up the yoga classes, but works out at home with 'one of those abdo things'. She's also thinking of moving from Spring Vale to a ground-floor flat, but a friend doesn't reckon the council will give her one: 'You won't get a flat, love, you've got to have a Zimmer. You're too fit.' Long may it last.

Leon Thorpe had a heart scare – 'my heart stopped, then started again' – and has now retired as secretary of the Chandos Club. He's had a couple of offers to manage and relief-manage pubs, but is presently looking forward to a cruise, so will no doubt end up as entertainments officer.

Frank Evans has stopped fighting bulls. The dodgy knee finally gave out and, in August 2005, Frank took part in his last corrida, at Benalmadena. The ritual cutting of the *coleta*, the matador's pigtail, to signify the end, was carried out by Juan Caparros, the torero who had been at Frank's first fight in Montpelier in 1966, and who had travelled from Venezuela to be there. Not a bad career, then, but Frank never did get to fight in Madrid, or Colombia, Peru and Ecuador, which was his ambition. Still, he's not taken his bullfighter's pension yet, and there's always a chance that Frank and a new knee might, as he puts it, 'pop up in Peru', even if, as he now concedes, he is in his mid-'60s. Oh, and he also revealed, in his Frankish way, that the other end from the coleta is a toupee.

Peter Yates was made an MBE in the Queen's Birthday Honours in 2005. When he met the Queen, she asked him what the award was for; Peter told her it was for his work at Carnforth railway station. 'That's where the film *Brief Encounter* was made,' she said. 'I do so much love that film.' A well-informed Duke of Lancaster, then. She has also said, by the way, that if she ever retired, it would be to the Forest of Bowland.

Roddy Wright emigrated with **Kathleen MacPhee** to New Zealand, where he died of liver cancer in 2005. Kathleen was at his bedside. I might have done the ex-bishop an injustice by suggesting he had no sense of irony: his alias on his travels was David Janssen, after the actor who played The Fugitive in the television series.

Sister Mary Lucy has gone to a convent in Slough.

Elaine Maudsley has been ill, but is not complaining: 'Only the good die young, I'll probably still be here in another 50 years.' And yes, people still want to talk to her about the 12 seconds.

Hoghton Tower is still standing, but the dream of a new theatre and library, the Lancashire Bayreuth and all the rest of it, seems fated to remain a dream for now, thanks to the usual suspects, like money. Still, as somebody once said, 'How poor are they that have not patience?' (*Othello*, Act 2, Scene 3). Meanwhile, while we're waiting, I'm sure Shakespeareans of all persuasions would enjoy **Mr Barrett**'s ghost tours.

Fleetwood has suffered a poignant absence. Love has flown: **Mrs Lofthouse**'s *Eros*, attacked in its aluminium by the bracing but salty sea air, was taken down and sent for repair in the summer of 2005. Close inspection concluded that it would never be able to withstand Fleetwood's robust humours. Fortunately for romantics everywhere, Mrs Lofthouse, as indefatigable as ever, thereupon commissioned a bronze version, which may well be there, lovingly triumphant, by the time you read this.

Charles Nevin has gone to live in Somerset, where he dreams of Lancs when he's not racing in from fully 80 yards at Knowsley Road. By day, he maintains his missionary zeal and, owing to his whimsical way with research, keeps discovering fresh and fascinating facets of the great county. Imagine, for example, his delight when he found out that the mighty Ashton Memorial, the biggest folly in Britain, with a dome that dominates the M6 just up from Camelot, is known as 'The Taj Mahal of Lancashire'! Indeed: it was built in the early 1900s by James Williamson, Lord Ashton, as a memorial to his wife, Jessie. An interesting figure, Williamson. Known as 'The Lino King of Lancaster' after his flooring business, he ruled the city like some baronial throwback, ordered the way his workers voted and bought his peerage from Lloyd George before falling out with him. Jessie was his second wife. The memorial, though, ran into a snag: by the time it was finished, Jimmy had married again. So he changed it into a memorial to himself. Not a very romantic solution, admittedly, but Nevin takes some consolation from another recent discovery: the boat which took the title role in *The African Queen*, the very vessel shared by Bogart and Hepburn and filmed by Huston, was built in Lytham. He would also like you to remember, the next time you are in Trafalgar Square, that the paving stones come from Bacup. Meanwhile, if you have any information on 'Syncopating' Sandy Strickland, the marathon piano player from Bolton, or, indeed, 'Manchester' Jack Gill, Britain's first lion-tamer, he would be most interested in hearing from you.

Acknowledgements

As you will know if you've come here the right way, many people helped me with this book and most of them are mentioned in the text. I should like to record my thanks to them and to those so far unrecognised, particularly the writers whose works I have cheerfully ransacked.

Chief among those not already credited are: *The Earls of Derby*, J.J. Bagley, Sidgwick & Jackson, 1985; *Roman Britain*, Peter Salway, OUP, 1981; *Anglo-Saxon England*, Sir Frank Stenton, OUP, 1971; *Stan and Ollie: The Roots of Comedy – The Double Life of Laurel and Hardy*, Simon Louvish, Faber, 2001; *Mr Laurel And Mr Hardy*, John McCabe, Robson, 1976; *Laurel and Hardy, The British Tours*, A.J. Marriot, A.J. Marriot, 1993; *Marx and Engels and the English Workers*, W.O. Henderson, Cass, 1989; *Friedrich Engels: The Shadow Prophet*, Grace Carlton, Pall Mall Press, 1965; *Karl Marx*, Francis Wheen, Fourth Estate, 1999; *George Formby: A Troubled Genius*, David Bret, Robson, 2001; *Jung: The Wisdom of the Dream*, Stephen Segaller and Merrill Berger, Weidenfeld and Nicolson, 1989; *David Lean: A Biography*,

Kevin Brownlow, Richard Cohen Books, 1996; *The Lancashire Cotton Industry*, ed. Mary B Rose, Lancashire County Books, 1996; *The Incomparable Rex*, Patrick Garland, Macmillan, 1998; *Between Ribble & Lune*, David Pownall, Victor Gollancz, 1980; *Hamlet's Divinity and Other Essays*, Christopher Devlin, Hart-Davis, 1963; *Saints in their Glory*; and *The March of the Saints*, Alex Service, Alex Service; *Shakespeare, The 'Lost Years'*, E.A.J. Honigmann, Manchester University Press, 1985; *Edmund Campion*, Evelyn Waugh, Longman, 1935; *Blackpool Tower*, Bill Curtis, Terence Dalton, 1988; *Romans And Britons In North-West England*, David Shotter, University of Lancaster, 1997; *Victorian Cities*, Asa Briggs, Odhams, 1963; *J.R.R. Tolkien*, Humphrey Carpenter, Allen & Unwin, 1977; *When Push Comes To Shove*, Vols I and II, Ian Clayton et al, Yorkshire Arts Circus, 1993, 1995; *The Golden Dream: The Biography of Sir Peter Hesketh-Fleetwood*, Bill Curtis, CF Publications.

The following gave permission for reproduction of quotations: Nicholas Evans for *Lancashire* by Walter Greenwood; David Higham Associates for 'Manchester' by A.J.P. Taylor, first published by Hamish Hamilton; John Murray Publishers for *Napoleon III and his Carnival Empire* by John Bierman; Sefton Council for *A History of Southport* by Francis Bailey; Harper Collins for *Feet of Clay* by Roddy Wright; Ann Law for *Oldham, Brave Oldham* by Brian R. Law; Random House for *My Autobiography* by Charles Chaplin, first published by Bodley Head; Lancashire County Books for *Four Centuries of Cotton* by Geoffrey Timmins.

Many of these books (but, sadly, neither of Mr Service's excellent volume) came from the shelves of the London Library, a marvellous resource. Drew Drake was a splendid guide to the more interesting aspects of Blackpool, and also an authority on Holland's Pies. Joe Riley and Philip Key of the *Liverpool Daily Post & Echo* were as helpful and delightful companions as I remembered; Joe's eye for the telling tale remains undimmed, unerring and, as you will have seen, most useful. Peter Elson kept me au courant de Scouse. Patrick Garland talked most entertainingly about Rex Harrison. David Bret was his equal about George Formby. John Knowles, secretary of the Noel Coward Society, provided the information on the Earl of Lathom; it will feature in his forthcoming biography, *The Lathom Angel*.

Other people who gave generously of their time were J.K. Walton, Professor of Social History at the University of Central Lancashire; his colleague, Dr Dave Russell, Reader in Social History; David Pearce, then Fleetwood editor of *The Gazette*; and librarians in Blackburn, Fleetwood, Ormskirk and the Lancashire County Archive, who proved as unfailingly helpful as their text-mentioned colleagues in Wigan, Ince, Southport, St Helens and Skelmersdale. As usual, all the mistakes are all mine; there would have been many more of them but for the scrupulous attentions of the Mainstream editorial team. Claire Rose and Deborah Kilpatrick are owed my particular thanks.

Other people who gave generously of their contacts were Ian Herbert and Paul Vallely of *The Independent* and William Leece of the *Daily Post*.

I must also thank my mother, for putting me up and putting up with me while I was wandering around Lancs (and during all the many years before); and my sons, Cristian and Luis, for providing a proper sense of proportion, and, in particular, steadfastly refusing to contrive the slightest enthusiasm for the fluctuating fortunes of St Helens Rugby League Football Club.

That last would also be the only conceivable failing of my beloved wife, who has provided an inspiring example of how to support a crazed obsessive and suggest some much-needed improvements while dealing simultaneously with rather more important matters, like championing and caring for other people. Thank you, Liv.

Thanks, too, in advance, for your forbearance, if I have passed by you or your passion or part of Lancs without so much as a glance, or stumbled or nodded or unaccountably ignored when I did visit. Blame it on the whimsy.